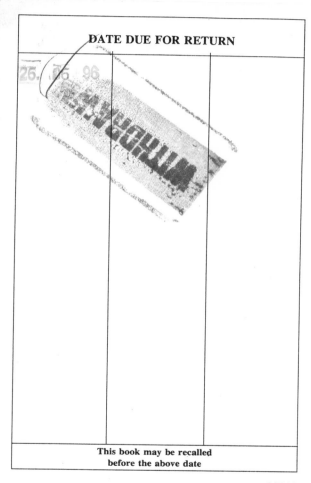

DATE DUE FOR RETURN

26. 06. 96

This book may be recalled
before the above date

90014

HAMILTON

The History of Canadian Cities

HAMILTON

An Illustrated History

John C. Weaver

James Lorimer & Company, Publishers
and
National Museum of Man,
National Museums of Canada
Toronto 1982

ISBN 0-88862-593-6 cloth

Design: Don Fernley
Cartography: Michael Doucet

Canadian Cataloguing in Publication Data
Weaver, John C.
Hamilton: an illustrated history

(The History of Canadian cities)
Includes index.
Bibliography: p. 214

1. Hamilton (Ont.) — History. I. Title. II. Series.
FC3098.4.W42   971.3'52   C82-095027-0
F1059.5.H2W42
100004871X

James Lorimer & Company, Publishers
Egerton Ryerson Memorial Building
35 Britain Street
Toronto, Ontario M5A 1R7

Printed and bound in Canada
6 5 4 3 2   83 84 85 86 87

This book has been published with the help of a grant from the Canadian Federation for the Humanities using funds provided by the Social Sciences and Humanities Research Council of Canada.

This book has been published with the help of a grant from McMaster University.

Credits
Photos and illustrations

Table of Contents

List of Maps

Appendix
List of Tables

Foreword
The History of Canadian Cities Series

The History of Canadian Cities Series is a project of the History Division, National Museum of Man (National Museums of Canada). The project was begun in 1977 to respond to a growing demand for more popular publications to complement the already well-established scholarly publications programs of the Museum. The purpose of this series is to offer the general public a stimulating insight into Canada's urban past. Over the next several years, the Museum, in cooperation with James Lorimer and Company, plans to publish a number of volumes dealing with such varied communities as Montreal and Toronto, Halifax and Quebec City, Ottawa and Sherbrooke.

It is the hope of the National Museum of Man that the publication of these books will provide the public with information on Canadian cities in a visually attractive and highly readable form. At the same time, the plan of the series is to have authors follow a standard format and the result, it is anticipated, will be a systematic, interpretative and comprehensive account of the urban experience in many Canadian communities. Eventually, as new volumes are completed, *The History of Canadian Cities Series* will be a major step along the path to a general and comparative study of Canada's urban development.

The form chosen for this series — the individual urban biography — is based on a desire to examine all aspects of community development and to relate the parts to a large context. The series is also based on the belief that, while each city has a distinct personality that deserves to be discovered, the volumes must also provide analysis that will lift the narrative of a city's experience to the level where it will elucidate questions that are of concern to Canadians generally. These questions include such issues as ethnic relationships, regionalism, provincial-municipal interaction, social mobility, labour-management relationships, urban planning and general economic development.

In this volume, John C. Weaver expands both the chronology and the geography of the series by examining one of Canada's heartland communities. This account of Hamilton's development makes clear that Canada had an urban dimension long before Confederation and that city-building — no less than farming — was the occupation of many of the country's "pioneers." Although Hamilton was bypassed in size by Toronto, it nonetheless remains one of central Canada's most important metropolitan centres. Dr. Weaver, a member of the history department at Hamilton's McMaster University, is a well-known urban historian. He brings to this study a wealth of evidence and thought about Canada's and Hamilton's urban development.

Professor Weaver's text has been enhanced by a fine collection of illustrations. This illustrative material is not only visually enjoyable, it also plays an essential part in recreating the past. While photographs and maps cannot by themselves replace the written word, they can be used as a primary source in a way equivalent to more traditional sources. The illustrations in this volume capture images of a wide variety of situations in Hamilton, allowing a later generation to better understand the forms, structures, fashions and group interactions of an earlier period.

Alan F. J. Artibise
General Editor

Already published in this series:
Alan Artibise, *Winnipeg* (1977)
Max Foran, *Calgary* (1978)
Patricia Roy, *Vancouver* (1980)

Acknowledgments

Many forms of assistance have been granted in preparing this book, including intellectual guidance, aid in locating source material and the provision of time for research and writing. I am grateful for the original work and points of view developed by Michael Katz, Bryan Palmer and Craig Heron. The inception of social and working-class history in Canada has a strong, even unique, connection with Hamilton. This condition impressed upon me the need to formulate observations about the movement of people through Hamilton, the struggles of workingmen, and the nature of an urban culture. Charles Johnston and Wayne Roberts, as colleagues with local interests, offered suggestions. Conversations with Wayne raised more questions than this volume can address. Michael Doucet read an early draft of the book and his thoughtful recommendations produced significant changes. His maps demonstrate his skill and his understanding of the city. Students in my urban history seminar deserve credit for their work on Hamilton topics; accordingly, I have cited a few of their papers in the notes. Alan Artibise has been a diligent editor, correctly insisting on topical and chronological balance. In a very general way, this volume would never have been possible without early encouragement from Jim Leith, George Rawlyk and Tom Plunkett, all of Queen's University. I hope they will take some pleasure in reading what they indirectly fostered.

It is usual to confirm the reputation of the Public Archives of Canada as a model institution, but institutions are exceptional because of interested and knowledgeable personnel. I was especially fortunate in being guided by Glenn Wright, Norman Ball and Jim Whalen. The staff at the National Archives in Washington directed me toward the extensive records of the Hamilton Consular Office. Brian Henley at the Hamilton Public Library gave generously of his time and devoted his knowledge of the visual records of the city to enhancing the book. Larry Nelson worked overtime to prepare the illustrations. Numerous photographers — many of them anonymous — have contributed to the visual documentation of Hamilton's history. The following were among the local masters of the craft: Robert Milne, Fred Sharpe, C.S. Cochran, E.M. Cunningham, Jessie Dickson, John Morris and Lloyd Bloom. Stanley Hollowell, in charge of records at city hall, and Tim Nelson, deputy registrar at the Land Registry Office, permitted access to civic documents and subdivision plans. John Bacher, David Burley, Peter DeLottinville, James DeJonge, Helen Carson, Peter Ward, Robert Fraser, Mel Bailey, Bill Rosart, Carolyn Gray and Matt Borsellino came to my aid or volunteered information. Harvey Lennox assisted by arranging for access to manuscript collections held privately. His good-natured enthusiasm was a bonus. Jim Lemon and Ted Mumford tried to impress upon me the need for clear and direct prose.

McMaster University and the Social Sciences and Humanities Research Council facilitated a sabbatical leave during 1980–81. Part of that leave was passed completing the volume. McMaster University's excellent research facilities and thorough support for scholarship and publication added to the enjoyment of writing. The National Museum of Man made it possible for me to spend a summer in Washington and two summers in Ottawa. Bill and Edelgard Tamorria have accepted me as a preoccupied houseguest on more than one occasion. Ora Orbach, Nancy Kent and Violet Croydon transformed draft chapters into a manuscript. To Joan, who helped with the research and the many chores associated with seeing a manuscript through to its published form, I offer my deepest appreciation.

This book is dedicated to the memory of Owen Adam Weaver and Orville Menno Weaver, who valued Hamilton's tradition of amateur athletics. Adam Carl is growing up in the tradition. It is his book too.

A romantic conception of the Dundas Valley in 1855, looking eastward from Dundas to Coote's Paradise, Hamilton, Burlington Beach and Lake Ontario. Artist Robert Whale included the newly constructed Great Western Railway on the left.

Introduction

The Head of the Lake before the Founding of Hamilton

The formative influences on the history of Hamilton concern non-indigenous peoples. For better or worse, events shaping urban space stemmed from European economic systems and settlers. Nonetheless, human history around Burlington Bay had notable dimensions before European occupation began in the late eighteenth century. From sometime in the sixteenth century until the middle of the seventeenth, an area within a twenty-mile radius of the bay held a comparatively large, flourishing and organized population. Comprising the Neutral nation, the natives may have numbered 40,000 during the early 1600s. French adventurer Etienne Brûlé visited the Neutrals in 1616 and again in 1624; at one point Samuel de Champlain was anxious to draw the 4,000 or 5,000 braves into an alliance. Aside from the Recollet missionary Joseph de la Roche d'Aillon, who visited in 1626-27, and the Jesuit Jean de Brébeuf, who came briefly in 1641, the Neutrals had unrecorded trade contacts with Europeans. In a region advantageously placed for trade with Europeans and supplied with excellent hunting and a decent horticultural base, the Neutrals flourished. Under warrior chief Souharissen, the Neutrals had held back pressure from the Iroquois confederacy south of Lake Ontario.

Plague and famine in the late 1630s weakened the Neutrals, and the chief's death at midcentury left the nation disorganized and vulnerable to Iroquois aggression. By 1650-51, the major palisaded villages had broken down and the population dispersed. Except for intermittent and limited native habitation, the region stayed depopulated for more than a century. Native association with the vicinity only revived after the American Revolution, when loyal Iroquois were relocated on a land grant along the Grand River.[1]

Early settlers came to the Head of the Lake by approaching Burlington Bay from Lake Ontario. A wide sand beach so completely sheltered Burlington Bay that early accounts described it as a lake. Five miles to the west a height of land rose 100 feet above the water. Behind this ridge there extended a marsh fed by streams descending from the Niagara Escarpment and the Ancaster Hills. The hills interrupted the escarpment and afforded a rough access for trails to the summit and the region beyond. The usefulness of this break was recognized by all who had to transport goods between lakeshore and settlement frontier. As well, the Niagara Escarpment curved sharply around Burlington Bay, concentrating the tumbling streams within a tight radius of a sheltered natural harbour. To early travellers, lush ravines and streams situated the area among the wilderness curiosities of Upper Canada. Adventurers and artists sought out the scenic locales, but others calculated practical benefits. In the age of sail and water power, a union of bay and rapid streams spelled opportunity to men engaged in commerce, milling and speculation in land. Individuals such as Richard Beasley, Richard Hatt, James Durand, James Crooks and George Hamilton were some of the men who grasped the potential and moved to organize the Burlington Bay economy. Thus the early history of the scattered communities which preceded the emergence of Hamilton consists of a meeting between a unique natural environment and men of ambition.

The influence of merchants and millers was conveyed by the names adopted for Head of the Lake clearings. Beasley's was interchanged with Burlington or Burlington Heights to describe the southwest side of Burlington Bay; Hatt's Mills, Coote's Paradise and Dundas Mills labelled the hamlet that became Dundas. Ancaster applied to both the township and the mill seats along Ancaster Creek. The array of names for locales with imprecise boundaries underlines the unconsolidated nature of settlement and the fact that the villages were unincorporated — circumstances that changed with the rise of Hamilton in the early 1830s. However, for many years the clusters of dwellings and mills grew slowly. The economy of the frontier was vulnerable to distant demands and uncertain sources of credit. No more than 3,000 lived around the bay in 1820.

The course of settlement was severely disturbed by the War of 1812, but the war also shaped the founding of Hamilton. See-saw military action directly touched the region in 1813. In contrast to 1812, when local militia companies had participated in triumphs at Detroit and Queenston Heights, in mid-1813 war broke into the bay area. Burlington Heights developed as a key defensive strongpoint. The crisis that carried the war so close began with the American attack upon Fort George on May 27. Brigadier-General John Vincent pulled in the Niagara frontier garrisons and retreated to the Heights. Richard Beasley's house became Vincent's headquarters. Vincent's senior staff officer, Lieutenant-Colonel John Harvey, reconnoitred the enemy position at Stoney Creek. He reported that "the enemy's guards were few and negligent; his line of encampment was long and broken; his artillery was feebly supported."[2] The British next had the good fortune to learn the American countersign. At two in the morning, June 6, the British used this countersign to surprise the American pickets. As dawn broke, the battle had degenerated into formless confusion, but a desperate attack had stopped the advance. On July 29, an American naval force landed several hundred men under the command of Lieutenant-Colonel Winfield Scott on the north end of the sand beach to reconnoitre the camp at Burlington Heights. Learning that the British were well organized, Scott retired. The final local encounter was a naval engagement that began near York on 18 September 1813. After an hour of indecisive action, British Commodore Sir James Yeo broke off to avoid the growing superiority of the American squadron. In heavy winds, he made a run for Burlington Bay. With the storm waves adding depth to the channel at Burlington Beach and having aboard a youth familiar with the local waters, Yeo escaped into the bay.[3]

As fascinating as these clashes were — the Battle of Stoney Creek had the added weight of repelling an American thrust — the significance of conflict is not to be found during rare interludes of combat. An understanding of this war must accent the responses of a diverse population. There were several reactions: loyalty to the Crown, sympathy for the American cause, neutrality and personal survival. Complicating matters, envy and business rivalry affected men's judgments about the loyalty of their neighbours. Among the colony's zealous defenders of the Crown was Allan MacNab from York, who was to have important future associations with Burlington Bay. At age fourteen, he had joined Sir James Yeo's flagship in May, 1813, and then had switched to the infantry. Bravery earned him an ensign's commission and the title "Boy Hero." Henceforth, militia, loyalty and an aggressive temperament would be rooted in his gregarious character.[4]

In a society that included numerous Yankee settlers, there were American sympathizers. A number left the colony. Other pro-Americans hoped to disguise their sentiments while hanging onto their assets. One would-be neutral was Abraham Markle, a partner in an Ancaster grist mill and Member of the Legislative Assembly. He was too prominent to have avoided a firm show of loyalty, but he tried. Accused of treason in the spring of 1813, he was ordered to York. He denounced his arrest as an act of malice perpetrated by political enemies, but upon release, he joined the Americans. Markle served capably with other turncoats and helped to guide a raid on Port Dover in mid-May, 1814. Destructive raids and questionable behaviour of settlers in sensitive areas forced the government to make an example of those captured while assisting the enemy or acting in open rebellion. Ancaster was chosen as the site for the showcase trials held in late May and early June, 1814. The attorney general and the court agreed that a few of the guilty should be spared. After weighing facts and petitions for mercy, eight of the fifteen suffered the prescribed punishment outside the military camp at Burlington Heights, 20 July 1814.[5]

James Durand is another who exemplifies the complex reactions of settlers to the war. Moreover, as an owner of what emerged as the Hamilton townsite, he ties together events in the years prior to its founding. Durand arrived at Montreal in early 1802 on behalf of London merchants who instructed him to press for the unsettled accounts of a group of mills and an iron forge on the Niagara River near Chippawa. Durand seized the works and decided to purchase the operation. Seeking a proper seat from which to supervise his enterprises, Durand began to acquire parcels of land in Lot 14, Concession 3, Barton Township. The

Bellevue was constructed for James Durand in 1805 or 1806. It was here that he hosted General Isaac Brock on the latter's journey to attack Fort Detroit in 1812. In 1815, Bellevue became the home of George Hamilton.

farm and the house that he built there in 1805 presented an attractive location and a well-situated base for commerce, close to a line of settlement leading from Lake Ontario toward the Grand River and Norfolk areas. He also speculated in additional land in Barton Township, securing fourteen acres in Lot 14, Concession 2, from Nathaniel Hughson in 1809. Together Hughson and Durand promoted Lot 14 as the site for a courthouse if a new district were formed.[6]

The War of 1812 presented Durand with shifting circumstances. The 1812 victories at Detroit and Queenston represented a high point. At the latter battle, Captain James Durand had commanded a flank company of the Lincoln Regiment. Within a year, tolerance for the conflict wore thin. War lingered and disrupted life in the areas where Durand had business interests. The flow of American settlers, essential to trade and land activities, had stopped. In the winter of 1813-1814, Durand had to billet troops. Soldiers camped in the Barton fields burned the rail fences for firewood and confiscated supplies. Durand did not escape the nearly universal damages. Aware of legal transgressions, distressed by mercantile upsets, and witnessing ruin inflicted on neighbours, he criticized the conduct of the war. Since Abraham Markle had defected to the American side, a vacancy existed in the assembly. Durand, standing as a candidate critical of the conduct of the military, was elected to the seat and entered the assembly in February, 1815. Speaking out in the midst of a garrison community intensified friction in Durand's daily affairs. "Times," he was warned, "were too dangerous for a man to open his mouth."[7] Thus, worried about his freedom, James Durand completed the sale of his Barton farm to George Hamilton in early 1815 and fled to the Trent River area. The farm became the townsite that is the subject of this history.

CONTINUITY AND THEMES

The sketches of a few incidents and individuals in the early era are not directly related to the urban focus of this history. They serve to introduce the significance of the area's physical geography, its position as a crossroad for British and American influences, and the role of land speculation. These remained important constants. Hamilton itself was a late addition to the Burlington Bay settlements, established only in 1816.

The following chapters concern this late addition; they examine essential periods in the development of a middle-rank Canadian city. Each chapter treats shocks, cyclical events and structural changes. The War of 1812, for example, was a major shock. In subsequent periods wars would alter the Hamilton economy, impose burdens, and disrupt population developments such as immigration. Cyclical events include the pattern of economic expansion and subsequent collapse. They also encompass population fluctuations: the influx of immigrants in good times and the exodus of residents in depressions. A further cyclical sequence has involved efforts by Hamilton's business elite to break away from Toronto's metropolitan influence and the failure of these determined efforts. This contest has shaped Hamilton in ways that have distinguished it from other medium-rank Canadian cities. Structural changes pertain to profound alterations in the economic and cultural life of the city. They may be thought of as great silent transitions that traditional local history has covered with a thick layer of events. For instance, the conduct of business in Hamilton has evolved from locally organized partnerships to joint-stock companies to integrated corporations with their headquarters outside Hamilton. The urban economy also has been the setting for another structural change as local industrial activity grew and commerce became less identified with the city's intrinsic character. Finally, civic culture has been altered by structural change involving the electronic media and the automobile.

This history of a Canadian city also examines power and the degree to which capitalists shaped the economic, physical and certain cultural features of Hamilton. The city has matured in an era of capitalism; its civic leaders have included land developers, ambitious business promoters, merchants and manufacturers. Those who acted directly and forcefully upon the city building process shared a commitment to growth. In part, the leadership of self-interested sponsors of a growth ethic rested upon their control of the instruments of local influence or authority: land ownership, credit, employment and domination of public offices. As well as the many levers of influence affecting the livelihood of citizens, the makers and shakers of Hamilton often acted with a measure of public sanction because their interest in community expansion with its promise of jobs could be embraced by all social groups. In pressing for economic advantage for their city, the business elite of Hamilton realized notable entrepreneurial achievements. They also have been responsible for the urban and work environments, many of whose aspects can be criticized.

Of course, the picture of a city dominated by a business class is a simplistic one. The labouring classes of Hamilton have not always agreed with the designs of a governing class. Protests and working-class action have made Hamilton's history far more than a story of manipulation by groups that have commanded rental accommo-dations, employment and patronage — the high ground of civic power. In addition, this study of more than 150 years has enough scope to allow an evaluation of geographic determinism. The loca-tion within North America, the proximity to Toronto, the role of the bay and of the escarpment represent obvious geographic determinants. This account, therefore, assesses both geography and human agency.

Constructed between 1827 and 1832, the Gore District Courthouse made permanent Hamilton's status as district town.

Chapter One
Hamilton, Upper Canada: A Frontier Town, 1816–1841

During its first quarter century, the town of Hamilton possessed features peculiar to the establishment of North American frontier towns. Above all, there was marked instability in commerce and population growth. As a gateway for settlement and farm-service activities and as a new community without accumulations of local capital, Hamilton was vulnerable to uncontrollable forces including immigration, climate and international credit fluctuations. The cultural contacts with the United States, the origin of some residents and the nature of transportation developments and land speculation locate Hamilton on the urban frontier of the Great Lakes and Mississippi Valley regions. On the other hand, many of its commercial and cultural linkages extended to the United Kingdom, especially to Glasgow. Whereas Buffalo, Cleveland and Chicago initially were outposts for the American cities of the eastern seaboard, Hamilton was part of a far more extended trade empire managed by Scots. Moreover, the government of Hamilton — first by appointed justices of the peace and then by an elected board of police with relatively high property qualifications — ran counter to a populist democratic approach in American local government. Hamilton was not a full participant in the experiences of new urban development in the United States; on the other hand, it was not as British as Kingston and York/Toronto, for it had neither the garrison nor colonial capital establishments.

What all of these general observations suggest is that Hamilton was an emphatically commercial centre. The commercial status was a structural condition expressed in the efforts of leading Hamilton politicians and business figures. It accounted for population changes and the seasonality of urban life. The seasons imposed busy and quiet periods that were more pronounced than in the railway and industrial eras. But to state that Hamilton became a commercial town, particularly during the 1830s, does not adequately describe its situation. The wheat staple was essential to the economy of the more settled parts of Upper Canada, including Hamilton. "Yet when one tries to translate the considerable body of research that has been done on Upper Canada's wheat economy into a framework or model that explains the extent and the timing of Upper Canadian growth, one encounters difficulties."[1] Certainly the wheat economy does not provide a model explaining Hamilton's growth in the 1830s. Not only wheat, but a settlers'-effects economy — the supplying of household utensils and farm equipment — explains many attributes of frontier Hamilton.

THE FOUNDING OF HAMILTON

After the War of 1812, the new occupant of the Durand farm acted with vigour and influence when he promoted a town on his property. George Hamilton had far more potential for establishing a community than had Durand. The son of the Honourable Robert Hamilton of Queenston, George was clever and well connected. From the early 1790s until his death in 1809, his father had been a force to reckon with on the Niagara Peninsula. A partner in a trading firm with Richard Cartwright of Kingston, Robert managed the interior business while Cartwright handled transshipments at Kingston and negotiated with Montreal merchants.

In 1794, Robert Hamilton was a judge of the court of common pleas, a Member of the Legislative Council, lieutenant of the county of Lincoln and part owner of the two largest schooners on Lake Ontario. Cartwright and Hamilton also held the contract for supplying the king's troops with provisions, and a portion of their wealth came from outfitting Loyalist settlements. At his death, Robert was found to have amassed one hundred and thirty thousand acres of Upper Canadian land; 200 debtors owed him an astonishing £69,000 in New York currency.[2]

George resided at Queenston after his father's death and helped manage the business. Early in July, 1814, during the battles along the Niagara River, the Hamilton family's property went up in flames set "by accident by our Troops."[3] This loss and the assumption that war could persist during 1815 forced George Hamilton to consider relocating away from the border. Well placed, he surely knew about early efforts to create a new district with a judicial centre at the Head of the Lake. The matter had been discussed in February, 1812, at the Legislative Assembly. James Durand became a willing vendor. Both parties came into this land transaction due to the fortunes of war, so that Hamilton was born in conflict and fathered by a shrewd man of influence.

Within a year of purchase, George Hamilton reached an agreement with the owner of adjacent land to the north, Nathaniel Hughson. The two prepared a scheme to increase the possibility of having the courthouse and jail located on George Hamilton's land, to the benefit of values on both men's property. Hamilton offered to grant the Crown the land upon which these public buildings could be constructed. Hughson and Hamilton empowered James Durand to sell lots on what would become the townsite. Durand was still the local Member of the Legislative Assembly, and the offers that he had been instructed to circulate at York coincided with the deliberation of the Assembly and Legislative Council on the formation of the new district. The new Gore District embraced twenty townships, most of which would eventually comprise Halton and Wentworth counties and parts of Wellington and Brant counties. There is little doubt about Hamilton's origins transpiring amidst a complicated private affair involving Hamilton, Hughson and Durand.

George Hamilton's town plan showed an awareness of land-use principles; it was not a random strung-out arrangement like neighbouring mill towns such as Dundas and Ancaster. Hamilton behaved like the founders of contemporary towns from Upper Canada south through the Ohio and Michigan frontier. His design was not original. It lacked the flair expressed in the radial street patterns attempted by town founders in Buffalo and Detroit or later in Goderich and Guelph. In effect, Hamilton was founded by a land developer. In that sense, it differed in purpose and character from British North American centres established under the aegis of a government, military or religious authority. Hamilton was the first speculative townsite to evolve into a major Canadian city.[4]

Hamilton's grid plan gave purchasers nearly identical arrangements; eighty lots all had frontages of fifty feet. Each faced a major street and backed onto a twelve-foot lane. All blocks had eight lots, with four placed on corners. As potential commercial sites, locations for shops, law offices or inns, none of the parcels had an inferior appearance. To this original core, Hamilton added more blocks around 1828-29 when construction on a permanent courthouse and the Burlington Canal brightened land-sale prospects. This time with assistance from land-surveyor Lewis Burwell, George Hamilton ordered the lot frontages to correspond to a presumed flow of trade. He added a market square, intending to strengthen commercial activity on his property.

Between 1816 and 1830, there were two phases to land sales on the Hamilton townsite and adjacent properties. An initial series of sales involved merchants, builders and speculators. To the west of the town, James Mills and Peter Hess purchased over 500 acres in 1817. Decades passed before their land was fully occupied with structures, but along with George Hamilton and Nathaniel Hughson they were the pioneer land developers. Sales fell off drastically during the depression of the early 1820s, although Peter Hunter Hamilton, George's half-brother, bought over 100 acres on the western edge in 1823. He would dispose of lots during the 1830s. From the mid-1820s forward, property sales increased with tradesmen, merchants, investors and lawyers settling around a courthouse.[5]

The district town did not immediately become the dominant centre in the Gore District. Only in the early 1820s was a temporary jail constructed. It was not until 1832 that a cut-stone jail and courthouse opened on Prince's Square, one of the two squares created in 1816. Significantly, the decision to construct a permanent public building was made while George Hamilton was a Member of the Legislative Assembly. Peter Hunter Hamilton received the contract for this work and hired a former Yorkshire mason to carry out the construction. The mason also built a home for Peter Hunter Hamilton in 1830. These details render an impression of a new community which in its first decade had aspects of a family affair, yielding opportunities and patronage for the Hamiltons. The courthouse attracted a handful of law offices; the earliest of these belonged to Robert Berrie and Allan MacNab. The latter hung out his shingle in 1826. Applying know-

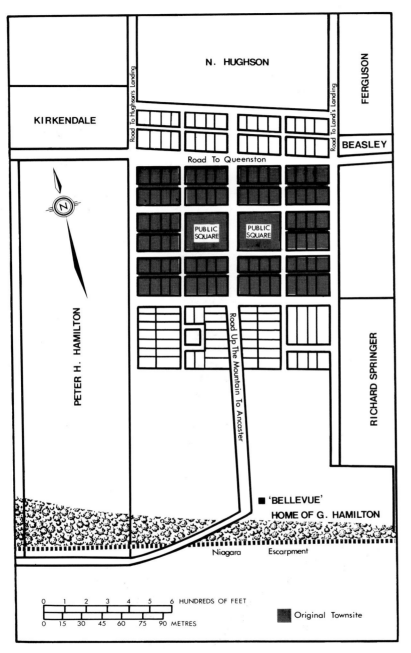

1 Major Property Owners and George Hamilton's Townsite, 1816-1829.

ledge of realty gained when acting as a land agent for the Hon. Henry Boulton of York, MacNab soon had a roaring land-agency business.[6]

A planned village where documents could be registered, law-breakers committed and courts convened, Hamilton was no hive of commerce and milling; the assizes only gave minor boosts to trade and hostelry. Industrial and commercial initiative during the 1820s originated around the mill seats and lakeshore wharves where men of drive truly managed settlements — men like Peter Desjardins and James Durand of Dundas, Job Lodor of Ancaster, James Crooks of West Flamborough, William Johnson Kerr of Burlington Bay and William Chisholm of Oakville. Most petitions for internal improvements originated from these Gore millers and merchants. They provided the district with its clusters of economic activity and lay leadership in congregations; they held district offices. Having interior land holdings and being engaged in commerce, their zeal in building up the population and amenities of the Gore District derived from self-interest.

A wish to strengthen development led several into opposition to the government. In 1817, James Durand, Richard Hatt, Richard Beasley and over sixty of "the principal farmers and gentlemen of leisure" associated themselves with the protest movement of Robert Gourlay, which presented demands for actions to hasten settlement. The Gourlay meetings implied that government resources had favoured a few individuals and that not enough had been done to serve the colony's development. The calling of assemblies by Gourlay's supporters came at a sensitive time when the British government perceived protest assemblies at home as tantamount to revolution. A new lieutenant-governor, Sir Peregrine Maitland, took heed of appeals for advancing settlement but cracked down on the Gourlay movement itself. Richard Beasley, selected president of a Gourlay convention, subsequently lost public offices. Interestingly, George Hamilton, as an advocate of greater zeal in the development of Upper Canada and as a cousin of Robert Gourlay, was likewise involved in sponsoring the Gourlay movement, attending the convention and defending its right to assemble.[7]

From 1820 to 1830, George Hamilton as the Member of the Legislative Assembly supported improvement schemes proposed by Burlington Bay community leaders. He was one of the colony's foremost advocates of measures to liberate commerce and land

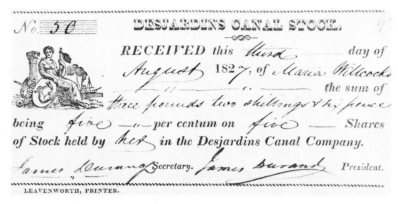

The Desjardins Canal, a notable example of an early joint-stock company, failed to raise Dundas into a commercial rival of Hamilton.

settlement. This does not mean that local merchants and millers were united on every scheme for development. Dundas and Halton County criticized the bestowal of funds for public buildings on the upstart townsite of Hamilton. Moreover, in 1821 the men of commerce and milling from the Dundas area began to discuss a transportation venture that would expressly benefit their enterprises. The driving force behind the project was Peter Desjardins. A former clerk to James Durand and Richard Hatt, he possessed a keen appreciation for the difficulties of getting bulky exports like flour, salted pork and lumber from the interior down to the lakeshore. Virtually on his own, Desjardins pursued a solution with paltry resources. In November, 1820, he had petitioned for and received a grant of land in the Coote's Paradise marsh that extended from Burlington Bay to Dundas "for the purpose of extending the . . . channel by cutting a Canal."

Thus began a tale of woe. The timing was inauspicious. Desjardins commenced his project in an era of chronic shortage of hard currency. From 1821 to 1823, the flour trade suffered a drastic reversal. Desjardins's resources fell short of the task, and after three years he was circulating a prospectus in order to draw in more capital. Until the 1820s, such ventures were financed by partnership and loan arrangements. By an Act of Incorporation, 30 January 1826, the Desjardins Canal Company became a joint-stock operation. Subscription books were kept at certain designated locations; investors could pledge a purchase of stocks, immediately paying an instalment on the face value of the certif-

icate. The remaining fractions were paid off in instalments, called in whenever the company required capital. Thereby the Desjardins Canal ceased being only a Dundas concern.[8]

The company officers over the years — William Chisholm, James Durand and Allan MacNab — came from the Head of the Lake elite, but important York investors also were drawn into the scheme. William Warren Baldwin and family came into the company in 1827; few Upper Canadians could match his prestige and influence. So the canal company was both a daring local commercial scheme and a pioneer joint-stock venture. The recent triumph of New York's Erie Canal served as a powerful example of commercial empire building. Thus at a public meeting in 1829, Desjardins advocates and local boosters envisioned a canal to the Grand River and a link with Lake Huron.

Within two years such dreams had been replaced with anxiety. There commenced a twenty-year period during which the "long frog marsh" swallowed private and public money. From the 1827 death of Peter Desjardins onward, investors bickered over construction contracts and remuneration for running the concern. All the same, investors like Baldwin had to answer the company's appeals or see it fail. In 1836, Baldwin was requested to exercise his political influence in securing a government grant, but the enhanced capital and political leverage of a joint-stock operation could not clear a lasting channel through silt. Moreover, a shallow and sheltered slip of water was of little use to lake schooners that could penetrate Burlington Bay by 1827. The failure of the Desjardins Canal coincided with the beginnings of a new commercial order that favoured Hamilton as the district town in fact as well as name.[9]

THE ECONOMY OF A FRONTIER BOOM TOWN

The promotion of the early townsite had little in common with the boom-town society of the 1830s. Transition from modest courthouse village to a centre of renown drew comments from travellers. British adventurer Edward Talbot could pass around the head of Lake Ontario in 1818 and record nothing about George Hamilton's fledgling townsite. Talbot described Dundas, Ancaster and Burford as "the only places, which from the multitude of their inhabitants, bear the least resemblance to villages."[10] As late as 1829, the roughly half-dozen farms that would comprise the town were "all in a partly cultivated state. Only a few lots had been sold off."[11]

Neglect was over by 1832 when the founder of the Grand River community of Elora, William Gilkison, wrote to his son Jasper, who worked in Hamilton as a merchant's clerk. The father commented enthusiastically on "thy celebrated town of Hamilton."[12] Montreal merchants and shippers considered it to be a superior transshipment point for serving the Upper Canadian settlement frontier. Methodists moved the centre of their work from Ancaster, settling their minister into "a convenient parsonage situated in Hamilton" in 1832.[13] Incorporation as a town followed in January, 1833. In sum, the courthouse village had sprung to life in a manner common to townsites along the North American frontier.

Emigration following the Napoleonic wars, the advance of the settlement frontier, transportation improvements and townsite promotion had joined to proliferate United States boom towns. Hamilton's growth was affected by similar circumstances. The community's situation within the British Empire, important in certain legal, political and cultural regards, makes Hamilton's initial period of expansion somewhat different from the growth of Buffalo, Cleveland, Detroit, Chicago and Milwaukee. Lake ports handling settlers' effects, the American cities flourished as intermediaries between Atlantic ports and a western agricultural frontier; they attracted a diverse population. Not just grain or timber exports but the influx of people and demands for household effects generated initial growth and defined the early urban society.

Hamilton's prospects and influence were oriented to the southwest, away from other settlements along Lake Ontario. Unlike Kingston and York, with their pre-1815 origins and garrison or government functions, Hamilton's instant society lacked the visible props of a United Kingdom presence. Trade, of course, long had had an American association. Yankee peddlers made their way to the Head of the Lake. Local merchants occasionally had falsified manifests in order to import without paying full customs duties.[14] The connections with Lewiston, Rochester, Oswego and ultimately New York coexisted with links to York, Kingston and Montreal.

Nonetheless, the mercantile credit source for Hamilton was more likely to have been Scotland than the United States.

American business connections extended to supplying capital and resources for industry. With rapid population increase, speculative excesses, grand commercial designs, young male population of diverse origins and a host of social problems, the boom town's ambience resembled that of sister towns and cities around the Great Lakes and down the Mississippi Valley. The Church of England, the Loyalty myths of the War of 1812, the patriot fervour of some community leaders, a courthouse establishment with ties to York and a certain envy of American material progress suggest that Hamilton was not entirely like the urban frontier of the United States. Americans were a portion of the Hamilton population, but they and vocal admirers of American progress like innkeeper "Yankee" Andrew Miller were regarded as different. In culture and political attitudes, Hamilton was not a carbon copy of a Buffalo or a Cleveland.

Hamilton was elevated into the paramount community southwest of York in little more than a decade from its founding. The essential consideration was location. The various mills as well as farm-service activities held limited potential for sustained and concentrated urban growth at Albion Mills, Ancaster, Dundas and Crooks' Hollow. Commerce, the organization of services and trades necessary for bulk movement of goods, was more likely to result in sustained urban development. The very factor which had made early village establishment feasible, the rugged streams, really impeded commercial advance. Mill sites lacked readily navigable connections with Lake Ontario. Even before the rise of Hamilton, regional commerce had concentrated on Burlington Bay. Miller and merchant Richard Hatt had leased government land on the Burlington Beach strip as early as 1802. Chief Joseph Brant and his heirs owned the property adjacent to the shallow natural outlet which opened onto Lake Ontario from Burlington Bay. In 1826, Brant's heirs described it as a highly valuable commercial tract. "Store Houses and Taverns were erected on the margin of the Outlet and made profitable returns in rent. — And land along the channel could have been readily sold for, from Three to Four hundred pounds an acre for the purposes of erecting Ware Houses, fishing Houses and Taverns." Forwarding agents processed outbound Durham-boat shipments of flour, pork, lard, potash and pearlash from this point. These goods were unloaded at the beach and transshipped to lake schooners. Inward shipments, bound for the landings on the southwest shore of Burlington Bay, occasionally cleared the sand bars and brought in salt, dry goods, utensils and luxury items. The value of imports appears to have exceeded that of exports.[15]

A surviving 1823 estimate of incoming traffic reported that approximately 100 boats under five tons entered the bay. The shallowness of the natural outlet limited capacity; hence, in the same year as this report on trade, there came the first merchants' appeal to open a canal. Petitioners James Crooks and William Chisholm had the ambition of trading in the western hinterland embracing the Thames River.[16] After completion of the canal, mercantile men would adopt steamboats as a commercial "open sesame" and form a local navigation company. In 1834, they pressed ahead with a proposal for a railway to London. In sum, the Burlington Bay merchant community not only embraced a booster enthusiasm like that of its American counterparts, but it did so with a parallel sequence of timing in promoting innovations in transportation. Hamilton gained from these efforts, for it was the one place where a relatively level shore met the bay. Further, it was reasonably close to where the Niagara Escarpment broke down into the Ancaster Hills. Through here teamsters could haul supplies to the Grand and Thames river regions. The locational advantages for trade at Hamilton exceeded those of its senior neighbours.

Actual construction of a Burlington canal went ahead by fits and starts. Work on a large scale commenced in the spring of 1825. Getting the canal into operating condition was difficult. Local investors operated with credit, not cash. As the Desjardins Canal was demonstrating, they could not afford to sponsor canal work. Internal improvements such as canals, roads and, later, railways required such large outlays of capital that financing efforts typically involved individuals, local government and the colonial government. This system of mixed enterprise was common throughout North America. The mixed nature of financing and of administration created problems. Conflicts among canal commissioners, the colonial government and the contractor, as well as engineering problems and cost overruns, delayed the opening of a channel until 1827. Piers required immediate reconstruction and the routine repairs and dredging would annoy steamboat operators into the mid-1840s. Nonetheless, trade with the southwest flourished. Consequently, north of the original townsite, the new community of Port Hamilton took form. The government of

Upper Canada and the Canada Company had anticipated a different turn of events and tentatively prepared a townsite on Burlington Beach; it was named Port Huskisson. However, the canal, along with steamboat ventures, roads and massive immigration, created a turbulent and economically vulnerable boom town which did not conform to government design.[17]

A steamboat craze flourished during the 1820s and 1830s, coinciding with the flurry of North American canal schemes. The first steamboat on Lake Ontario was launched in 1819, and by 1825 service began locally as steamboat whistles sounded at Burlington Beach twice a week. Later, with a canal finished, they churned into the bay itself. To guarantee service to Hamilton, the bay area merchants took another initiative. In October, 1831, William Chisholm, the founder of Oakville, Job Lodor, the leading Ancaster merchant, and Hamilton businessmen Allan MacNab and Colin Ferrie sponsored a meeting to form a company that would place a boat on a York, Hamilton and Niagara run. Their action represented the further use of the joint-stock corporation. Soon many of the same men met at the courthouse to discuss incorporating a bank. By the summer of 1833, the boat company operated a vessel on a Rochester-Hamilton route, tapping into the emigrant traffic on the Erie Canal. Concurrently, William Johnson Kerr, a War of 1812 hero, Burlington Canal Commissioner and merchant, secured a modest stern-wheel steamer that had failed in its Rideau Canal operation. It began to make trips to York in 1833. Using a high-pressure engine, Kerr's vessel, *John By*, roasted its passengers. In August of the next year, William Chisholm commenced daily runs on the same route with his *Oakville*. There were several significant points about the local steamboat ventures. First, such enterprises required government aid in the form of canal funds. Second, investors identified business aims with the advance of the community. They expected profits from freight and passengers, but they also regarded steamboats as necessary for promoting their community and thereby enhancing commerce and land speculation.[18]

Events inland also benefited the Hamilton economy. Crude statistics indirectly connect the growth of Hamilton with the settlement of its hinterland. From the end of the Napoleonic wars, the Gore District's settlement frontier shifted from lakeshore townships to ones further inland, particularly in the Grand River Valley. The decline of sawmills in Ancaster Township, eleven in

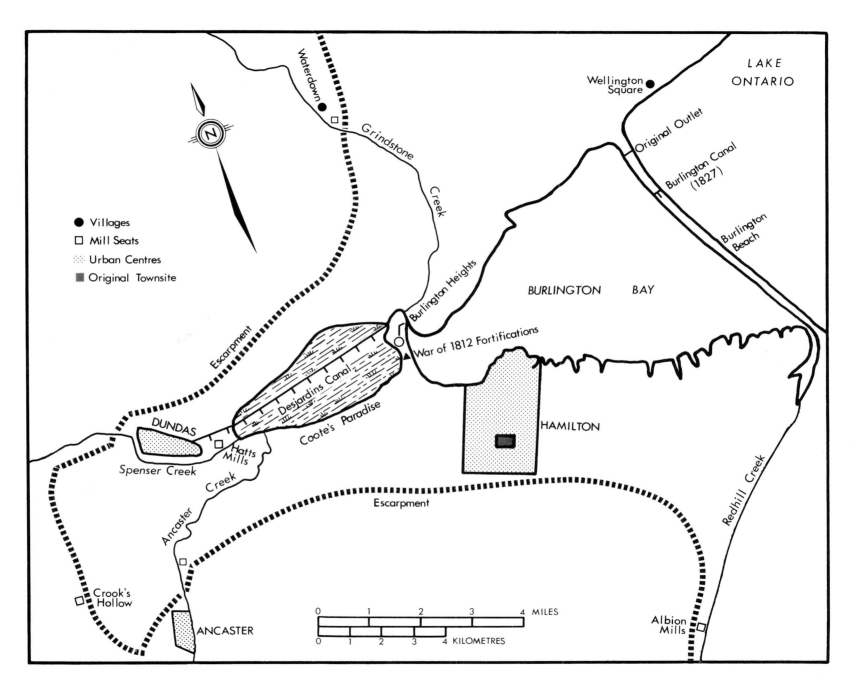

2 The Head of the Lake, c. 1835.

*"If a vessel was to be built for roasting passengers the **John By** might have furnished useful hints."* The high-pressure engine made
William Johnson Kerr's vessel unpopular on the run between Toronto and Burlington Bay.

1819 and six in 1834, taken into account with the appearance of new mills in Dumfries and Waterloo (nine and twelve respectively in 1834), indicated shifting land clearance. Townships like Dumfries had remarkable growth. Hamilton's rates of population also increased during the period, hinting at an association between interior lands with their new villages and the rise of the port on Burlington Bay. Brantford, Paris and Galt, boom towns in their own right, served as outposts for the mercantile houses, artisan shops and manufacturers setting up in Hamilton. The hinterland is likely to have extended to Woodstock.

It was the operation of importers and manufacturers along with the structure of credit that linked Hamilton to the villages and farms to the west. Emigrant guidebooks cautioned settlers against carting their furnishings and personal effects, advising that they make purchases upon reaching their destination. Help from the old country, meagre savings, credit and wages enabled the purchase of settlers' effects. Necessary funds were sometimes obtained by inheritance or by the family in the old country helping to sponsor a member's emigration.

A common method for acquiring capital was by employment as a farm labourer. Teams of choppers were in demand around the Gore District. Farmers and land speculators had to clear land to satisfy the Crown's settlement requirements. A good chopper cleared an acre a week, for which he received eight to fifteen dollars, depending on the terrain. Harvest labour was hired by the day, while some farm labourers were taken on for eight or ten months. Payment varied according to whether the terms of employment called for board and lodging. Unmarried labourers probably saved a share of their money wages. Urban employment and work on roads and navigation improvements also allowed for some savings, but necessities were expensive in the towns and so were "entertainments" — gambling, drink and brothels. The seasonal character of rural employment and the expense of town life often frustrated the labourer's pursuit of the savings to launch him as a farmer. Rural and urban opportunities and limitations, not to mention the yearly economic fluctuations, kept some of the Gore District population churning about in a quest for better situations. Whatever an emigrant's personal struggle for employment and savings, his reliance on the goods and credit of the general merchant was a certainty. The general merchants eventually were replaced by specialized merchandising, but until midcentury the general merchants were a link between rural settlement and Hamilton.[19]

During the 1830s and 1840s, Hamilton beckoned as an Upper Canada site with great advantage for merchants keen to outfit a swelling population. Montreal merchant Adam Ferrie, whose experiences as a Glasgow capitalist added weight to his sense of where opportunities lay, recounted how he and other Montreal traders rushed agents down to Hamilton in the 1830s. In 1835, Isaac Buchanan, extending the family's Glasgow operation into Upper Canada, decided to open a Hamilton store, joining those run by Colin Ferrie, John Young and Samuel Mills. In 1840, during a depression, Buchanan had enough trust in Hamilton's future to take out a lease on a large brick establishment constructed by Samuel Mills. Until that decision, Colin Ferrie's white clapboard store was the largest commercial house. By 1830, Ferrie kept a branch store in Brantford; in 1833, he purchased another in Waterloo. The next year he opened one in Nelson. Like his fellow merchants, Colin Ferrie offered credit and accepted barter payments of lumber, potash or farm produce. Samuel Mills advanced his shelter and construction enterprises by advertising that he would accept lumber in trade. Typical of a frontier town, Hamilton's commercial affairs were a matter of improvised exchange.[20]

Judging from the character and volume of activity at the Gore Courthouse, rural defaulting on mercantile debts was pervasive even in good times. Allan MacNab, William Notman and George Tiffany, the area's prominent lawyers, were busy enough to have the printers supply them with blank forms. By illustration, from October to December, 1835, seventy-five of these summons forms came into the hands of the court clerk. One complaint, a sample of the kind, contained a list of the purchases made from Colin Ferrie. In January, 1835, John Vollick had procured the following from the store at Nelson: pots, plates, knives, forks, spoons, cups, bowls, blankets, ticking, food items and minor luxuries like tobacco. Learning that Vollick had difficulties and knowing that spring thaw inaugurated the moving season, Ferrie filed for court action in April. It was a feature of colonial society to have many would-be settlers fleeing from indebtedness. Creditors routinely stated concern about debtors departing Upper Canada or being "concealed within." Flight and concealment seemed sensible actions, better than a debtor's cell, where roughly 1,000 Gore residents spent time during the 1830s.[21]

The merchant group, embracing marginal operators who teetered on a slim credit base and fear of defaulting clients, had its own men on the run. An anecdote of the era tells of a man who failed to meet his debts. His neighbours sympathized, but he laughed "pity my creditors." Farm failure tipped over the first domino, and not long after rural crises the town merchants faced lean times. Shopkeeper J.M.A. Cameron wrote to his acquaintance William Lyon Mackenzie in 1830 and humorously recounted his six weeks in the debtor's cell. Interestingly, failure did not completely tarnish his reputation. Cameron expected to be engaged "as a Poll Clerk for the Sherriff [sic] at the election having acted twice with him in that capacity before he is extremely desirous that I should act again."[22] A man with friends, Cameron did not flee, but others did. The packed boxes in Thomas Baker's shop in 1840 tipped a friend. "I did not learn from him that he was about to abscond but I did suspect it."[23] Debt and inability to cover outstanding demands need not have brought irreparable disgrace, especially for men of public station having a coterie of associates, lodge and militia comrades. Moreover, it was a rare merchant who would have been exclusively a debtor or creditor. A merchant who found himself short likely had the bad fortune to be caught with delinquent accounts and could not liquidate stock or land fast enough to bridge the hard times.

A quest for status could exacerbate crisis. Adam Ferrie, remarking in the depression year of 1838 on son Colin's new estate of Westlawn, warned another son that "the cost of it and furniture, and living like the House requires will keep him from ever becoming a rich man."[24] Colin Ferrie had succumbed to a competition for prestigious display, with Allan MacNab as his aggressive rival. The latter had coveted land on Burlington Heights and, when complex financial circumstances forced Richard Beasley to sell his farm there in 1832, MacNab tenaciously pursued the property.[25] By 1834, Allan MacNab had begun construction of Dundurn Castle. Married to a daughter of Richard Beasley, Ferrie had to assert position and family pride with Westlawn, constructed adjacent to Dundurn. Prestige of domicile eroded the assets of both men.

For all of these considerations — the nature of commerce, luck, display — the indebtedness of Hamilton's town fathers, and even their occasional embarrassment, formed accepted and recognized circumstances of frontier business. No less a figure than Peter Hunter Hamilton, half-brother of George, found himself over-extended in 1834-35 due to his land, iron forge and Desjardins Canal speculations. Unlike Ferrie and MacNab, both of whom had brushes with collapse, Peter Hunter Hamilton was brought closer to the brink. Because he lacked liquid assets, creditors placed all his household goods up for auction.[26] Notoriously indebted, Allan MacNab kept his head above water by juggling loans, pleading for extensions and leaning on associates. Crises for MacNab, a land jobber, came when settlers or town residents who had purchased property from him could not meet payments. Demands for payments of his debts followed hard upon announcements of his public honours. William Notman of Dundas congratulated MacNab "on the distinguished honor our young and virgin queen has conferred upon you...now for business." Notman held £417 in outstanding notes; the year was 1838 and times were hard. Notman's request had a hint of panic: "let me hear from you on the subject; will you?"[27]

Sheer prevalence of debt built a certain immunity against despair, especially among men familiar with the conduct of affairs on the frontier and able to count upon sympathetic colleagues. Sales of land and supplies to settlers entailed the risks of credit extension for both vendor and client, but to describe this only as an economic fact would be to ignore an emotional dimension exaggerating frontier lifestyles. For the immigrant, anonymity extended possibilities for escape. This worked for a few lesser merchants too, while major operators relied upon the building of contacts in political, social and business circles to cushion a fall. Isolation and transiency on the one hand and gregarious outreach toward respectability on the other — these extremes defined preparations for handling possible collapse.

At their most complex, mercantile activities involved unloading cargo, sorting contents, auctioning, advertising, cartage and recording transactions. The considerable handling involved with imports, more likely to be concentrated at one point than was the moving of bulky staples like grain, pearlash and lumber, had employment potential. Grain and the highly regarded local flour were handled through Hamilton, but along with lumber they were high-bulk items that did not require special care in shipping. Thus small lake schooners could pick them up along the Lake Ontario shore, which was amply provided with inlets and docks.

Settlers' effects required care and occupied stevedores, ware-

Son of a respected but deeply indebted government officer, Allan MacNab (1788-1862) yearned for the stature of a Scottish Laird. Dundurn Castle, a Regency mansion in the romantic Italianate style, was central to his fantasy, but also to his many financial problems.

house labourers, clerks, printers and teamsters. Each had pleasures, frustrations and manners related to their work. Some clerks entered service by the intercession of a father who wanted a son to gain experience before taking over a family enterprise. William Gilkison placed his son Jasper with Colin Ferrie. What Jasper learned about credit — who to trust, how to establish contacts — would serve him later as a land agent and in his promotion of railways in the 1840s. Clerks had a social cachet, but there were tensions with employers. Clerks were driven hard in this commercial boom town. As a young gentleman, Jasper Gilkison was irked that his New Year's Day responsibilities prevented courtesy calls. In 1840, the clerks petitioned the town to have the bell rung at 7:00 p.m. to guarantee a uniform closing time and deter merchants from working them longer than prescribed. Town council refused.[28]

Not genteel aspirants, teamsters present a contrast to the clerks. With a salt-of-the-earth reputation, "Paddy the Driver" could entertain or offend. Strong language accompanied a task that suffered slow-witted animals, fellow drivers and abysmal street and road conditions. That so many drivers were Irish struck English visitors as the basis for the frequency of oaths, "a profusion of 'Ochs,' 'murderers,' and 'spalpeens.'" Street contact between teamsters and ladies were occasioned by the locations of Hamilton's winter firewood market on Main Street. A plank crosswalk with heavy pedestrian traffic conflicted with wagon movement. An 1843 complaint specified "the annoyance to which pedestrians especially females crossing the sidewalk are exposed from the rudeness and incivility of the Teamsters."[29] Both clerks and teamsters were typical elements in a swelling commercial population; both were worked long hours in difficult circumstances. Culturally, they were worlds apart and so were their prospects.

A few awkward settlers' effects had to be constructed locally, including furniture, wagons, farm implements and stoves. A commonplace durable, the stove, had a propitious influence on Hamilton's long association with the iron trade. It established another precise connection between settlement and concentrated urban growth. Introduced in western Europe in the late eighteenth century, the cast-iron stove provided enormous advantages. For heating efficiency, it exceeded the fireplace and cooked food as well. Not exactly a necessity, it figured prominently on a list of immigrant purchases. Hamilton acquired several stove warehouses. During the mid-1830s, iron merchant and pattern maker Alexander Carpenter may have stocked as many as 1,000 at a time; Daniel MacNab, another 500 and ten tons of iron bar for country blacksmiths. At first, the stove trade involved merchants who shipped in the assembled stoves or assembled the plates, bolts, rods and sheet metal supplied by various manufacturers in the United States, the forge at Trois Rivières, and the Normandale Upper Canada ironworks. Typical of stove manufacturers throughout North America, Alexander Carpenter shifted away from mere assembly of imported parts and designed an improved model. Altogether, five patents on improved stoves were taken out by Hamilton founders between 1832 and 1844. Peter Hunter Hamilton, who had a hand in most development ventures, had plunged into an ironworks at Norwich in the expectation of serving Hamilton's iron requirements. Pig iron, as Peter Hunter Hamilton recognized, had a growing market in town as the stove trade evolved from assembling parts to casting plates, parts for stoves, steamboats, farm machinery and water pumps. Flexibility fitted diverse needs in a settlement region.

The stove was not the sole item of early local manufacture that illustrated the international reach of iron technology. The threshing machine, like the stove, was a practical convenience purchased by established settlers. When farm acreage in wheat was small, the grain was stored in a barn and threshing postponed until winter. Hired hands and family members flailed, separating kernels from the straw. Storage of wheat for the winter was accompanied by loss from insects and rodents; it also meant a crucial delay in marketing. Threshing machines, owned by larger farmers or by teams which undertook custom threshing, grew into a near necessity during the 1830s and 1840s. Simple machines, hand- or horse-powered, had probably appeared in Scotland as early as the 1780s. A few crude beating devices were used in the United States at least as early as the 1820s. To clean the grain, another implement, the fanning mill, came into use on a few American farms during the 1820s.

Inventive activity concerned with these two iron machines became noteworthy after 1830 with manufacturers contributing to design innovations. John Fisher of Batavia, New York, and Joseph Janes of Rochester were such enterprising mechanics.

Moving to Hamilton in 1835, they set up a small furnace. Fisher discovered that he did not have sufficient capital to keep the foundry in operation. His remedy for the limited cash flow and high overhead — appealing to his cousin Calvin McQuesten — pointed toward urban growth as a function of external injections of capital and not just local revenues generated by staple exports. A partnership was formed among Fisher, Janes and McQuesten. The partnership specified that the furnace could be used in manufacturing various kinds of castings. Plows and threshing machines were the main products, but stoves and pumps were also produced in the late 1830s.

During the first few years of the partnership, Fisher resided in Hamilton and operated the foundry. McQuesten remained at Brockport tending to his pharmacy, but also recruiting skilled labour, purchasing parts and helping Fisher to secure supplies of iron and coal. Coal shipments came through the New York centres of Oswego and Lewiston; iron often arrived from Ogdensburg, Rochester and Ohio. The best iron came from Scotland and was shipped as ballast. Patterns and skilled labour were brought in from the American iron-foundry centres along the Erie Canal. By the early 1840s, the enterprise achieved stability. In 1857 McQuesten would turn over the business to his nephews Luther, Samuel and Stephen Sawyer. What began as a boom-town foundry would develop as the Sawyer-Massey Company.

The early foundries altered names because of frequent partnership reorganizations. Not until the post-Confederation decades did foundries become organized as joint-stock companies. Bank, insurance, canal and railway companies were organized much earlier as joint-stock companies and received government charters because they were considered to be enterprises in the public interest, serving the community. Foundries were more explicitly private affairs. Foundry operators and owners were not necessarily the same people. Owners secured capital from an assemblage of friends and relatives, not from the impersonal sale of shares. Investors and craftsmen moved into and out of partnerships in reaction to death, retirement and financial crises. These partnerships were typically limited to a specific time period, at the end of which a settling of accounts among partners was made.

The same factors that had brought the McQuesten-Fisher foundry to Hamilton — an expanding agricultural hinterland and proximity to the New York State iron-trade centres — would attract other American foundrymen. In December, 1842, Edward and Charles Gurney arrived after having been trained in Utica. Eventually a few employees left these pioneer furnaces and organized their own shops: James Stewart (1845); Burrow, Stewart and Milne (1864); Copp Brothers (1867). The early success of foundries operated by Carpenter, Fisher and the Gurney brothers initiated cumulative growth in the iron trades.[30]

By 1837, Hamilton's first great boom, replete with an atmosphere of vigour, risk and deceit necessary for promotion, came crashing down. There was more than one reason for the crash. Apprehension in the United Kingdom that credit extended to North American private and public ventures had gone too far set fiscal arrangements tumbling. In the financial panic, the government of Upper Canada's banker, Thomas Wilson and Company, went under and took with it assets which the colony had held on deposit. The colonial debt, limited revenue and the panic meant that one of the ambitions of the Hamilton elite, a railway from Burlington Bay to London, had to be set aside. The initial step to organize a company was taken in 1834 and rewarded in early 1837 with passage of a bill of incorporation. On 1 March 1837, the town's houses were illuminated in celebration; "a large Cannon" was produced for the occasion and everything was "in preparation for a great demonstration of joy." Pride had preceded the fall. Funding for existing public works also dried up; turnpike and canal work was halted. Contractors were compelled to dismiss their employees. Many departed to work on canals in Michigan and Illinois. Merchants and land jobbers were forced to press payment of accounts, causing many farmers to lose property through foreclosure or to flee from their debts.[31]

In the countryside the distress had begun even before the 1837 panic. The 1836 crop had not been good. Food prices had soared. Meetings around the Gore District deplored the "enormous price" of grain. Some attributed it to distillation of "ardent spirits"; others blamed exportation. Three hundred Hamilton residents signed a petition warning the government of possible starvation conditions. The fiscal, agrarian and political setbacks had immediate commercial and land-sale implications that claimed a wide circle of local victims in an international liquidity crisis. Allan MacNab's Port Hamilton lots came back to him as purchasers defaulted. All businessmen scraped to secure the hard cash to meet obligations. William Johnson Kerr, well practised in posturing as a loyal Indian chief, appealed to the Trustees of the Indian Fund to grant him a £1,500 loan. Colin Ferrie suffered losses when his country clients defaulted. He cleared stock by discount sales and disposed of his country stores. The newspaper columns, once filled with advertisements for businesses and requests for labourers, now contained announcements of distress sales and sheriff's auctions.[32]

THE POPULATION OF A FRONTIER TOWN

Until 1834, the town's population was not recorded separately from that of Barton Township. Therefore it is impossible to accurately determine the rate of growth before the first town census in 1834. It appears that there was modest growth from 1816 to 1821, followed by stagnation until 1827. From 1827 to 1831, Barton's population rose by 25 per cent, likely a reflection of the commercial activity generated by the Burlington Canal and the arrival of newcomers. The urban population increase of 133 per cent from 1834 to 1837 was most definitely due to new arrivals.

From the immense emigration out of the British Isles came an impetus for urban growth, the character and conflicting values of the town's workforce and the burdens that had to be borne by an unprepared local government. Unskilled Irish formed a definite element; literate and skilled artisans with sophisticated outlooks came too. So did Americans who recognized an opportunity for their trades or capital. It is impossible to establish the proportions of national groups among Hamilton's residents. Jail records and a census of religious denominations in 1839 reveal something about the mix. From 1831 to 1833, jail committals indicate a plurality of Americans; from 1834 forward the plurality was Irish. The census, taken in a year of recession, did not portray the Hamilton of growth years. Still, Roman Catholics were 15 per cent of the population, while in the surrounding townships they were merely 7 per cent. These meagre facts show the Irish to be visible especially after 1832-33.[33]

In Ireland tenant farmers and their labourers, neither of whom had security of tenure, were the victims of the post-1815 fall in the price of grain. Landowners substituted pasture for tillage. Equally important, Ireland's population had risen remarkably. Independently, or assisted by societies and landlords, Irish tenants and subtenants emigrated. The population movement that affected Hamilton owed much to actions taken to channel the Irish. One emigration agent, Englishman William Cattermole, had resided in Upper Canada for several years before returning to the United Kingdom in 1830. The Canada Company sponsored his tour and arranged for publication of his 1831 lectures, *Emigration: The Advantages of Emigration to Canada*. All in all, Cattermole claimed responsibility for superintending the passage of 6,000 to Canada on British vessels. As he departed from England in March, 1832, he was accompanied by 700 or 800 passengers due to arrive at the opening of the St. Lawrence navigation season. The bulk of these newcomers continued on to York. Only 100 were thought to have been English; the remainder were Irish. Upon his return to Upper Canada, Cattermole settled in Hamilton, where he operated the Cambrian House hotel in conjunction with a land office and employment agency, where labourers paid fees for having their names listed.[34]

The backgrounds and routes taken by newcomers cannot be reduced to confining description. George Martin, a Hamilton carpenter in the late 1830s, departed England in 1834 and landed at New York. He travelled by steamer to Albany, by railway from Albany to Schenectady, on a canal barge to Rochester, and from there to Cobourg via a steamer. Toward the end of this costly journey, Martin and family ate one meal a day and slept in a Genesee warehouse.[35] Rather than incurring the many charges of Martin's route, thousands landed at Quebec and took cheap river and lake boats, like those of McPherson, Crane and Company of Montreal who kept a wharf at Hamilton. Open Durham boats were inexpensive, but as a Hamilton journalist outlined, the trip inflicted hardship. "Densely packed and exposed to the scorching sun by day and mists and cold by night," passengers could not depend on a scheduled arrival at Hamilton, "the place where the Tide of Emigration may be said to break."[36] Newcomers had to trust weather and boatmen. Storms were an obvious hazard, but being caught in a calm was also a problem. Steam vessels rescued stranded boats and levied a towing charge. As for boatmen, they were abusive characters. An emigrant from County Kerry who arrived in Hamilton in 1831 announced his indignation. "Poverty and lawless depredation" were bad enough in Ireland, but he had suffered treatment by St. Lawrence boatmen "of the most brutal and barbarous description."[37]

The scale of the "tide" was astonishing, considering that Hamilton appeared as little better than a ramshackle town, barely capable of housing its extant population. The *Queenston*, in one landing in June, 1832, disembarked 140 passengers. That was likely an unusual incident. Typical lake schooners of under 100 tons could carry about 50 passengers; the modest steamers operating into Burlington Bay conveyed about twice that number during the peak of the emigrant season. Such an extraordinary time came between 17 June and 25 June 1833, when more than 300 newcomers landed. The seasonal swelling of population was evident in local records. The assessor recorded the September, 1834, population at 2,100. In May, 1835, the count reached 2,600. The difference between these figures showed the sudden spring onrush of newcomers.[38]

At Burlington Canal, wind-driven ice could clog the channel into April, forcing vessels to land passengers at Wellington Square. In whatever fashion this phase of the trek ended, the rush of people extended from April to July, an event recognized and welcomed by merchants and innkeepers. The first weeks of navigation brought new wares, but just as important as replenishing stock it was greeted as "the season for emigrants, which enlivens the towns and villages of this Province, and increases the circulation of money." Emigration figured as a critical ingredient in the growth ethic of Hamilton's promoters. They deplored tales of distress, fearing that rumours would frighten traffic. In the words of Hamilton's *Western Mercury*, "all will rejoice to see them [immigrants] except the grievance monger fraternity, who being opposed in every way to the prosperity of the country, represent them as paupers."[39] On one occasion the journal did admit to difficulties, mentioning that a few arrivals were "obliged [in 1831] to encamp at the edge of the lake, exposed to the night air and thunder showers."[40] Hamilton promoters essentially regarded arrivals from the same vantage point that they considered transportation measures — as an aspect of economic development.

Cholera came as one unhappy derivative of emigrant traffic. The disease, carried out of Asia by trade and army contact, had reached England in 1831. It crossed the Atlantic via emigrant ships, progressing westward from Quebec City during June, 1832. By July 7 cases were reported at Burlington Bay, and by July 21 there were several deaths in Hamilton. The crisis peaked in August. On one day early in August, seven people died. There was great difficulty in procuring persons to attend and bury the dead bodies. A temporary Board of Health met but could do little beyond preventing vessels from landing. An emergency hospital for the dying occupied an old War of 1812 barrack. The government of Upper Canada responded to York and Hamilton fears about the spread of disease from emigrants and the expense of keeping sick emigrants. One remedy was a scheme to employ emigrants in the countryside. From May 15 to December 31, 412 men laboured at road construction between the Credit River and Burlington Bay; 281 women and children were supported in nearby camps. Another epidemic struck in 1834. Hamilton again tried to meet the health crises by keeping "indigent strangers" beyond the town limits. The fear was not exactly that newcomers would spread the disease, for there was only a vague concept of contagion. Instead, many believed that cholera afflicted the dissolute as a punishment. A prohibition on strangers was meant to limit the town's welfare costs.[41]

Growth of Hamilton's population depended on continued immigration, a healthy rural economy, credit arrangements and a mood of optimism; the rebellions and depression upset each condition. Between mid-December, 1837, and mid-January, 1838, in response to the Upper Canadian uprisings, 125 Gore District residents were committed to the jail for high treason. In most cases, prisoners were pardoned or released. The roundup added to dissatisfaction. John Fisher's closest friend, Yankee merchant John Parker, was arrested for high treason, a fact that nearly caused Fisher to sell his foundry and return to Batavia. His wife Catherine wrote to the McQuestens about the persecution of Americans in 1838. "We are all very well, happy and contented and as pleasantly situated as we could desire if the patriots would only let us alone. We do hope and trust that we shall be no longer molested."[42]

For some, the situation was too oppressive to bear so patiently. It is impossible to determine the number of local people who left the colony for political reasons or in disgust; some certainly did, among them town clerk Charles Durand, who found the New York State and Chicago of his exile years sprinkled with former Canadians. New arrivals did not balance the loss of population from Upper Canada. Only about 3,000 emigrants landed at Quebec in 1838. Alarmed by an abrupt decline that affected Upper Canada as late as 1840, Lieutenant-Governor Sir George Arthur wrote Governor-General Charles Poulett Thomson. "I am anxious to inform you that not more than between 5 and 600 im-

An early and shrewd investor in land, James Mills (1774-1852) made his fortune in land development and as a landlord.

Christina Mills (1787-1867) raised a Hamilton mayor (George) and a Canadian senator (Samuel). Like their father and their brothers, George and Samuel were prominent holders of landed wealth.

migrants have yet reached this Province, and all these have been absorbed at, or before they arrived at Toronto."[43]

Hamilton civic leaders attempted to administer their own tonic for depression and the population decline long before the restoration of confidence had improved credit. Looking to the early 1830s as holding the elements of a pattern worthy of imitation, they called a public meeting in February, 1837, and endorsed a petition which Allan MacNab forwarded to the lieutenant-governor's office. The document requested the sponsoring of agents to recruit emigration from the British Isles. This assembly also proposed the creation of a receiving agency at Hamilton.

Concerned parties attempted to haul William Cattermole back into service, promising to finance his trip to England. The veteran recruiter recognized altered conditions and would consent to go "provided employment is found for the working class, a Hospital for those who needed it and land as cheap as in the states." Cattermole's last point registered as a real consideration, one that made settling in Upper Canada less attractive than in Ohio, Michigan and Illinois. During the 1830s, the United States Congress forgave illegal trespass on public land, granted preemption rights and auctioned land to squatters. United States land distribution beckoned as a more open process.

Direct recruitment and publicity became urgent matters. Unable to send Cattermole, the Gore District nominated Dr. Thomas Rolph to travel to the United Kingdom.[44] There in 1840 he met with estate owners and officials from the colonial office. In the meantime, Hamilton's young male population had been dropping. In 1837, the town's residents numbered in the vicinity of 3,200. The number slumped to roughly 3,100 and 2,900 in 1838 and 1839 respectively. Many of these fleeing transients had crossed the border. Eventually, during the early 1840s, public works resumed and emigrants again trekked into the Hamilton vicinity. Over 44,000 landed at Quebec in 1842, and the Welland Canal and navigation improvements to the Grand River stimulated Hamilton business into a convincing recovery during the 1840s.[45]

THE PHYSICAL ATTRIBUTES OF A FRONTIER BOOM TOWN

Accommodations for what was a young transient male population were rudimentary and scarce. Taverns and shanties were thrown up hastily. A few men lived at the place of employment, and there was a doubling up of families in dwellings. Surviving statistics point to overcrowding; the average number of inhabitants per Hamilton dwelling was seven to eight during the 1830s. In late 1831, the *Western Mercury* estimated Hamilton to have had "about one hundred inhabited houses, besides stores, shops, outhouses." Population was thought to have reached 900 "as several of the dwelling houses contain two families, and there are six taverns and two private houses which receive boarders at present."[46] Jasper Gilkison complained to his father in 1832 that he had to share warehouse lodgings with other employees, whereupon his razor, brushes and other personal belongings vanished. As late as 1840, Isaac Buchanan had an area of his warehouse set apart as rooms for the clerks to sleep. In part this was a condition of employment and training.

English travellers in Upper Canada during the 1820s and 1830s were aghast at overcrowded inns. Beds were shared and clients requested to receive a companion if necessary.[47] A June, 1832, report alleged that beds could not be obtained in Hamilton "and every sort of shake down has been put in requisition."[48] Plummer Burley's Promenade House may not have participated, for as the stage inn — also the site for auctions and public meetings — it cultivated respectability. Other taverns, more rustic, welcomed all trade. Across from the Promenade House, Andrew Miller ran a rickety, unpainted establishment. Near the haymarket stood a wooden farmers' hotel. At the eastern margin of Hamilton, on the corner of King Street and a road leading down to Land's wharf, widow Price kept a country tavern. Chatfield's house near Port Hamilton was remembered as "where all the big bugs put up . . . they nearly ate us."[49]

Demand made the provision of shelter an attractive venture. Allan MacNab had had a tavern and twelve houses constructed by late 1831. Samuel Mills emerged as the town's paramount builder and owner of frame rental dwellings, holding a score or two of wooden houses. The number of dwellings doubled between 1830 and 1834, when cholera temporarily frightened off trade and speculation. During 1831 and 1832, the construction boom kept every carpenter, mason, plasterer and painter that could be obtained in full work. Housing stock doubled again from 1835 to 1838. Over a third of the dwellings in any year during the 1830s were single-storey frame dwellings with a single fireplace. At best, during the 1830s, frame houses were two-storeyed, painted and with additional fireplaces. At worst, supporting frames consisted of posts driven into the ground. A few miserable shanties lacked proper floors.

Such an urban environment was laden with risk. Fear of fire quite properly kept town authorities on edge. The want of sanitary drainage, the overcrowding, and the arrival of undernourished newcomers pushed up the town's mortality rate. Despite a very young population, it had an estimated 65 deaths in 1840 for a mortality rate of 23 per 1,000. Three-quarters were believed to have been infants and young children. A British officer who had made an investigation into the health of Hamiltonians concluded that "the number of children that die are mostly of the poorer class."[50]

Demand for housing made land appear to be a foolproof investment, but there was a further set of explanations for gambling in real estate. Land holdings, perhaps because of the old-country connotations that equated land with power and prestige, were assumed evidence of worthy character. Understandably, merchants, lawyers and innkeepers indulged in a mania of land and building speculation. Attorney Miles O'Reilly purchased a large tract on the east corner of George Hamilton's townsite and had it surveyed with a distinctive street plan and large lots. When a statement of Peter Hunter Hamilton's real and personal estate was prepared for his creditors in 1835, the list included fifty-eight town lots for sale. Tales of success quickened prospects for speculative gain. An 1831 issue of the *Western Mercury* circulated the claim that the Burlington Canal had tripled the value of building lots. It was speculative greed, therefore, that prompted George Hamilton to petition the governor in council in 1831 to buy back the public square opposite the courthouse, two acres that he had transferred in 1816. The town's founder could reverse what little planning had been made fifteen years earlier. The undermining of land-use plans due to avarice would recur, but this was the first concession.[51]

During a March, 1837, trip to Hamilton, John Macaulay caught a glimpse of the last days of the real-estate binge, renewed by expectations that Hamilton would be connected by railway with London. A repetition of the canal miracle was anticipated: "The speculation that is going on in Hamilton is extraordinary.... The Americans flock in to buy, and they all feel confident the Railroad will go on. If it should, Hamilton will be a flourishing place."[52]

Hostler Plummer Burley joined in the speculation and stretched his credit. To his creditor, the Niagara banker Samuel Street (who held the Promenade House mortgage), Burley had to report a November, 1836, default. "I regret that owing to my having been engaged in building a good deal this summer it was not in my power to meet the whole amount due, and have now to beg the favor of a few months indulgence for the Balance."[53] The worst was yet to come. The frenzied excitement soon deteriorated into distress sales.

Analysis of North American towns and cities of the early nineteenth century has led to the notion that their small scale and the desirability of residing close to places of work promoted a cheek-by-jowl contact between rich and poor. Residential segregation lacked the clear patterns evident in cities during the age of mass transit; however, there were divisions of a sort. The quality of a dwelling, especially in a crude town without sewers, was profoundly affected by drainage.

Corktown constituted one of the least desirable Hamilton areas developed in the Thirties and Forties. Several streams crossed the property and swelled with the spring run-off from the escarpment. This area was home to a concentration of Irish Catholics. Considerably lower than the sand ridge running from Burlington Heights to the escarpment, a rise where the better homes were found, the existence of Corktown points to geographic segregation. If low-lying property was least desirable, lots on heights of land were prized. In 1834, James Mills advertised 100 lots, describing them as "sufficiently elevated to command a fine view of the dense part of the town." Part of the appeal derived from the desire to have a vista; the notion that an elevated situation secured good health was also a consideration.[54]

The waterfront fostered a community apart from the old townsite. Early Hamilton was a community divided. A cedar swamp and an inlet pinched between the two population centres. With a military engineer's eye for terrain, Major Thomas Glegg marked down in his diary of 1841 that "the space between the part of town most built upon and the wharf is intersected with small streams and ravines."[55] Briefly in the 1830s, the two halves were far enough apart in geographic and social terms that a rivalry developed; Port Hamilton endeavoured to secure its own bailiff and marketplace. Like other North American ports, the waterfront district had an unsavoury reputation, containing rough

Like all of the early industries, the foundry owned by John Fisher and Calvin McQuesten (1801-1885) was located at the centre of the city.

hotels, boarding houses, gaming and drinking establishments. Well-heeled visitors stepped onto the dock, into a wagon, and rode to proper establishments distant from Port Hamilton.

At first glance, frenzied construction would seem to offer happy circumstances for the rising number of town carpenters. In fact, boom growth led to extension of work hours and the challenge of unskilled labour. The construction of a dwelling, tavern or commercial property began when the owner of a vacant lot decided to build upon the property rather than seek a speculative gain from its resale. The construction decision could have been made by a tradesman or prospective home-owner; often an investor made the decision, looking toward rental income. The tradesman or capitalist approached a master builder or master workman. The master builders took journeymen carpenters into their employ and possibly took on a boy who would be indentured as an apprentice to work for two or more years at low wages. Masters would contract work out to other building trades: masons, plasterers and painters. They also laid down the wages and hours. Given the demand for shelter and a short construction season, the incentives for masters to cut corners and stretch the working day placed journeymen under a three-fold stress. Long work hours were pressed; the rush to throw up four walls meant crude techniques; the crude methods permitted the encroachment of unskilled labour. Masons and plasterers could not be so easily threatened, but carpenters attracted a casual fringe.

In response, carpenters from Quebec City to Philadelphia organized during the 1830s. In Hamilton they established the Hamilton Carpenter and Joiners Society in February, 1832. All master builders were first to offer work to journeymen, who in return agreed to discount their scale of prices by 25 per cent. Violators faced expulsion. In the event of a journeyman's arriving in town and not finding work at the scale set by the society, the society would provide an amount up to twelve shillings and sixpence "to aid the said journeyman (should he be in want) to proceed to the next town." The threat to employment security by unskilled labourers likely came from impoverished Irish arrivals, thus reinforcing with economic concerns a cultural and religious antipathy that led to the occasional rumblings of disorder between orange and green on Hamilton and Dundas streets.[56]

Whatever had been their original belief in colonial opportunities,

carpenters from England may have had little reason to celebrate life in the colonies. The boatloads of Irishmen hard on their heels exacerbated narrow concepts about fraternity; fraternity was served by lodges and craft associations — distrust was directed toward the unskilled Irish. By way of illustration, carpenter George Martin would recommend a bigoted artisans' remedy for the Irish problem. "Give justice to Ireland, and this is, make her free and hang every Irishman you find in Great Britain after 6 days notice."[57] Martin can be forgiven for frustration; he had not had an easy time in Upper Canada. Writing to family in England from Rochester, New York, in 1844, his despair testifies to the insecurity of his trade: "I have for the first time in ten years had a steady winter's work."[58] During his Hamilton residency, from about 1836 to 1838, prospects for security had come within grasp only to recede. At the peak of speculative fever in property George boasted to his father and brother that he could afford furniture now that he received rent from a boarder. An offer of $600 for his house and lot inspired confidence. He gloated about the sudden advance in prospects, hoping to hold the house a while longer. "I would not sell it for less than $800 . . . and if I can keep it for 2 or 3 years it will be worth $1000 or more."[59]

All manner of people had been smitten by speculation. Indeed, during 1837, the town's building activity soared. As would happen in later growth periods as well, supply had caught up with demand, but optimism pulled construction beyond immediate needs. A perceptive but anonymous diarist detected what neither the mighty like MacNab nor the lowly like Martin would have wanted to hear in 1837. "There has [sic] been too many buildings going up these last two years for the demand." Merchant Adam Hope also recognized telltale signs of gambling in property. "Speculation in town lots is rife and some will burn their fingers for all this some day." That March, 1837, warning was prophetic.[60]

BOOM-TOWN CULTURE AND CIVIC AFFAIRS

Until the 1837 collapse, Hamilton had presented the very picture of a footloose frontier society. From the mid-1820s until the slump, the male proportion of the population hovered at approximately 20 per cent above that of females. If we consider individuals over sixteen years of age, the population that could have moved independent of parents, then the male proportion stood closer to 40 or 50 per cent above the female. A balance between the sexes existed in the surrounding townships, and a balance came to the town during the economic slump when single men moved out and toward opportunity. Several considerations account for these population circumstances. Many newcomers travelled without their families. Carpenter George Martin went against the grain and moved his wife and children with him. Sojourners without family had the flexibility necessary for shifting around North America, following opportunities signalled by word of mouth, letters from relatives or by the press. Uncertainty about employment prospects and housing conditions dictated caution. Prudence involved flexibility, travelling light to appraise conditions and accepting a loss of domestic arrangements. In turn, scarcity of female companionship encouraged prostitution, drinking and brawling.[61]

Concern about morals led to occasional antivice campaigns. One in April, 1843, resulted in the collection of sixteen women whom town authorities placed aboard a Toronto-bound steamboat. A number of merchant shops sold liquor by the drink and allowed gambling. The quadrupling of the number of assessed shops and warehouses between 1830 and 1838, therefore, can be seen in relation to trade and population increases, but also in terms of a proliferation of vice and frontier sociability. Joseph Case maintained one of these multipurpose establishments, and his 1836 brush with the law implied how they functioned. He stood accused of keeping his "grocery and beer shop in a disorderly manner. Witnesses swore that the defendant allows common women of the Town to get drunk in his house." Comparable places included Daniel Tolliver's "notorious house," Nancy McDonald and Marianne Ravelle's "Bad House," Mary Ann Lavill and May Lilly's "house of ill fame," and Thomas Livers's "gambling house." Mr. and Mrs. Luckey, failing to have the good fortune of their surname, came before the authorities twice during the summer of 1835, charged with keeping "a disorderly house."[62] On occasion, the immoral lurched onto Port Hamilton streets, where open pleasures provoked arrest.

> On Saturday [July, 1844], about 7 pm Jacob Bishop swears he saw June Ellis walking through the streets with her breasts exposed and drunk. Henry Masiah was pointed out to him as the man who was walking arm in arm with her and playing with her breasts as they walked.[63]

Both were given twenty days in jail. Another response to the conditions of vice came in campaigns for moral reformation. Charles Edwin Furman, minister of the American Presbyterian Church in Hamilton from 1835 to 1837, acted as agent for the American Tract Society and circulated its pamphlets on life's temptations and the bliss of virtue. The message turned few heads. Expulsion, fines and jail sentences indicate that trust in the printed word to reshape social reality was misplaced.[64]

Workingmen squeezed all manner of excitement into the hours after sunset and before sunrise, as well as Sundays. Ironically the Sabbath, the only day for relaxation during the busy season, became the day for furious driving of horses, drinking to excess and profanity. To contain the bowling rage that swept the town in the 1830s, a September, 1833, regulation forbade playing "either earlier than 6 o'clock in the morning, or later than 9 o'clock in the evening."[65] Requests for bowling licenses were denied. These concerns of a municipal government disclose an interest in controlling leisure activities, keeping labourers quiet and tame after work and on Sundays; some workingmen, on the other hand, were devotees of boisterous pleasures and the secular Sunday.

Spontaneous activities were of a different order for the men of property. Some activities required capital. Accounts of hunting are confined to reports about the rural gentry or town leaders — men like Elijah Secord, who shot 300 pigeons in one field, or Peter Hunter Hamilton and the Durands, who rode down to Norfolk County to hunt fowl. A genteel activity such as the carriage excursions onto Burlington Beach or along Burlington Heights provided opportunity for flaunting status. After George Jeffers opened his wagon works in 1834, a variety of carriage styles could be built locally, but imported carriages conferred greater prestige. Town founder George Hamilton wrote to the government of Upper Canada to prevent settlement on Burlington Heights. With carriages, the affluent were "feeling alive to the Drive" as Hamilton phrased it. The heights and the beach, he asserted, were "the two great Public Promenades." In a subsequent appeal, he proposed how settlement of Burlington Heights would, "as the country improves [and] all other places

In the frontier boom town, lodges, cultural groups and educational associations like the Mechanics Institute met in Hamilton's first town hall (1836-1839) on King William Street.

being shut up," offer "a place of general resort and recreation to the Townspeople." It was an appealing notion, even if it came from a self-serving party who had purchased a town square for subdivision.[66]

Amateur bands and the militia afforded additional occasions for outdoor display with connotations of social distinction; instrument and uniform costs made these associations exclusive. Another self-recruiting circle of men, the first volunteer fire company, picked only Orangemen. The debating club consisted of "young gentlemen." Farmers and artisans gathered at rustic inns. Workingmen had their own occasions for coming together, for sober discussion or rowdy ceremony. Artisans and clerks had founded a Mechanics Institute by 1839, meeting at the town hall for lectures on technical matters, natural history and literature. In direct contrast to the formal setting of an institute lecture, there were occasions for social diversion that involved a form of protest. The charivari, a nocturnal and noisy visitation of men in costume upon an unpopular town figure, represents the blend of hell-raising amusement with the serious matter of enforcing unwritten codes of behaviour. A victim may have deviated from sexual standards, marrying an older widow or absconding with someone's wife; he may have transacted business that gave offence to the community. Charivaris and showers of stones directed against persons or dwelling places were serious enough in the frontier town to be the subjects of an 1842 bylaw.[67]

Commercial spectator events demonstrated the shared interests among the town's social elements. The steamboat conquered cultural isolation, bringing in the entertainments of New York and even London. Popular spectacles like a panorama of the Battle of Trafalgar came to town, but the most routine events were the troupes that followed the Erie Canal and Lake Ontario circuit. Exhibitions of wild beasts or circuses with performers — gymnasts, jugglers and boxers — made the summer rounds. One can imagine that more than an interest in the art of juggling lured men to an 1829 circus where "a very beautiful woman" appeared "as a ball thrower." Nearly seventy years later, upright Charles Durand had fond recollections of that exhibition. Gambling in many forms appealed to men of all rank. Local lotteries were conceived for all manner of objectives. When Andrew Miller's tavern burned, he financed reconstruction by selling lottery tickets with town lots as prizes. A bookseller re-

sorted to the same measure to stimulate business, giving book prizes. American lotteries frequently were advertised in local papers, attesting to the popular culture links with the United States.[68]

The balls, militia, bands, fire company and clubs upheld exclusivity; commercial entertainment necessarily made a more open appeal. Politics and organized religion functioned with great complexity somewhere in between. They aimed at numerical support and assembled individuals from assorted backgrounds; yet party and denomination did not entirely crosscut social distinctions. It is far too simple to assume that a local elite embraced Tory politics and the Church of England, or that farmers and artisans were dutifully reform-minded Methodists. The new society was too diverse and fluid for that. All the same, this crude division has utility, although neither Reform nor Tory factions had a precisely defined social composition. Indeed, politics made strange bedfellows. One important local consideration in Hamilton was the town leaders' interest in development through public works and chartered companies. Hamilton reformers like George Hamilton and later Colin Ferrie avoided radical opposition to the executive in the 1830s, since government policy now coincided with their economic outlook.

A further complication was that local Tories like Allan MacNab and William Johnson Kerr balanced social climbing with a flair for the common touch. They could rally a rowdy element. Their businesses made them promoters of emigration and employers of newcomers. Thus they could pose as workingmen's friends. As War of 1812 heroes, MacNab and Kerr adhered to the lessons of their youthful accomplishments. They conducted themselves with dash and a penchant for attack. Even so, it is misleading to dismiss them as mere bullies, thereby underestimating their understanding of an element in common society that admired strength, praised gusto and appreciated largesse. Although there are several episodes that connect MacNab and Kerr to assaults — the 1827 tar-and-feathering of reformer George Rolph and the 1832 beating of William Lyon Mackenzie on a Hamilton visit — one incident of political harassment can illustrate the use of force and "the rabble." During a political discussion in 1838, MacNab lost patience with his opponent. "Sir Allen [sic] called into the room several of the labourers and common people with whom he had business, and began a settlement of accounts with them: — And in this way he got rid of the presence of the Gentleman."[69]

On the Reform side, Methodists did figure prominently. A devout Methodist, Charles Durand, son of James, wrote for Hamilton reform journals and was the Hamilton agent for William Lyon Mackenzie's *Colonial Advocate.* The secular cultural values of Methodism, including its opposition to privilege, its concern for temperance and its interest in education, set it at odds with the rough panache of Hamilton Tories and their adherents. Members of each faction certainly knew their opponents, for the Upper Canadian newspapers were open in their denunciations. However, the radical reformers in Hamilton, deeply sympathetic to Mackenzie, seem to have been a relatively small group.

Residents in the townships closer to Hamilton did not have the isolation that permitted leeway for radical assembly or uprising. The fact that there was no Hamilton-area counterpart to the Mackenzie and Duncombe rebellions does not testify to total loyalty, for there were important exceptions. In one shadowy episode, Charles Durand met Mackenzie on Yonge Street during the latter's march on York. It may have been a contact to signal an uprising in the Gore District.[70] Proximity to Hamilton, not sentiment, kept much of the Gore District in line.

Farmers around Hamilton had economic grievances. For some, the Gore Courthouse was the bane of existence; the Hamilton merchants, land jobbers and lawyers stood for ill-gained riches. Hamilton, after all, was a town with imperial designs and commercial power. It was also a community with a different religious bias. A disproportionate number of Anglicans and Roman Catholics resided in Hamilton; a disproportionate number of Methodists and nonestablishment denominations lived in the immediate countryside. It is tempting to see an urban denominational inclination toward the churches of formality and hierarchy and the countryside in sympathy with informality and evangelical religion. In terms of political and denominational inclination, the metropolitan reach of Hamilton into the hinterland of the southwest townships was incomplete. The town's economic influence caused tension. In short, the connections between the town and its district were complex and included rural hostility, dissent and trepidation.

After the ill-fated 6 December 1837 attack of Mackenzie's followers on York, Hamilton Tories, dominant and prone to action, seized the occasion to initiate their mayhem. Armed with muskets and bayonets, the militia set up pickets. Minor outrages came from the erstwhile forces of law and order; an overzealous search party visited Charles Durand's house, jabbing at furniture and wainscotting in its undisciplined hunt for seditious material. The American John Fisher, McQuesten's foundry operator, sensed peril and would have fled, except that he feared threats to burn down the foundry would have been realized if he had left.[71] As members of the Tory bulwark in a reform countryside, Hamilton Tories — the men of Gore — had to quell turbulence in the western townships during the weeks after the Mackenzie rebellion. With support from Kerr's friends on the Six Nations Reservation, MacNab's militia cheerfully advanced. Adam Hope, who participated in the roundup of rebels, observed that "there were numbers of Orangemen with us in high spirits at the prospect of a little fun."[72]

The militia romp into the countryside to suppress the rebellion had an additional dimension. It was a financial godsend, injecting hard currency into a faltering economy. MacNab and Kerr submitted expense sheets, while Colin Ferrie was rescued by sales to the Third Gore Militia. For £850, Ferrie provided blankets, boots, socks, gunpowder, shot, camp ovens and a gallon of whiskey. Teamsters prospered because the militia required a supply train to victual the troops on the march to Brantford and on their later expedition to the Niagara River.[73]

Due to the colonial political excitement of the 1830s, it is tempting to interpret Hamilton politics as an extension of broader controversies. In part, that would be accurate. However, there were other significant features: the special patronage opportunities, the power to influence property values and the local family cliques. Prior to its 1833 incorporation, local government throughout the Gore District, including Hamilton, had been handled by the appointed justices of the peace meeting in the district court of quarter sessions. The 1833 act created four wards, each represented by an elected councillor; candidates had to possess property assessed at sixty pounds, and voters had to be freeholders of a lot and dwelling or tenants having paid one year's rent. In a town which had roughly 220 houses and shops assessed at sixty pounds or more in 1840, the number of possible candidates was likely to have been less than 25 per cent of the adult male population.

When four councillors, called members of the Board of Police, had been elected, they appointed a fifth from among qualified town residents; the fifth member served as president of the Board of Police. The board's powers related primarily to regulatory action: inspecting and licensing food production and sales, regulation of wharves, inspection of weigh scales, enforcement of fire prevention measures, keeping the streets clear of obstructions and maintaining public order. The construction and management of a market building constituted the largest municipal undertaking of the 1830s and early 1840s.[74] There were enough patronage opportunities to make the scramble for office an occasionally bitter affair. The board appointed at least five officials; a clerk and assessor, a collector and treasurer, a high bailiff, an inspector of highways and chimneys, and an inspector of weights and measures, who also served as clerk of the market. In addition, the board awarded contracts for printing and assorted materials like lumber for boardwalks or pumps for civic wells.

It also could make decisions affecting real-estate values. Town founder George Hamilton offered to grant land for the market place to attract businesses and inns, thereby increasing the demand for adjacent land. The choice of the market site became the town's first major civic issue. Hamilton's site was rejected because it degenerated into a quagmire in periods of heavy run-off. A compromise brought the market place to James Street, and George Hamilton's location became the haymarket. Unfortunately, this incident and fragmentary evidence on other contests in civic affairs do not result in a complete picture of early town politics. The 1836 election riot involving the supporters of "Yankee" Andrew Miller and those of his opponent, complaints against Allan MacNab for obstructing a street with building materials and the appointment of Reformer Charles Durand as town clerk probably expressed partisan cleavages that merged with the colonial situation.[75]

The payment of the town's regulatory officials was drawn from the fees that they collected; expenditures on municipal improvements came from the tax revenue based on property assessment. The 1837 collapse reduced this latter source when defaulting and appeals for reduced taxes became commonplace. An April, 1838, resolution of the board conveys the distress.

> Ordered that 100 handbills be circulated informing defaulters in their Taxes that the Police in consideration of the pecuniary distress so prevalent throughout the past year, have hitherto forborne in most instances to levy them as authorized by law but that warrant of execution will now be issued against the goods and chattels of all who shall not have paid within 10 days from date.[76]

The town's declining revenue inhibited its ability to hire constables, repair streets and assist the needy. In truth, at this stage of development in North American municipal government, town services remained inexpensive so that the situation did not herald civic catastrophe. Municipal action had yet to enter a period of heavy spending for public utilities and professional fire and police protection.

CONCLUSION

In terms of Upper Canadian history, Hamilton's prominence came late and in a manner that challenges impressions about the era. Partly because of the British imperial patriotism of Ontario, expressed during the late nineteenth century and through two world wars, it has been assumed that Hamilton was steadfastly British during its first century. Symbols of the myths which have pervaded the town's history are visible today in the form of the Loyalist monument at the courthouse and the statue of Queen Victoria in Gore Park. Emphasis on political events and a few personalities — the Rebellion of 1837 and the character of Allan MacNab — also has reinforced a limited perception of Hamilton's situation in North America. A civic pride in Dundurn Castle and in the local son who became a prime minister of the Canadas reduce awareness of the blatant greed and hardships prevalent in Hamilton's boom-town years. A full appraisal of Hamilton, one that considers the common man's plight as well as the actions of the elite, discloses class contrasts and some American influences.

Property may not have guaranteed the fiscal security of the elite, for businessmen could err. However, their handling of debt, relation to the law, dwelling places, and forms of entertainment confirm the presence of a divided society. The governing class of Hamilton also had a strategy for economic development and recourse to patronage and intimidation when it confronted opposition. What unfolds is a picture of a community whose founders and builders were self-interested, whose economy and culture drew heavily on United Kingdom and American connections, and whose residents were often part of a transatlantic drama of distress. The expansion of Hamilton brought together people, ideas, technology, expectations and antagonisms that were all a part of the North Atlantic world. Participation in international economic, demographic and cultural trends would remain apparent in each of Hamilton's subsequent eras.

The Dakin, named after a director of the Great Western Railway, is seen here in the summer of 1864. The poses and clothing reflect the sense of pride felt by businessmen and railway operatives.

Chapter Two

Hamilton, Canada West: From Lakeport to Railway City, 1841 – 1870

On St. Patrick's Day 1840, parties unknown burned down a surviving War of 1812 blockhouse on Burlington Heights.[1] During the next thirty years there would be many more alterations, a few overt and physical, others invisible and social. From garrison, to courthouse town, to an immigrant distribution centre and commercial lakeport, Hamilton was about to advance into its railway era and to begin its longstanding history as a medium-rank Canadian city. The decades from 1840 to 1870, combining as they did both change and continuity, stand as a complicated pivot in the city's affairs. Community leaders and economic designs evident from the 1820s and 1830s persisted into the 1840s and 1850s. Navigation, public works, immigration and mercantile operations recovered after the 1837-40 depression; they remained important to Hamilton's prosperity and continued to give a transient and seasonal life to the community.

However, the original booster strategy of forwarding Hamilton as a commercial city, supplying the Grand River Valley and London areas, betrayed weakness. The city had neither the capital nor the political leverage to surpass Toronto, although some efforts were not complete failures. As for early industries, they persisted while the settlement frontier that they originally served receded westward, ultimately into Manitoba. By the 1870s, when Hamilton had been forced to relinquish grand commercial aspirations, industry had assumed a critical role. On the side of continuity, several of the foundries opened in the late 1830s and early 1840s endured into later decades; Edward Jackson, Calvin McQuesten, John Fisher, Luther Sawyer, Alexander Carpenter, Edward and Charles Gurney and Dennis Moore, names synonymous with iron work, remained prominent. At midcentury approximately a third of the tonnage entering Burlington Bay through the canal consisted of iron, much of it destined for city foundries. The iron industries founded in the 1830s were joined in the 1850s and 1860s by machine shops manufacturing precision items. As well, textile industries came to the region at midcentury.

The city as an administrative and physical entity moved in fresh directions at the outset of the railway age. Until then, local government proceeded with essentially regulatory functions and depended upon voluntary responses to health problems, fire, welfare and law and order. A major reorientation came in the 1840s and 1850s as the city considered relief for indigent immigrants, policing its streets, and providing water and sewer services. The significant turning points came when the city undertook responsibility for operating such public services as a waterworks, sewer system, police force, and extended a franchise to a gas company. As well, the practice of raising capital by bonds became an increasingly adopted technique for expanding the activities of local government.

Boom periods, particularly the early 1850s, recast Hamilton. Streets were opened, hills were cut and marshes filled. In addition to all other forms of change, familiar individuals passed from prominence. Richard Beasley, pioneer of the area's commercial activity, died in 1842. Colin Ferrie had a heart attack after meeting directors of the Gore Bank in 1856. George Hamilton's son, Robert Jarvis Hamilton, brought the family land and banking business to bankruptcy in 1864. Allan MacNab passed away in 1862 and John Young in 1873. Issac Buchanan outlived his glory days, dying in 1883. Bankruptcies had forced him to leave his estate of Auchmar on the escarpment and move into the city by 1876.

New men began to make their mark. Richard M. Wanzer, the sewing-machine entrepreneur, had been raised in the United States. William E. Sanford, an innovator in the new industry of ready-made clothes, had not even been born when the men of Gore had rallied to suppress rebellion in 1837. By the 1870s, economic life had lost more than its older men of enterprise; the structural change from commerce to industry was well under way and so was a significant growth in the activity of local government. All the while, the city encountered cyclical episodes: boom and depression, fluctuations in population and incidents in a rivalry with Toronto.

THE COMMERCIAL ECONOMY OF A LAKEPORT

Around the Great Lakes, navigation remained fundamental to commerce, even while American and Canadian capitalists scrambled after funds for railways. Schooners served as major carriers of bulk goods and immigrants. Among the former cargoes, grain for export became enormously important during the 1840s. The wheat boom was one significant factor in boosting port activity at Hamilton and aiding rapid growth from 1844 to 1847.

Vessels trading into Hamilton ranged from 15 to 650 tons. Most sailing vessels fell into one of two general categories. Those of 50 to 100 tons, carrying three to six crew members, belonged to small local operators like the Edward Zealand family of Hamilton. Edward Zealand had come to Lake Ontario as a member of the British naval forces during the War of 1812. Afterward he served on lake vessels, eventually operating a wharf and forwarding business at Port Hamilton. The family's schooners, the *Concord, Hope* and *Dove,* were typical of farm-produce collectors and mercantile-goods distributors. Calling at larger centres, they also stopped at country wharves and secondary ports where merchants assembled the inland production of grain. Zealand's vessels visited Lewiston and Rochester. In the years of tension between Great Britain and the United States, with talk of war in the mid-1840s, their names reflected the sentiment of a trading community which appreciated peaceful contact with American ports. Surviving fragments of port records for the mid-1840s illustrate the prominence of Oswego, Rochester and Lewiston in Hamilton's import trade. Typical shipments originating in these centres included settlement essentials: boots, shoes, harnesses, fabrics and tools.

The next class of vessels, schooners of 150 to 250 tons, carried about ten men. Generally, the owners of these were not Hamilton men. The merchants of Hamilton handled extensive overland trade, but the Atlantic and St. Lawrence forwarding activities were concentrated in Montreal and Toronto, with some Kingston concerns involved.[2]

The initial Burlington Bay ventures into steamboat ownership during the 1830s had not persisted. Land transit issues, the financial panic of the late 1830s and the persistent zeal of Toronto steamship entrepreneur Donald Bethune all had a part in wiping out Hamilton-based ownership. That created minor problems for the town, since outside operators could and did treat Hamilton with contempt. Two groups of steamers called at Hamilton. The 350-ton vessels, like Bethune's *Eclipse*, had a complement of eighteen men and carried passengers and a higher quality of cargo than schooners. Their ratio of crew members to tonnage as well as costs of fuel and repairs to engines meant that as freight carriers they were not an immediate replacement for sailing vessels. Bethune discovered this during three bankruptcies. A second cluster of steamers, consisting of the more recent 50-ton propeller-driven craft, like Bethune's *Scotland*, were inefficient as general carriers. However, speed gave them specialized roles as packet boats, catering to luxury and mail traffic.[3]

Shifts in steamboat ownership and technology concerned Hamilton's business leaders, although not to the same degree that railway affairs were to focus their energies. There were unsuccessful attempts in 1850–51 to organize Hamilton companies that would break the pattern of outside control. Except for a brief period when the Great Western Railway (GWR) operated vessels, the city had to depend on lines managed elsewhere. Mild interest in a locally controlled line revived in 1860–61 but soon faltered.[4]

Ultimately, Hamilton's ease of access to the Atlantic depended less on ownership of vessels than on the state of the Burlington Canal. Throughout the 1840s problems disrupted its operation. The size of steamboats and the silting up of the channel from fourteen to eight feet created unfortunate situations that threatened Hamilton's reputation as a port and furthered the advantage of Toronto. The 1843 Report of the Board of Works of Canada described the canal as "in such a wretched state of dilapidation, as to threaten the stoppage of navigation." Certainly from 1842 to 1848 lake ships were held up by dredges, regulations which insisted that vessels enter the canal with a three-quarters

The west side of James Street looking south from King Street (1860). The craftsmanship expressed in a few structures like St. Andrew's (later St. Paul's) Presbyterian Church and the head office of the Canada Life Assurance Company (three buildings right of St. Andrew's) contrasted with the majority of city structures, which were frame dwellings and shops.

The Gore Bank (here pictured around 1871) outlived its Toronto rival, the Bank of Upper Canada.

load and construction operations which temporarily narrowed the canal. Year after year Donald Bethune complained about conditions and altered his schedule of runs to Hamilton, blaming risks at the canal.[5]

Import and export trade were not the sole considerations behind the transportation innovations at Hamilton. Like the settlement and boom-town years, immigration figured in the development schemes of the 1840s and 1850s. In concert with locally sponsored recruitment of emigrants from the British Isles, the government of Canada collected information to inform potential emigrants about the prospects for labour and farming. The aim was to allay fears that might have arisen as a consequence of the 1837 Rebellion and financial collapse. The resurgence of arrivals in the early 1840s, however, owed more to the revival of public works in the colony and the continuing agricultural and demographic problems of Ireland. Locally, work on the Burlington Canal, Welland Canal, Grand River navigation scheme and turnpikes restored immigration. This renewal included exceptional periods when the promoters of growth got much more than they had anticipated. Faced with Irish famine migrants, Hamilton and colonial officials engaged in a dodging of responsibility for temporary care of impoverished arrivals.

In addition to the frustrations experienced with the Burlington Canal and immigration, there were the problems faced by mercantile interests when they tried to enhance the city's financial services by promoting banks and insurance schemes. Hamilton had several banks and one insurance company of local origin in the midcentury. Most so-called banks were small private enterprises that invested deposits in mortgages. Stinson's Bank was founded by merchant and land developer Thomas Stinson in 1847. The Stinson family had arrived in Hamilton by 1830 and prospered. Thomas successfully expanded the family business into land development and mortgage banking. The son of the town founder, Robert J. Hamilton, ran comparable operations until he failed to cover withdrawals in 1864.[6]

In contrast, the Gore Bank was a chartered bank with diversified interests and a network of agents. Stinson's bank and Hamilton's partnerships had no metropolitan ambitions, but the Gore Bank did. However, the latter did not approach the stature of the Commercial Bank (Kingston) nor the Bank of Upper Canada (Toronto). In fact, it was a tribute to Hamilton boosters that they had secured a charter for such a small community. The bank's inferior status derived from a lack of large sums of capital. Chartered in 1836, the stock was not taken up quickly. The government could have helped by placing customs-revenue accounts or public-works funds with the Hamilton concern rather than favouring Toronto and Kingston banks. The denial of government business had serious consequences, since without it the Gore Bank could not expedite overseas business for Hamilton merchants as readily as could the Commercial Bank. Government funds raised in London and deposited with the Bank of Upper Canada or the Commercial Bank allowed them to charge lower foreign-exchange rates. The Gore Bank made pointed overtures for business generated by the government. In 1841 and 1843, the bank notified the receiver general that it had agents in Guelph, Woodstock, Simcoe, Saint Thomas and Chatham — a fair description of the extent of Hamilton's hinterland. In any case, the appeals failed and business went to the local branch of the Commercial Bank.

In an era of suspicion about a merchant's or a bank's resources, this action had a serious side effect. According to the cashier, it had "a tendency to induce the public to think that there is some good reason why the Gore Bank was not treated as well as the other Banks of the Province."[7] The Gore Bank's president from 1839 to 1856, merchant Colin Ferrie, was powerless with respect to improving the bank's stature. In fact, he was part of the problem. After an 1844 purchase of land from Ferrie, the bank was located directly beside his store and warehouse. That fact made tangible a strong financial connection, for Colin was a heavy borrower and not always a sound risk. The troubles confronting the Gore Bank — especially its undercapitalization — betray the vulnerability of Hamilton's bid to control the economy of its southwest hinterland. It did not have the inherent strength to combat Montreal and Toronto. The harsh truth finally had to be confronted when the city's greatest bid for commercial dominion, the GWR, produced overwhelming Toronto and Montreal competition rather than a Hamilton mercantile victory. As for the Gore Bank, it limped from crisis to crisis until 1870, when it was taken over by the Toronto-controlled Bank of Commerce, but it had outlasted both the Bank of Upper Canada and the Commercial Bank.

Fire and life assurance firms developed across North America

Land speculator, railway official and civic politician Jasper Gilkison (1815-1906) epitomized the brashness and self-interest behind Hamilton's boosterism. His fortunes followed those of the city into decline.

This portrait of Sir Allan MacNab, railway entrepreneur and politician, was taken not long before his death in 1862.

from the 1830s to the 1860s. The convenience of their services and the local investment potential of their accumulated capital were much desired in a maturing community. Several proposals to form insurance companies had been raised at Hamilton in the 1840s, but only one of these led to a major institution. Hugh Cossart Baker, manager of the Hamilton branch of the Bank of Montreal, was aware of the capital-raising potential of an insurance company. Thus he organized a joint-stock company in late 1847 and early 1848. Along with sixty-two other investors from Hamilton and Toronto, Baker established the Canada Life Assurance Company. Potential clients were reluctant to insure with an unproven company, but Baker countered with lectures delivered in various Canadian towns. The business prospered. Policy sales represented a coverage of £59,650 in 1848 and £762,031 in 1857, when the company moved to its own building. It was such a success that it readily survived the depression of the late 1850s. This most successful of several local ventures into the field of financial service would end its association with Hamilton in 1899. Directors voted to move the head office to Toronto. These particular efforts to establish independent and indigenous financial institutions ended with concentrated financial might in Toronto, although there were local building societies and later ventures such as the Hamilton Provident and Loan Company (1871), the Bank of Hamilton (1872) and the Federal Life Assurance Company (1882).[8]

THE ECONOMY OF THE RAILWAY CITY

Compared with the steamboat companies, the Gore Bank or the Canada Life Assurance Company, capital requirements for a railway were enormous. Shortly before the financial panic of 1837, the assembly of Upper Canada had incorporated the London and Gore Railroad and agreed to provide a loan of £200,000. In the short term, the railway charter meant little to Hamilton. The government funds were never advanced "owing to the money embarrassment which overspread this country and the United States, together with the subsequent Provincial disturbances."[9] The government held back, fearing that the company's investors did not have the assets to cover defaults on loan payments. During the early 1840s railway talk revived and included speculation about a straight line from Albany to Chicago, with Hamilton at the midpoint.[10]

The men who renewed the railway were familiar figures who had hitched ambitions to Hamilton from its boom-town years. Isaac Buchanan desperately wanted the rail connection with the western part of the colony to justify his decision to concentrate wholesale activities at Hamilton. His associates Robert Harris and John Young were equally committed. Allan MacNab and George Tiffany, frequently in debt because of real-estate speculations, held potential residential property and a section of the waterfront appropriately situated for a railyard. Jasper Gilkison likewise had land investments. All of these men served at some time as company officers and promoters. Unable to collect funds locally, they knew where to look: London, Glasgow, the government of Canada and American financial centres.[11]

The journeys to the British money markets often ended in disappointment. In late 1845, excessive speculation in British railway stocks discredited all railway financing schemes. Deteriorating relations between Britain and the United States over the control of the Oregon territory likewise made it difficult to convince potential investors of the security of North American ventures. MacNab made the rounds of London investment houses in the summer of 1846; conditions remained unfavourable. Over a year later, toward the end of 1847, only 5 per cent of the par value of the GWR stock had been paid up. The Canadian board of directors feared that a demand for an instalment would force many shareholders to cut losses, forfeiting their shares and burying the company.[12] Apprehension came perilously close to being realized in 1848 when another "great panic in Railway and money matters" took place in England, making it impossible to compel payments on subscribed stock.[13] After a decade, all that had been achieved was a series of surveys which had used up the limited capital raised by subscription payments. Contractors had been approached and agreed to take a portion of their payment in company stock. These were irregular financial arrangements, but at this moment the government of Canada and the city of Hamilton assisted the foundering private enterprise. The Guarantee Act of 1849 specified that the government of Canada would guarantee the interest, at a rate not above 6 per cent, on half the bonds of any railway over seventy-five miles. The GWR then secured participation of New York and Boston investors.[14]

In Hamilton itself, the railway promoters intensified capital-raising drives throughout 1849 and 1850. Jasper Gilkison organized public rallies; prominent gentlemen were appointed to

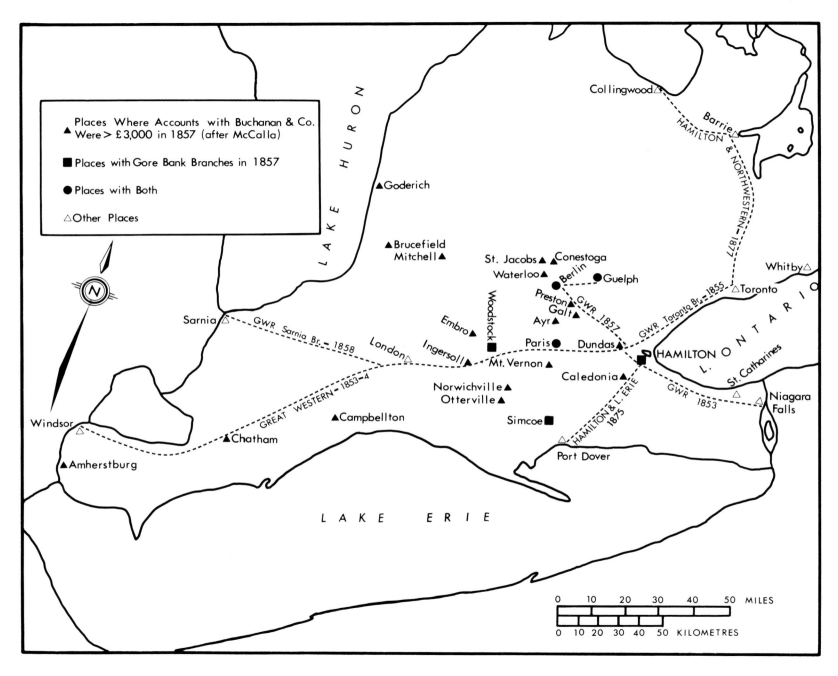

Places Where Accounts with Buchanan & Co.
▲ Were > £3,000 in 1857 (after McCalla)

■ Places with Gore Bank Branches in 1857

● Places with Both

△ Other Places

LAKE HURON

Collingwood △

Barrie △

HAMILTON & NORTHWESTERN — 1877

Whitby △

▲ Goderich

▲ Brucefield
Mitchell ▲

St. Jacobs ▲ ▲ Conestoga

Waterloo ▲ ● Berlin ● Guelph

△ Toronto

Woodstock

Preston ▲
Galt ▲

GWR 1857

GWR Toronto Br. — 1855

Sarnia △

GWR Sarnia Br. — 1858

London △

Embro ▲

Ayr ▲

Ingersoll ▲

Paris ● Dundas ▲

HAMILTON L. ONTARIO

Mt. Vernon ▲

Caledonia ▲

St. Catharines

GWR 1853

Norwichville ▲
Otterville ▲

HAMILTON & L. ERIE 1875

△ Niagara Falls

Windsor △

GREAT WESTERN — 1853-4

▲ Campbellton

Simcoe ■

▲ Chatham

△ Port Dover

▲ Amherstburg

LAKE ERIE

0 10 20 30 40 50 MILES

0 10 20 30 40 50 KILOMETRES

3 Hamilton's Hinterland and Railways, 1853-1877.

canvass their wards for subscriptions.[15] Civic patriotism and avarice built up a mood of excitement, although doomsayers appealed for caution. Nehemiah Ford, a shareholder who supported the railway, spoke against municipal support at a public meeting. He worried about the city debt and maintained that the city needed "sewers, good water and such like."[16] The city council chamber became a setting for debate and decision. On the essential question of whether or not the city should purchase stock in the GWR, an August, 1849, vote came to a tie. The ever-present Gilkison, an alderman, helped to present the railway position. So did alderman Robert McElroy, a contractor who had his eye on the construction possibilities. The mayor broke the tie, siding with the railway interests. The entire affair had to be aired again during deliberations on the report from the Committee on Finance. Interestingly, the committee's recommendation took into account the possibility that stock might not make a sound conventional investment.

> Even were the road likely to be somewhat unremunerative to the stockholders the manifest advantage of its construction to this City is such that as jealous guardians of the interests of the ratepayers the Council would act wisely in incurring the risk of a possible pecuniary loss when they are assured so large a general gain.[17]

Against a background of long yearning for a transportation link running westward, and amidst the pressure of the GWR campaign, the bylaw approving purchase of stock was swept through its readings at a special meeting of council on 29 August 1849.

The boost to the Hamilton economy came immediately. Hamilton's status as the centre of a major North American construction project attracted skilled and unskilled labourers who had to purchase or, more frequently, rent shelter; it filled warehouses with contractors' supplies; it gave a lift to the cartage and shipping business. Railway construction had slowed in New York State, so equipment from Rochester and Buffalo flowed into Hamilton during the summer of 1850 and 1851. Contractors Moore, McElroy and Pierson, building the line through Hamilton, imported two steam excavators used in New York State. Sam Farwell, who had constructed a portion of the New York and Erie Railroad and had contracted to build the GWR section from the Desjardins Canal to the Grand River, brought his equipment through Port Hamilton.[18] The Hamilton waterfront, recently familiar with emigrant suffering, now funnelled the light and heavy equipment of steam and iron technology. Scottish carpenter Peter Crail wrote to his brother in 1852, "this is a very flourishing city this season, there is employment for any man that is willing to work".[19] His qualified optimism — this season — thrust realism into speculative excitement.

To expedite shipment of construction equipment, most heavy machinery was exempted from import duties. Dock workers and teamsters benefited directly. As construction began, the iron-moulding and machinist trades grew. Foundrymen bid to construct roughly 450 railway cars between the summer of 1852 and 1853. An object of pride, a luxury coach forty-three feet long and nine feet wide with McQuesten ironwork, went on display at the 1853 Provincial Fair held in Hamilton. Contractors who built the cars rented the buildings of the railway company and provided their own machinery. The GWR supplied the central steam engine and shafting that would drive the contractors' lathes. This enormous shop, the city's largest enterprise, required a host of subcontractors to supply fittings for rolling stock. In addition, the equipment used for building the roadbed and laying track required repairs and parts. All of this demand stimulated local foundries and lured skilled machinists like Benjamin F. Smith, a "boomer" who moved his tools from one railway boom town to another. A capable and independent man, he departed from Rochester and leased "premises consisting of a workshop and steam power near the city of Hamilton," bringing with him his machine tools, lathes, vises, chucks, drills and castings. Whereas in the frontier years the stove had been the object of inventive activity, the railway city of Hamilton held machinist-inventors who took out patents for railway improvements.[20]

Traditional trades, distinct from the metal crafts, likewise swelled with newcomers. In Buffalo, news of Hamilton's splendid employment prospects encouraged Alex Main, a Scottish rope-maker, to move to Hamilton. The railway city, as Main recognized, created employment for more than just mechanics and navvies. Haulage demands in railway construction actually stimulated other modes of transportation: wagons and navigation. This in turn broadened wagon, harness and rigging manufacture. As a participant in the production of these traditional items, Alex Main is an illustrative counterpart to mechanic Benjamin F. Smith. Apprenticed as a ropemaker in Glasgow, Main emigrated to Boston in 1846. In 1851, he arrived in Hamilton after a sojourn in Buffalo. Receiving backing from Isaac Buchanan, Main constructed a rope-walk in the north end. Until its destruction in 1902, the ropewalk sheltered a wholly manual process. The enterprise provided ship's rigging, harnesses and hemp items for the GWR. Hand labour and old skills endured.[21]

In 1854-55, Hamilton passed into the Indian summer of its com-mercial history. A shrewd observer of North America, British traveller Isabella Lucy Bird, visited Hamilton in 1854 and described the mood that swept Hamilton into a frenzy of building.

> It is, I think, the most bustling place in Canada. It is a juvenile city, yet already has a population of twenty-five thousand people. The stores and hotels are handsome, and the streets are brilliantly lighted with gas. Hamilton has a peculiarly un-finished appearance. Indications of progress meet one on every side — there are houses being built, and houses being pulled down to make room for larger and more substantial ones — streets are being extended, and new ones are being staked out, and every external feature seems to be acquiring fresh and rapid development. People hurry about as if their lives depended on their speed .... Hamilton is a very Ameri-canized place.[22]

The GWR explains the bustle and optimism, but precise clues to its impact were found in Clifton, near Niagara Falls. The his-torical connections between the Head of the Lake and the Niagara frontier ran deep, but the link of the 1850s, the Niagara Sus-pension Bridge, involved an extraordinary engineering achieve-ment. Like so many transportation ventures, it began as a chartered company in the 1830s. Revived in the mid-1840s, the bridge company proceeded cautiously. In 1847 a number of em-inent American engineers were asked to prepare designs and estimates. The successful competitor supervised construction of a seven-and-a-half-foot-wide roadway. It was possible for loaded wagons to cross by January, 1849, and the mounting toll revenues convinced the company that expansion could yield enormous returns. Therefore they hired the most successful suspension-bridge engineer in the United States, John A. Roebling. Commenced in 1852 and completed in 1854, Roebling's two-level bridge carried pedestrians, carriages and trains until 1897.[23]

Completion of the suspension bridge and an agreement with the New York Central Railway enabled immigrants to journey by rail from Boston and New York directly to the American Mid-west. In the Troy-Albany-Schenectady urban area, feeder lines from Boston and New York made connections with the NYC trunk line. This railway then joined the GWR at Clifton, and the GWR carried passengers to Sarnia using twenty "immigrant cars" constructed in 1853 at half the cost of regular passenger cars. After a ferry crossing of the St. Clair River, travellers could board the Michigan Central Railroad (MCR) and continue to Chicago. An alternative involved inland navigation from Quebec to Hamil-ton and thence by GWR and MCR to Chicago. However, by 1856-57 it is likely that the railway alternative had replaced nav-igation as the principal means of immigrant travel. Beginning in 1856, Clifton surpassed Quebec City as a port of entry for Cana-dian immigration. Passengers from the NYC disembarked on the American side of the suspension bridge. GWR cars were backed across the bridge onto the American side, loaded up and started out for Hamilton. The peak year (1857) saw 32,000 immigrants entering Canada by the suspension bridge; the bulk of them con-tinued to the American West.

An international depression starting in 1857 slowed the pace of immigrant traffic and exposed fissures in the local economy that had been obscured by railway construction. Politicians and businessmen in other centres would not allow Hamilton to retain an edge over Toronto. Merchants in the hinterland, London for example, did not passively accept Hamilton ambitions to dominate the commerce of the southwest. A number of them encouraged the idea of a rival for the GWR. American railway promoters were not about to concede control over a vital segment of through traffic to a Canadian railway. Routes south of Lake Erie were being constructed. The hostile blows fell in rapid succession; the city was vulnerable to every attack. Hamilton's anomalous posi-tion, being a colonial city and a part of the American frontier, had been at the heart of its boom in the 1830s and its prosperity from 1850 to 1857, but it left the city exposed during talk of economic patriotism.

Montreal and Toronto railway promoters criticized a rail sys-tem that bound the United States together but did nothing to fuse Upper and Lower Canada. Therefore a rival line, running from Portland, Maine, to Montreal and from Montreal to Toronto and

The death toll was estimated at sixty after the railway bridge over the Desjardins Canal collapsed on 12 March 1857.

Sarnia was completed in 1859. This Grand Trunk Railway bypassed Hamilton. Prominent politicians were among the GTR board of directors, arranging investigation of railway accidents on the GWR and damaging its reputation. The GWR had little defense since its contractors had been guilty of shoddy work. In a notable catastrophe, a GWR train plunged through the bridge over the Desjardins Canal on 12 March 1857, killing sixty. Meanwhile, syndicates of railway promoters secured charters for two railways that if united would parallel the GWR, provide a shorter route between the Niagara frontier and Detroit, operate with easier grades and bypass Hamilton. This assault on Hamilton's metropolitan ambitions eventually presented the spectacle of Hamilton's business community, once largely united by the GWR projects, bitterly divided.[24]

At first glance, the proposed rival scheme would seem to be so hostile to Hamilton interests that the merchant railway promoters of the city would rally to oppose. On the surface that happened. In the murky depths of Canadian railway corruption, however, affairs had greater complexity, for while the GWR sponsors had appealed to civic patriotism, they also were dedicated to personal gain. Their ambitions intruded into the GWR's affairs. Contractors charged excessive rates for inferior materials. George Tiffany and Allan MacNab unloaded waterfront property; the prices paid for MacNab's lands included acknowledgment of his political services in securing government loans for the GWR. If civic patriotism glimmered, it only did so through greasy layers of self-interest. This harsh judgment also must apply to impetuous Isaac Buchanan, who plotted an ambitious plan for squeezing the GWR.[25]

Buchanan had always taken risks. He had defied advice when he made Hamilton rather than Toronto his business headquarters. In the summer of 1856, his ambition drew him into a series of unethical acts. Through stock purchases and a bribe, Buchanan secured control of the two railways that if joined would have completed a southern route. His unconsulted partner Robert Harris fumed. Harris's rebukes were private and pertained to the risk that Buchanan had loaded upon the firm. Soon GWR investors and Hamilton residents launched public complaints, accusing Buchanan of doubledealing. What lay behind the takeovers was open to several interpretations. Buchanan alleged that his control was benign. There had been discussion of double-tracking the

GWR to improve service. Buchanan proposed that if the GWR would purchase control of the southern route from him, it would eliminate the possibility of a hostile rival and would acquire a double track between Niagara and Detroit. A hint of threat accompanied the plan. If the merger were rejected, Buchanan threatened to construct the southern route. The English investors denounced him as an opportunistic scoundrel and Hamilton opposition, centred around pioneer Judge Miles O'Reilly, branded him a false friend of the city. The English board of directors of the GWR defeated the merger. Buchanan continued a campaign for the southern line and his integrity. Public vindications, possibly unfounded and certainly generous, did not result in Buchanan's making a fortune. The 1857 financial panic meant that the southern lines could not raise capital. For Buchanan and Hamilton, seven years of plenty (1850-56) now were followed by more than the proverbial seven lean years.[26]

Most North American cities have endured bleak times when they lost businesses and population. Nonetheless, the demise of Hamilton as a commercial and railway centre was a startling reversal. A reasonable estimate of population loss between 1858 and 1862 would be 20 per cent. The city had to suspend interest payments on its bonds. A preliminary ripple of impending disaster came in January, 1857. Ever-hustling Jasper Gilkison had gone to London in late 1856 authorized by Hamilton Council to sell city debentures up to £300,000. Capital so raised had been designated to assist the GWR with a branch line to Galt and to build the Hamilton and Port Dover Railway (H and PDR). This latter scheme had originated in the mid-1830s to secure for Hamilton a subsidiary port on Lake Erie, thereby extending competition with Buffalo. Gilkison had great difficulty placing any debentures except at a discount of 10 per cent.[27]

At the same time, GWR and city revenues declined. A fall in GWR traffic, loans to the Detroit and Milwaukee Railway and the replacement of inferior iron rails on 250 miles of the main line trimmed company profits. The city's tax base shrank as "boomers," sojourners and failed retailers left for superior employment and entrepreneurial frontiers. Wholesale grocer James McIntyre reported in August, 1861, to his brother-in-law John Young that there was "no life or activity...everyone seeming paralyzed and indifferent it is like a God Forsaken city." A depressed Buchanan admitted that "all would leave who could."[28]

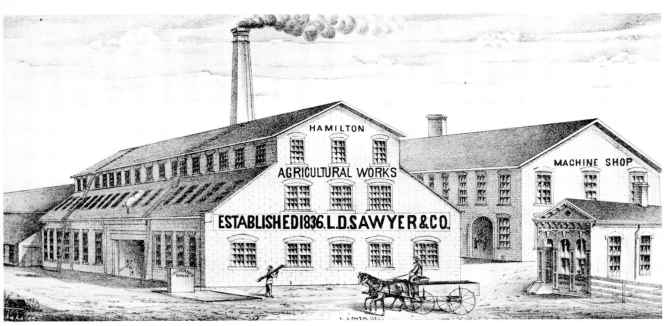

L.D. Sawyer and Company abandoned the McQuesten foundry site and became the first major industry, in 1857, to move to the railway on the city's northern periphery.

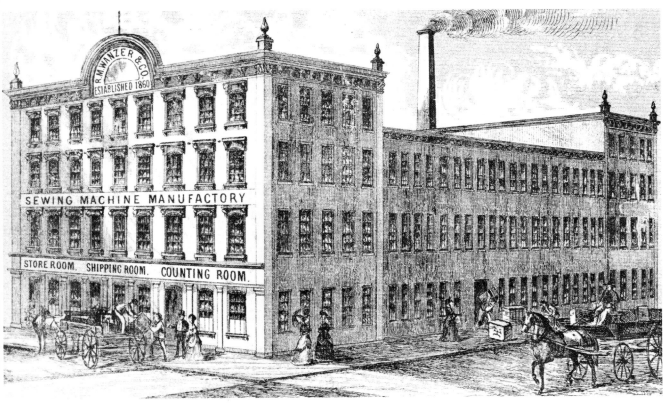

The Wanzer sewing-machine factory, like many of the city's manufacturing enterprises, combined industrial and commercial functions by the 1870s. It remained close to the city's core and to the homes of its employees.

Indeed, in 1861 21 per cent of the city's housing stock had become vacant — most of it cheap frame cottages. That compared with a slim 3 per cent vacancy rate during the boom of 1852. The American Civil War, tension between the United States and Great Britain, and especially the announced intention of the United States not to renew a reciprocal trade agreement with Canada upset the important trade links.

Vacated dwellings were not being filled with newcomers; immigration had slowed to a trickle. William Fruehauf, who had acted as the German immigration agent since 1854, requested another posting in 1861 "owing to the great decrease in the Emigration from Germany." The loss of population snowballed the crisis, since the only means of meeting civic expenses and the interest on the municipal debt in a shrinking city was to raise taxes. That action encouraged more residents to depart. A desperate council had to meet interest on a debt of roughly two million dollars of which almost half had come from the purchase of railway stocks. In August, 1857, the municipal government took initial steps to cut spending. The police-force expenditures soon were reduced and in 1861 gas lighting on some streets was discontinued. "The place is as dark as a dungeon," wrote one worried resident who believed that darkness in conjunction with police retrenchment would encourage the criminal element.[29]

To finance its earlier "splurges," Hamilton had issued two types of bonds. The waterworks bonds were distinct and interest payments eventually were to be met from the household water rate. Interest on the general bonds which had financed the stock acquisitions came from tax revenues. In early 1861, the shrinking tax revenue would not cover this obligation; the reduced expenditures were insufficient to balance accounts. The Canadian government stepped in temporarily to cover interest coupons. The colony's banker, Baring Brothers, was instructed to deposit £7,155 to the credit of Hamilton's account with the City Bank of London. The government hoped that this would prevent the colony and municipalities from losing the respect of London bankers. At the same time, the government made it clear that it would not pay the next instalment due in January, 1862. Therefore the city requested bondholders to permit a brief suspension of interest payments. The appeal for a breathing spell confessed distressing information about investments in railway stock. The city held $150,000 of GWR shares, $500,000 in the H and PDR,

$40,000 in the Galt and Guelph and $200,000 in the Preston and Berlin. The H and PDR was entirely worthless, being unfinished and burdened with debt. The Preston and Berlin could not be used in consequence of a bridge failure. The Galt and Guelph line had been mortgaged to the GWR. In sum, the stocks had depreciated to a fraction of their purchase price.[30]

The way in which the city kept creditors at bay had elements of *opera bouffe*; Hamilton outmanoeuvred bondholders and the county sheriff. As a consequence of a special meeting of London creditors, about 100 bondholders refused to forfeit an interest payment. They secured a court order forcing the sheriff to raise the interest payments by a special tax levy. The sheriff, who would receive a portion of the claim for executing the order, pressed for civic action, applying for the right to examine the assessment rolls so that he might estimate an appropriate charge on each property. However, the clerk and several aldermen prevented him from using the records. Contempt of court proceedings ended obstruction and by December, 1862, the sheriff had drafted the tax charges. Now he had to find willing tax collectors. The clerk and council refused to help; collectors never were appointed. In 1864, the affair came to an end with passage of the City of Hamilton Debenture Act which reorganized the city debt.[31]

The collapse of the railway boom struck down a number of industries supplying rolling stock and, to a minor degree, locomotives. Daniel Gunn's locomotive works, which had constructed four engines for the GWR using English patterns, was one victim. Cessation of railway expansion and the importation of most locomotives for the GWR and Grand Trunk forced Gunn to close, leaving creditors and ending employment for 100 to 150 men. Foundries and machine shops producing consumer durables — stoves, hardware and farm machinery — survived the crisis by reducing their labour force. McQuesten and Sawyer (farm implements) and Gurney and Company (hot-air furnaces and stoves) endured and were expanding by 1867.

One investor defied a bleak business climate and actually set up a shop in 1859. Sometime between 1856 and 1859, Richard M. Wanzer had discovered a loophole that permitted him to break into the manufacture of sewing machines. In 1856, leading American manufacturers formed a patent pool that controlled access to the industry. Canada was not affected. Small entrepreneurs could vault over the border. Wanzer made the move and opened a machinists' shop with a dozen employees. His product gained a decent reputation, winning an award at the Paris Exhibition of 1867. Recognition encouraged orders and Wanzer became one of the largest employers in the city by the 1880s. William E. Sanford also began his business at a low point in Hamilton's fortunes. Sanford had worked with New York wool dealers and through them became familiar with ready-made clothes. The sewing machine had made possible high-volume production of ready-to-wear suits. Sanford grasped the concept and initiated his scheme with merchant Alexander McInnes as partner. In the immediate post-Confederation years, Sanford carried their trade into Manitoba and the Maritimes.[32]

Employers whose businesses and industries endured the depression had one compensation during the early 1860s; they benefited from a surplus of skilled labour. "Laborers now are more abundant than the demand." Like the appearance of sewing-machine manufacturers, the phenomenon of skilled Americans in abundance derived from Hamilton's proximity to the United States and the city's situation in a British colony. The Civil War and the United States draft law of 1863 encouraged a fair number of Americans to move to Canada. An estimated 400 out of 500 Americans arriving in Hamilton in 1864 found employment, and their presence drove down wages. Thus even while the city's fiscal plight remained an obstacle to confidence, a peculiar alignment of international events began to rescue prospects for industrial capitalism.[33]

The transition toward an industrial city that originated in the railway boom and progressed even in the depression — witness Wanzer's decision — was captured in Canada's first industrial census, taken in 1871. According to it, the city had no fewer than seventy-six steam engines ranging from four to eighty horsepower and a labour force of between 4,500 and 5,000 who were employed in establishments with ten or more operatives.[34] The *Spectator* of 18 August 1871 made this appraisal of the industrial successor to the old commercial city.

> Then we traded; now we manufacture. Then we over-traded and over-speculated, and ran into debt and we became bankrupt; now our industry is steady and calculating, and we are getting out of debt. Our prosperity rests not on the money we make as agents...but upon manufactures which cannot fail of a market.[35]

Still, steam technology and places of manufacture that were larger than artisan shops did not create an industrial order with assembly-line methods producing specialized products. There remained numerous small shoe and harness shops, carriage and wagon works, and hat and garment establishments. Main's rope-walk, mentioned earlier, retained primitive methods for fifty years. The metal-working shops, moreover, produced a variety of articles in competition with other firms: stoves, wagon parts, saddlery hardware and scales. The Wanzer sewing-machine shop was an exception, for it specialized and organized production in individual departments, but artisan skills were essential at each step.

Much of the economic and labour history of Hamilton as an industrial city can centre on the erosion of traditional crafts by technology. However, for many decades after the railway boom, the speed of the new order and the manual pace of unskilled tasks and crafts could be viewed together on shop floors. Similarly, the introduction of steam power and machinery into the railway city serves as a convenient and conventional image for progress. However, there were many areas where manual labour remained entrenched: construction, haulage, manufacture of clothing, and numerous aspects of metallurgy. The pride of Hamiltonians in the shift from commerce to industry should not be taken to prove marked advances in the workplace and reduced burdens on the city's workingmen. Work hours were not reduced. Drudgery and danger persisted. Indeed, the industries exposed large numbers to occupational hazards: the inhaling of dust particles in the cotton mills, accidents, and the problem of intense heat and cold drafts among iron moulders. From the perspective of the city's economic fortunes, industry would prove as susceptible to business cycles and competition as commerce had been. Proof was soon in coming, for the industrial spurt of the late 1860s and early 1870s ran into difficulty during the international economic downturn of 1873-74.

POPULATION CHANGES AND INSTABILITY

Like the description of life in the earlier boom town, one means of understanding the urban society is to examine the mobility of the population. Who moved into or away from the city? Why did they choose to do so? What resources did they carry? How did they respond to the uncertainties that compelled or enticed their movement?

During the years of recovery and into the period of Irish famine immigration (1841 to 1848), Hamilton's population rose from roughly 3,400 to 9,900. Scattered newspaper accounts during the 1840s describe a thriving agricultural service centre that gained enormously from the grain trade. Some of the growth also followed from the famine immigration. The prospect of railway construction and the lift that such an anticipated project gave to the building trades in conjunction with commercial and housing construction also added to the appeal of Hamilton as an employment centre. The lack of annual census data comparable to the reports of the 1830s and the fact that few newspapers survive from the early 1840s make it difficult to separate the contributions made to Hamilton's growth by the prefamine and famine newcomers. One source has placed Hamilton's population in 1843 at 4,860 and at 6,478 in 1845. A sudden 35 per cent gain is not inconsistent with an impression formed from the rare newspaper. Compared with the business advertisements of the early 1840s, those of 1845 were extensive, listing a variety of professionals, importers, commission agents and craftsmen. The arrival at Hamilton of Irish famine immigrants in the 1840s offers a more detailed picture of population growth.[36]

The conditions that forced approximately 400,000 to emigrate from Ireland in 1846 and 1847 resembled the causes for the exodus fifteen years earlier, with the addition of a novel urgency. A blight destroyed the subsistence potato crop in 1846 and forced thousands to depart from rural Ireland as a matter of survival. Those who chose to cross the Atlantic placed themselves in other forms of peril. Finding cheap passage aboard empty timber vessels returning to ports like Saint John and Quebec, they exposed themselves to the risks of storms and disease. From port cities immigrants moved out in the summer months in search of work. Meanwhile the towns and cities along the major arteries of navigation braced themselves for relief expenses and a threat to health. Hamilton was to become an overburdened centre requiring assistance.[37]

Mayor Colin Ferrie detected a parallel between the problems anticipated in 1847 and the cholera epidemics in 1832 and 1834.

Ferrie had been on the 1832 Hamilton Board of Public Health. Drawing on this experience, he called council's attention to the expected Irish tide and recommended formation of a board of health. Ferrie also corresponded with the government about assistance for the sheltering of arrivals and the prevention of disease. In the first season (1847), the crisis was well handled. A special committee of council administered aid, recommending the following ration system: three-quarters of a pound of bread and three-quarters of a pound of meat every day for no more than six days; children were to receive half a pound of bread and half a pound of meat. To finance this, Ferrie requested a £1,500 grant from the Canadian government. He received £1,155 and the government reluctantly managed an immigration hospital in sheds near the waterfront. Cooperation and decency were exercised because the small numbers involved and their health had not yet strained resources.[38] The impending crisis was foreshadowed in a few cases of typhus and smallpox during 1847. Hamilton was in an unusual and unenviable position.

> Emigrants who feel unwell are frequently induced to conceal the state of their health from the agents, from dread of going into a Hospital and being separated from their friends and thus continue their journey until they can travel no longer and hence it commonly happens that the Toronto and Hamilton agencies have a larger number of sick in Hospital than we have at Kingston.[39]

Nonetheless, the Canadian government was not about to accept responsibility for any city residents who became ill due to contact with immigrants. Therefore in November, 1847, the Hamilton immigrant hospital was ordered closed.[40]

The narrow interpretation that the government placed on its responsibilities forced Hamilton into a variety of hidden expenses. Policemen had to be hired to attend at the wharf. The 1847 and 1848 tides left behind orphans; the traditional solution, putting out the children as apprentices, could not function on a large scale. As civic authorities discovered in the winter of 1848, it did not absorb everyone. "It is not likely to take place at present as the subject of this report is a weakly female." A Ladies' Benevolent Society came to the rescue, creating the Orphan Asylum which received municipal support as well as voluntary contributions. It also reacted by establishing a paupers' hospital and poorhouse, the House of Industry. To gain admission to this institution below the mountain at the head of the present Ferguson Avenue, the applicant had to present a certificate from a clergyman, magistrate or physician. The city council also found it necessary to reassess its support of the "casual poor." Traditional methods, including the provision of food and shelter, threatened to involve the city in "endless and ruinous expenditure." Council members resolved that henceforth priority would be given to residents fallen upon hard times but who once had enriched their community "by rate-paying and labor."[41] As well, council threw the problem of indigent immigrants back at the government with a rebuke. "While we find in the index to the Revised Statutes of Canada that the words Education and Schools occur 38 times, we search in vain for the words Poor, Pauper, Destitute and Afflicted."[42]

Bad enough in 1847 and 1848, problems multiplied in 1849. By mid-July, 1849, almost 900 immigrants had landed. In the four weeks preceding a July 16 report, 134 had been admitted to the Emigrant Hospital, although many were "children or relatives in attendance on the sick." On the day of the report, 264 persons had taken up shelter in emergency sheds. By August 27, the arrivals for the season had exceeded 1,900; a month later, the season's total had jumped to 4,000. By then, 700 lived in the sheds. During two extraordinary days in September, 1849, 900 had stepped ashore at Hamilton. The influx added to civic expenditures, challenging but not eliminating the perception of immigrants as an economic stimulus. Mayor George S. Tiffany happily detected a lowering of wages in the city, which pleased him because cheap manual labour was a requisite for railway construction.

Even so, there was such a surplus of labour that municipal officials reacted to immediate relief problems by trying to reduce the number of newcomers. They pleaded with the government to stop granting free tickets to Hamilton. The city's own program of forwarding came into force in August, 1849. A special Emigration Committee of Council had recommended "the plan of sending the emigrants to various places is the best, for if they remain here, they must be fed." At the very moment that they condemned the forwarding of the destitute to their own centre, Hamilton authorities distributed tickets and bread, thrusting the poor onto Brantford, Caledonia, Fergus, Galt, Guelph, London, Norwich, Port Dover, Simcoe and Woodstock.[43]

Irish emigration declined in the 1850s. Agriculture in the United Kingdom began to recover. Violent expressions of anti-Irish prejudice in the United States held down the numbers of Irish immigrants entering the United States and taking the NYC-GWR-MCR route to the West. Canadian immigration authorities claimed that three-quarters of the immigrants were now relatives joining families. Germans became a significant enough element to warrant the posting of an immigrant agency translator at Hamilton in 1853. Most Germans merely touched Hamilton in transit to the West. A few fell out from this migration and stayed awhile, so that in 1857 the city had a German community with supporting institutions. The Reverend C.L. Haesel used Christ's Church for German-language services and the Methodists established a mission. The German proprietor of the Waterloo Hotel, the name itself a symbol of English-German fraternity, published the semiweekly *Canadian Zeitung*. Moreover, it was in 1853 that a few German Jews founded the Hebrew Benevolent Society of Anshei Shalom, eventually to be known as Anshei Shalom Temple.

Many who increased Hamilton's population from about 9,900 in 1848 to 25,000 in 1857 were sojourning rather than settling. Some Irish famine immigrants stayed around the region only so long as their labour was needed in construction. Of the Germans who broke their journey at Hamilton, many did not conceive of it as a final destination. A temporary opportunity or sense of adventure had interrupted their migration to Chicago, Milwaukee and the West. A flight from Hamilton by individuals from all ethnic and trade groups soon would begin, cutting the city's population to about 19,000 in 1861.[44]

In addition to receiving large numbers of immigrants, many of whom were poorer than those who came in the waves of the 1830s, Hamilton had to absorb a young population. In 1851, the age group between fifteen and thirty embraced 37 per cent of the people of Hamilton. These ages marked the stage of life when young men and women were able to move about relatively unencumbered. The fact that these ages were so strongly represented indicates the impact of the famine Irish on the city and the attraction of Hamilton for opportunity-seeking adolescents and young adults. The statistics take on added meaning when contrasted with those for 1861, in the midst of a depression. In that year, the fifteen-to-thirty age group had fallen to 26 per

Private charities received municipal grants to aid victims of an industrial society. This 1870s photo shows the Aged Women's and Orphan's Home.

cent and the percentage of those aged sixty and over had more than doubled from its 1851 proportion to 5 per cent. In numbers proportionately greater than other age groups, youthful Hamilton adults fled in search of employment elsewhere. The older people stayed on; so did more women than men. It seems that adults with children may have found it awkward to move, accepting reduced wages, partial employment or a shift to a new line of work. In the depression, Hamilton was a suitable place to remain and raise children; the vacant dwellings created rental bargains. The depressed city was not as desirable for independent young labourers.[45]

If adolescents and young adults — able to endure and perhaps relish a shifting about on the employment frontiers of North America — were transient, then it is important to note that their family situation differed from the population which moved through Hamilton in its boom-town years. In the 1830s boom, the town had attracted many more men than women due to the uncertainties of life in a strange environment when the interior of the continent was considered raw and where transportation had its discomforts. Improvements in transportation made it appear feasible for the whole family to move toward employment by the late 1840s or early 1850s. There were also distinctions between the prefamine Irish immigrants (1829-1837) and those who fled to North America during and after 1846. The early movement was largely male; the latter one included young adult females. At the same time, Hamilton had become a different community. In 1851 its population was about triple that of the boom year 1836. A much larger professional and mercantile element was able to absorb female servants. All of these points suggest that in the new growth period of the 1850s there was no widely disproportionate number of males. When men now trekked toward a bonanza of jobs, they were more likely to include female family members.

When the financial blight struck in 1837, a portion of the floating young male population of Hamilton departed, restoring a male-female balance. The panic flight from the city in the late 1850s and early 1860s had a similar male composition. In the young-adult age group of twenty-one to twenty-five, the ratio of men to women sharply declined between the census years 1851 and 1861. The decline was most marked among the Irish, suggesting withdrawal of young unskilled male labourers; it was accompanied by a rise in the proportion of spinsters and deserted wives. The hallmark of the population was motion, but that motion was different from the motion of the 1830s. By the late 1860s and certainly by the 1871 census, the city's population was back to the level of 1857.[46]

THE PHYSICAL SETTING AT MIDCENTURY

Viewed from atop the escarpment, the Dundas Valley and Burlington Bay imparted rustic tranquility amidst economic transformations. "Swelling hills, masses of forest, and in the distance the broad waters of Ontario." Robert Whale's romantic vistas painted at midcentury extolled the natural beauty of the city's setting. Nonetheless, the romantic artist's vision had had to come to terms with buildings, roads and railways. Down on the city streets, the man-made environment was generally uninspiring. Only the diversified topography of Hamilton and a number of exceptional buildings rescued it from a commonplace appearance. Roughly three-quarters of the dwellings in the 1850s and 1860s were frame. Vacant lots were a feature of most city blocks. In summer dry spells, the street dust mingled with "road apples" deposited by horses. The mixture blew into windows and doors. Spring run-off or a heavy rain disrupted traffic. Across the city, on the south side, the access up the escarpment was difficult to maintain. Streams running off "the mountain" in the spring prevented wagons from making an easy transit up or down the John Street access. In the late 1840s, travellers on this original road through the Hamilton family farm had encountered so much difficulty that the city built a second route using a macadamized surface. This gave a measure of relief, but the annual run-off soon encumbered it with fallen trees, stumps and loose earth.[47]

One outstanding feature of the rough man-made urban environment was an increase in housing construction during the lakeport period of the 1840s and the railway boom of the 1850s. The phenomenal increase in dwellings from 1841 to 1848 (200 per cent) indirectly suggests that construction was a well-established leading sector in the urban economy. The 100 per cent gain in the number of dwellings between 1848 and 1861 was a feature of the railway boom, but the impressive expansion of the earlier period testifies once more to the prosperous state of

Hamilton as a lakeport servicing an agrarian hinterland and public-works projects. The recovery of the late 1860s produced further construction that in terms of the absolute number of new dwellings represented the greatest period of construction to date.

The construction activity produced a social geography that was not too different from that of the frontier town. Rich and poor lived close to each other, but elevation and drainage considerations influenced their precise relationship with respect to housing. Most of the city's better estates, those in the southwest at the bottom of the escarpment, maintained elaborate gardens at mid-century. Here were the homes of merchants like John Young and Archibald Kerr, hardware merchant and nail manufacturer Richard Juson, spice and grocery wholesaler W.P. McLaren and the Hamilton family estate occupied by Robert J. Hamilton. Another sprinkling of estates occupied the "hogsback," the distinct ridge meandering from Burlington Heights south across York, King and Main streets. Upon it were the homes of the Mills family. In politics and in property ownership the sons of James Mills dominated the west end of the city. Banker Thomas Stinson and Judge Miles O'Reilly maintained estates in less fashionable parts of town. O'Reilly, living in his Corktown estate "The Willows," stayed close to his ancestral countrymen and political supporters. All of these landscaped estates were cherished marks of status; they contrasted with a public landscape composed of crude streets and vacant land.[48]

The lowland in the city developed into residential areas primarily inhabited by poorer folk, renting frame or rough-cast dwellings. Corktown and James Mills's survey south of Main Street in St. George's ward were relatively low districts vulnerable to spring run-off and noted for inexpensive houses and, along with the old Port Hamilton area, a disproportionately large number of Irish and labourers. The north end or old Port Hamilton, while not generally low-lying, was interspersed with ravines and vacant lots. Close by the new railyards, it was a place of residence for the working class. All working-class areas in the city sheltered a mixture of people. Skilled and unskilled labourers mingled in Corktown; ships' carpenters, sailors, mechanics and dock labourers lived together in the north end. This mixture and the relative proximity of the elite can be considered spatial hallmarks of the commercial or early industrial city where extreme class segregation was not apparent. In an otherwise stratified society, spatial distance between the elite and other social groups was moderate. Despite the overrepresentation of the Irish in Corktown and Port Hamilton, there was no real ethnic ghetto.

Industrial and commercial location likewise draw attention to patterns of urban land use which seem appreciably more mixed than in the industrial city. One expression of segregation was the virtual absence of industry from the "hogsback" and its extension at the foot of the mountain near James and John streets. Most foundries and boilermakers present in 1871 had located in an area just north of King Street on the fringes of the central business district. Specialized marine foundries were found in the north end and adjacent to the GWR yard. Along York Street near its intersection with Bay Street, the carriage makers and related trades — axle and spring producers — congregated. A region of closely related new activities had formed in the 1860s along King Street just east of Gore Park, including several of the city's largest employers: the Wanzer factory, the McPherson shoe factory and the Sanford-McInnes clothing operation.

This positioning of plants of related or like activity was an expression of their sharing resources and the provision of complementary services. Moreover, few Hamilton industries by the 1870s had sufficiently high ratios of commodity inputs per worker to have to locate near transportation terminals. Eventually, the costs of intermediate haulage from factory to railyard or dock and the bulk of materials used in new industries would lead to the city's being pulled inside out when factories moved nearer to the harbourfront and the railways. Sawyer-Massey pioneered the shift when it left the downtown location of the old McQuesten foundry and moved to the periphery around 1857.

Meanwhile at the heart of the city, the peculiar wedge of vacant land known as the Gore was evolving from a firewood market and a rubble ground for building materials into an embellished park. As a meandering trail, King Street had not conformed to the grid survey of concession lines. In about 1816 George Hamilton and Nathaniel Hughson had proposed a joint development of their properties which might have corrected part of the irregularity by forming a town square into which King Street would be absorbed. The scheme fell through, guaranteeing the eccentricity of King Street and leaving in doubt the ownership of the triangle of land that George Hamilton had pledged to form a square. The am-

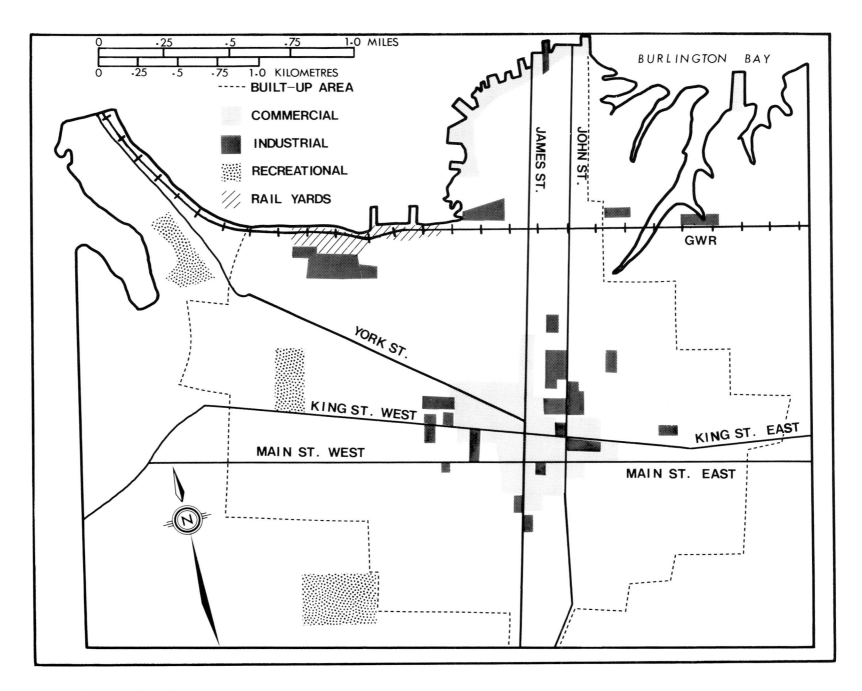

4 Land Use in Hamilton, c. 1870.

Scale:
0 · .25 · .5 · .75 · 1.0 MILES
0 · .25 · .5 · .75 · 1.0 KILOMETRES

Legend:
- - - - BUILT-UP AREA
COMMERCIAL
INDUSTRIAL
RECREATIONAL
RAIL YARDS

BURLINGTON BAY

JAMES ST.
JOHN ST.
GWR
YORK ST.
KING ST. WEST
KING ST. EAST
MAIN ST. WEST
MAIN ST. EAST

N

Embellished as a park in the early 1860s, the Gore (here shown around 1865) evolved as a unique geographic and civic heart for Hamilton.

Stone buildings comprised the typical central-core business block. These shops on King Street included the partnership that launched the ready-made clothing empire of W.E. Sanford.

biguity about ownership continued until the city's worries about its revenues in the economic slump of 1847 and 1848 led to speculation about the sale of civic property. A committee of council investigated the sale of Gore land. Robert Jarvis Hamilton, George's son, had a reasonable claim but no deed. After a battle of fences, the city and its founding family agreed to subdivide the land and to share the proceeds.

Over seventy property owners petitioned the government of Canada to halt the sale, alleging that it would "destroy one of the chief ornaments of the town and that the revenue which is said may be derived out of it will not in the opinion of your Memorialists prove an adequate compensation to the inhabitants of the City generally for being deprived of the enjoyment of it as a Public Square." They also feared "a decrease in the value of their property." The solicitor general of Canada recommended that the city and Robert J. Hamilton not go forward with the sale. Eventually the city gained clear title and revived the notion of a land sale. Perhaps hoping to raise capital for railway investments, council sought legislation that would enable it to sell lots on the Gore. As with the prior effort, this attempt was resisted. Thus the Gore survived as public land, no thanks to elected representatives.[49]

Hamilton's business district took form around the disputed Gore. The central area was not the jumble of confusion that historical geographers have seen in other midcentury cities. There was "differentiation of activity within the central area." Retail stores dominated the north side of the Gore; wholesale establishments were more prominent on the south side. Banks clustered near the wholesalers. Lawyers located on Main Street close to the courthouse. Artisan shops and manufacturing establishments dominated the outer central area, while hotels and boarding houses intervened between that area and the city centre. Hamilton at midcentury was not clearly divided into economic sectors and socially distinct neighbourhoods, but its space had elements of segregated land use and was far from being a disorganized mix of estates, shanties, stores and industries.[50]

Aside from the Gore, there were no successful attempts to embellish the city's public areas. Several land developers tried and failed to convince the city to purchase public squares that would have enhanced property values. Hamilton was redeemed from a total want of stylish adornment by a few splendid stone structures. Sandyford Place, comprised of four town houses with a Palladian facade and constructed in the mid-1850s, was one of the finest examples of a terrace structure in Canada outside of Montreal. Only slightly less distinguished were Herkimer Terrace (1855-60) and the commercial terrace on James Street known as the Murison Block (1854-60). The Commercial Block (1858), a mercantile palazzo with finely crafted stonework, would survive as a monument to the city's trading status at midcentury.

The Hamilton elite built impressive churches. Christ's Church, Anglican, had the patronage of many elite families; MacNab Street Presbyterian was virtually in Calvin McQuesten's backyard; the renowned St. Paul's Presbyterian (originally St. Andrew's) was the favoured church of the Scottish merchant families. Samuel Mills established All Saints Anglican Church in 1872. Often sponsorship of a church building program ripened from sincere theological interests. Calvin McQuesten and Isaac Buchanan were serious students of theology. As well, there were men and women who organized fund-raising ventures to build churches because they considered them the *sine qua non* of a civilized community. Piety and culture had their role in building campaigns, although the magnificence of Christ's Church and St. Paul's likewise expressed a sectarian version of Hamilton boosterism. Churches and railways may have been cut from the same cloth so far as the city's promoters were concerned. Samuel Mills, a keen real-estate investor judged avaricious by peers, tried to persuade Presbyterian Isaac Buchanan that a contribution to Christ's Church's expansion would help to complete a structure advertising Hamilton as a community of substance. It is impossible to say how many civic leaders accepted such notions, but it is plausible to see secular ambitions underpinning sacred ideals in the movements to build inspiring places of worship.[51]

In addition to churches, four secular achievements made architectural statements about Hamilton's material progress. The Hamilton Central School epitomized the advanced thinking of the era on education. The School Act of 1846 established a system of funding and administering primary education. A debate about neighbourhood schools versus a central school tied up the Hamilton school trustees from 1847 to 1850. The decision to build an impressive central facility was a tribute to a highly motivated Hamilton reformer, Dr. William Craigie. Educated as a medical practitioner in Edinburgh, he came to Ancaster in 1834 and settled

Central School was a pioneering venture in centralized public education. Farm and city families who could spare children from labour sacrificed to send them here. The elite employed private tutors.

The Crystal Palace at Victoria Park was constructed to help arrest Hamilton's sliding economic fortunes by attracting provincial fairs.

The industrial future was prefigured in the extensive buildings at the Great Western Railway yards. This 1863 view captures none of the grime and noise of the yards.

In the 1860s, the railyard bridged the commercial past and the industrial future; the grain elevator, small sailing vessel and steamer indicated a continuing agricultural service function.

in Hamilton in 1845. In numerous public campaigns, the energetic Craigie was a staunch advocate of forceful state action in health and education. He admired efficiency and authority; he dearly wanted Hamilton recognized as a progressive centre. Erected on a ridge near the centre of the city between 1850 and 1853, the symmetrical schoolhouse, designed along Greek Revival lines, came to express Hamilton's ambitions in the years just before its fall.[52]

Craigie's civic-reform interests extended to public health and advocacy of a civic waterworks, leading to the construction of a remarkable pumphouse. Initiatives came from several directions. Noted business leaders like Isaac Buchanan, Robert J. Hamilton and Calvin McQuesten requested the government of Canada to assent to a bill to incorporate a joint-stock company to supply water "for domestic uses and for extinguishing of fire." A charter was granted in 1852 but dissension impeded development. Concern increased in the summer of 1854 when cholera swept through the city. The virulence of the epidemic "unfolds a frightful, as well as a Calamitous Tale." Between June 29 and August 16, 533 died of cholera. GWR officials reported that navvies on the Hamilton-to-Toronto line of the GWR were dropping so fast that construction had all but stopped. The cholera crisis and a rash of fires convinced civic leaders that they had to improve water supply without waiting upon private ventures. Like other North American urban centres at midcentury, Hamilton had begun environmental reforms that were to increase public safety.[53]

In August, 1854, Hamilton was authorized to construct a waterworks. A design competition was held, although no submissions were used. Thomas Keefer, who assessed the competition, prepared his own report and recommended, with the support of Dr. Craigie, that Lake Ontario rather than Burlington Bay would provide the cleaner water. Contracts were let during 1857 and 1858 for construction of the various components of the system. Construction in hard times provided work for some of the area's idle shops and unemployed labourers. In October, 1858, the first water was pumped from the lake into the reservoir. The pumphouse structures and a 150-foot chimney were architecturally appealing. The interior overwhelmed visitors with immense flywheels, iron Doric pillars and walking beams rocking on their bearings. Traditional masonry had been blended with iron and steam technology. The complete moment of civic achieve-

ment was attained when the Prince of Wales officially inaugurated the waterworks on his 1860 tour of Canada.[54]

During the prince's visit, work progressed on another public structure, a Crystal Palace which had had its origin in near despair and shallow boosterism. Until the city's two Members of Parliament, MacNab and Buchanan, intervened, it seemed that legislation would have limited the movement of a provincial fair to the regional centres of London, Toronto and Kingston. The fair had become irrationally attached to economic hopes when the commercial-railway economy faltered. Buchanan was only one of many who desperately believed that "the Exhibition here for next year...is thought everything to prevent property going further wrong in value."[55] To compete as a fair site, the city built a glass-walled building with dome. This Crystal Palace was condemned and razed in 1891.

The fourth monument in the railway city, though privately owned, qualifies as a creation of civic promotion. The GWR yard did not embellish; rather, its renown derived from mass and energy. The *Canadian Illustrated News* (1863) turned a blind eye to the collection of very plain buildings and praised the yard solely for size and functions. "The spirit of improvement has made sad work of the old bathing ground...on this 'made ground' the workshops are erected, some twenty buildings in all, embracing an area of over forty acres. They are by no means remarkable for beauty of architecture nor symmetry of arrangement, but then they were not built to please the eye." Identical words could describe the next hundred years of development on the bayshore, since the GWR shops were forerunners of an industrial waterfront. Yet for all their sooty atmosphere, metallic racket and hazards, the GWR shops were accepted by city boosters as signs of well-being; the absorption of the GWR by the GTR in 1882 and the subsequent removal of the shops in 1888 were taken as civic defeats.[56]

SOCIETY, CULTURE AND CIVIC AFFAIRS

The unsettled state of the population was an indirect expression of the material circumstances of the common residents. Property ownership in the working class was quite rare. Reports on Canadian wages for 1843, 1865 and 1870 confirm that opportunity for savings and acquisition of property were limited to the very few. In all of the reported years, common labourers received about $1.00 a day. Skilled tradesmen such as carpenters, masons and blacksmiths earned more: $1.25-$1.50 per day in 1843 and 1865 and $1.75-$2.75 by 1870.

It is difficult to assess what this meant since consumption patterns and information about family resources — inheritance, assistance from relatives, the taking in of a boarder, additional wage earners in the household — are not available on a routine basis. Even a crudely fashioned estimate is a revelation. If wages paid without board are subtracted from those that included board, it appears that food would have cost twenty-five to thirty cents a day per person; a family buying in bulk would have been able to reduce this cost. Rents fluctuated with the turns in the economy; however, $6.00 a month for a modest dwelling is a fair estimate. They could have gone higher in the early and mid-1850s, thereby reducing real wages. Therefore, a guess at the cost of food and shelter for a family of four for a year amounts to between $250 and $300. Assuming that the head of the family could find work for the whole year, he could earn annually between $300 (labourer) and $450 (tradesman). The wife might work and it was not uncommon for children over ten years of age to find occasional employment. Families with adolescents had access to greater income.[57]

Illness could absorb these meagre income supplements. Then there was unemployment, both seasonal and cyclical. George H. Mills recalled how in 1858 he saw "strong men begging for work, asking for food, clamouring for some kind of municipal measure that might better their condition."[58] Layoffs were widespread; as for men who held their jobs, they frequently were subjected to wage cuts. The GWR reduced pay so that employees were to receive four-and-a-half days' pay for six days of labour. It is possible that a few working-class households were ground into poverty by the vises of a family member — drink or gambling. More likely, distress was locked into step with the frequent recessions and the rough survival practices of employers.

The strategies of family maintenance were varied, but available information strongly suggests that workingmen and their households in Hamilton eked out a marginal living which, under good conditions, would make acquisition of property possible but extremely difficult. Home mortgages were usually available for relatively short terms and principal often had to be paid in a lump sum at the end of term. The transiency of the population, the presence of many poor immigrants from Ireland, the wages and the system of home financing meant that in the 1850-to-1870 period only about one-quarter of the city's dwellings were owner-occupied. Home ownership was far greater among elite professions than among labourers.[59]

Property ownership was concentrated in the hands of a business and political elite that had clear interests and worries. During the midcentury, the following were prominent as landlords or land developers: Colin Ferrie, Allan MacNab, Calvin McQuesten, Samuel Mills, Thomas Stinson and Hugh Willson. Among the owners of multiple properties in 1861, four aldermen held twenty-seven properties, the high bailiff owned six, the two Members of Parliament had 11. These pieces of information, coinciding with incidents in the promotion of railways, relate public office to the pursuit of private gain. The vigorous promotion of Hamilton evolved from the self-interest of merchants, contractors and property owners. The handful of men who controlled property and public offices were able to use their influence and the cry that Hamilton must progress for the promotion of private ends.[60]

Occasionally, opposition had disturbed the railway and real-estate promoters even in the robust years. Resistance to the city's purchase of GWR stocks had been lively. What is more, certain consequences of economic expansion — the swelling of the labour force and labour protest — unsettled the civic elite. The response was not to renounce growth, for that would upset the all-important property values. Rather, education and police were accented as the means by which growth and order could be reconciled. In the frontier era of the commercial town, a degree of turbulence had been accepted; serious political disturbances were to be put down by the voluntary militia. Events in the railway city forced a reappraisal of such a loose approach and a stiffening of a resolve to police the city beyond the degree that had accompanied the moral-order concerns of the 1840s.

At once the civic elite sought to stimulate growth and to control the social turbulence that progress seemed to promote. Expression of this dual ambition came in the 1846 Act of Incorporation that gave Hamilton city status. It established five wards, each with two elected councillors. Much of the act repeated earlier powers spelled out in the 1833 act, powers like market regulation and control of fire hazards. New aspects dwelt upon a balancing of change and stability. To codify the commitment to growth and to enable the municipal government to promote enterprise, the act gave Hamilton the authority to enter into contracts. For example, the city could extend franchises like that granted to a gas company in 1849. A blanket clause allowed the council "to provide for the permanent improvement of the said City in all matters as well ornamental as useful." To further stability, the act created the position of stipendiary police magistrate and confirmed the authority of the municipality to arrest rogues and vagabonds. The concern for stability extended to the qualifications for voters and councillors; the former had to be local residents for twelve months and the latter for two years.[61]

The arrival of Irish famine immigrants constituted one source of fear, but labour incidents next mobilized the elite to insist upon a large police force. In the era of the industrial city, after 1870, a sequence of labour-reform movements would emphasize social criticism and promote ideals of commonwealth and justice. However, in the mid-nineteenth century, labour organization was sporadic. In Hamilton it had been initiated by the skilled carpenters in 1831 or 1832. It is likely that the next group was Hamilton's journeymen stonecutters who, in April, 1845, formed a society for benevolent purposes and for the establishment of regular wages. In one of the first Canadian strikes against mechanization, the tailors at a Mr. Lawson's establishment resisted the introduction of the sewing machine in 1853. These were exercises built on craft concepts; there were many more.

Meanwhile, direct action with resort to force was evident in the region's political economy. There had been the 1837 uprisings and violent incidents associated with strikes by canal labourers on the Grand River navigation project and Welland Canal in 1843-44. Doubtless there were numerous disputes with a violent edge and assaults on authority. Sporadic actions involving a few men did not stir deep fear among the city's propertied families. It was success in securing a railway that introduced an awesome threat. A militant display by railway navvies in early 1851 rocked the civic elite. Roughly 900 labourers, more than anticipated, had arrived to work on the GWR in the Dundas vicinity. Work had been underway for less than a year when men who had "twice left their employment on a demand for higher wages and armed with bludgeons by threats of violence [had] drawn off and effectually prevented the peaceable and industrious labourers from

earning their livelihood." On 5 February 1851, a party of the striking navvies marched through Dundas "to the great consternation and alarm of the peaceable inhabitants." Fifty Hamiltonians, essentially the major businessmen, petitioned the government of Canada to send in troops. The government, not wishing to incur expense, demanded that local officials first form an effective police force. Dundas, Hamilton and the GWR jointly supported a temporary force, not exceeding twenty-seven men, and the government dispatched two companies of troops to Hamilton where they stayed from July, 1851, to the spring of 1852. The railway city, unlike the frontier town, harboured a major employer with an enormous labour force. The joint-stock company introduced a level of labour strife that initiated a local and colony-wide debate about security. The clashes between large enterprises and workingmen contributed to the founding of professional police forces.[62]

The 1857-1864 depression, bringing layoffs and forcing abandonment of the city by many labourers, reduced prospects for strike action. However, it added to the store of bitterness. One labourer questioned, in a letter to the *Hamilton Times*, "why should the artisan and the mechanic suffer" for the folly of the "merchants, storekeepers and landgrabber?"[63] The recovery of the late 1860s and early 1870s as well as the 1871 struggle for an eight-hour day in the United States and for a nine-hour day in England emboldened Hamilton workers' organizations. Indeed, the nine-hours movement in Canada originated at a meeting in the Hamilton Mechanics Institute, 27 January 1872. A unanimously approved resolution declared the nine-hours movement to be a matter of social necessity to enable workingmen to improve their education and better meet their duties as fathers and citizens. Hamilton men then organized a league to draw the support of labourers in other cities. A few Hamilton employers seemed sympathetic and instituted the nine-hour day. However, 144 of the city's manufacturers and contractors signed a resolution on 13 February 1872 opposing it in principle. By mid-May workers had struck or been locked out at the Sawyer farm-implements plant, Wilson, Bowman and Company (manufacturers of sewing machines) and all of the foundries except one. Roughly 1,000 men were out of work. Adequate financial support for their struggle failed to flow from the Montreal and Toronto labour movements.

By the summer of 1872, workers had drifted back and shops that had instituted the nine-hour day reverted to ten hours. Like the carpenters' organization in the mid-1830s and the militant deeds of railway navvies in the early 1850s, the 1872 nine-hours movement had significance even in failure. Local workingmen shared in a fraternal experience of meeting and struggle; the organized resistance of employers confirmed a class cleavage. An impression of unrelenting friction, however, is a narrow one. Workingmen could accept booster promotion of the city and unite with employers in advocacy of a protective tariff as an ingredient in the city's new industrial strategy. The attitudes of workingmen of various origins, faiths and skills prohibit any conclusion other than that at midcentury and the years ahead there were critical points when class considerations became particularly vivid.[64]

The economic fallibilities of Hamilton during the midcentury were consequences of a shortage of investment funds in a colonial community, the lure of quick profits in land speculation, and the waste of resources connected with a ruinous duplication of railway lines. One effect of this formula for crisis was that a growing urban labour force was alternately pressed into long hours or cut loose in reaction to the needs of free enterprise operating in a realm of capital shortages. The merchant princes, real estate speculators and early industrialists had their own problems stemming from this awkward stage of economic life. To be sure they established estates with stone mansions, hired gardeners and employed servants, entertained and travelled abroad. A few men, John Young being the prime example, founded successful business dynasties that adapted to changing opportunities, but failures were plentiful in the context of competitive capitalism. The risks of commerce and speculation could terminate with a wearing down of the proprietor's health, a loss of assets and status or the leaving of an impoverished estate. The careers of four men — Colin Ferrie, Jasper Gilkison, Sir Allan MacNab and Isaac Buchanan — ended in these circumstances. That shopkeepers, blacksmiths and others failed is not surprising, but it is the fall of the mighty which bears witness to the risk-laden economy.

Colin Ferrie had survived the 1837 collapse by selling off branch stores, sacrificing real estate and clearing stock at discount prices. When other merchants detected a return of prosperous times in 1840, rival John Young could dismiss Colin as a spent force whose old debts "will be worse and worse to collect." Costly repairs to a family milling operation, heavy losses sustained by his father's business and the competition of Isaac Buchanan had rendered Colin taciturn and anxious. He withdrew from politics. Only as his businesses recovered did he reenter civic affairs and serve as the city's first mayor in 1847. A tightening of credit from 1848 to 1851 precipitated his final withdrawal from public life. In this difficult period, he quarrelled with family members over business affairs. He had to pursue debtors, clear off stock and mortgage more property in order to meet his debts. The family recommended that he exercise more caution in future dealings and that he sell off lots from his estate. In 1855, just when he and the city had recovered and benefited from the railway boom, the firm suffered when winter collections turned up more than the usual number of bad accounts. As well, two vessels carrying company goods sank in Lake Ontario. Rumours about his losses weakened confidence in the Gore Bank. The anxiety undermined his health. Following a November, 1856, meeting with directors of the Gore Bank, Ferrie collapsed. He died at home a few days later from "an enlargement of the heart."[65]

Jasper Gilkison, a former clerk in Ferrie's store, made good in the late 1840s as a land agent, speculator and officer with the GWR. The depression erased his gains; he was reduced to touching associates for loans and employment. His 1859 letter to Alexander Tilloch Galt, Minister of Finance, requesting patronage is a pathetic appeal.

> In these times my business has fallen off so very seriously, and having met with severe losses, I am reduced to the necessity — for the sake of my family in particular — of seeking some office of employment.
>
> I therefore venture to trouble you with this note, trusting that you will give me your friendly interest should anything suitable present itself either in the gift of the Government or otherwise.
>
> My business has been that of a law and general real estate agent, arbitrator as well. I have filled the offices of Secretary and Director of Railways, and have much experience in Municipal and local affairs.

The presentation of colours to the Thirteenth Battalion in 1863. The attachment to military traditions was strong in Hamilton and could be traced to the militia companies organized during the War of 1812 and the rebellion of 1837.

Social glitter in the midst of an economic collapse: a dinner to honour Lord Lyons and the other aristocrats and officers who visited the city in 1863. Such affairs displayed the patriotic attachments and social ambitions of the local elite. Both Sir Allan MacNab and Senator Samuel Mills had daughters who married into the aristocracy.

I have also for the last 20 years been an active politician, and am a supporter of the Government.[66]

For three years Gilkison sought a patronage appointment and eventually was appointed Indian agent at Brantford, where he died in 1906. Daniel Gunn likewise pleaded and friends found a position for "the poor fellow" with the GWR.[67]

Sir Allan MacNab kept up appearances even in the depression. Occasionally he had turned a profit on land sales or traded on his political influence to extract favours from the GWR; often he kept ahead of creditors by floating new loans. Several times demands by creditors forced him to sell off property at a disadvantageous price. The dearth of assets behind the knight was apparent after his death when claims on his estate forced the sale of Dundurn Castle's furnishings.[68]

Between interludes of anxiety, elite pleasures were ample and kept apart from common socializing and recreation. A tight elite circle was not only a matter of taste and pretension; it hived rumours of profits or failures which might have deflated the public image of selfless men shrewdly guiding the city. Through the seasons, merchants, respectable clerks and professionals followed a formal pattern of social contact. The summer brought carriage rides, garden parties and cricket. The popularity of yachting led to the organization of one of a growing number of exclusive associations, the Royal Hamilton Yacht Club (1860). In the same year there was talk of forming a racquet club for gentlemen. In winter there was curling at the Ontario (Thistle) Club, organized in 1853; later the Mechanics Curling Club was formed to cater to a different class of enthusiasts. The officers of the militia formed an exclusive company. A series of balls held in private homes were understandably discriminatory, but so were a number of so-called public balls managed on a "subscription" basis which screened ticket seekers.

Moving from strenuous to passive recreation, the gentlemen of Hamilton were avid purchasers of *Blackwood's Magazine*. The works of Sir Walter Scott led among fiction imports. The steady demand for Jane Porter's *Scottish Chiefs* is equally suggestive, for the Scottish background of the merchant princes and their pride in stone dwellings and shops dovetailed with the old-country books they chose to read and display. Homes were decorated with romantic or religious paintings.[69]

Business trips to London and Glasgow as well as routine correspondence with family and associates in the United Kingdom reinforced cultural yearnings and a need to feel informed about politics and letters in the metropolitan community across the Atlantic; that community, after all, supplied much of the money for the heavily capitalized projects of the railway city. Hamilton's elite could conceive of their city as more than an isolated outpost of the old country. The 1855 marriage of Sir Allan MacNab's daughter Sophia Mary to William Coutts Keppel, Viscount Bury, confirmed the intimacy of a transatlantic elite — as did an 1862 visit of no less than sixty military officers including Lord Alex Russell, Lord Edward Clinton, Lord Cecil and Lord Cavendish. The balls, courting and gossip of the latter occasion kept the ladies diverted while the financial collapse preoccupied husbands and fathers. Barbara MacNab could not contain herself: "I hear such a lot of news of one kind and another," she wrote to Mrs. John Young, "that I must add another sheet."[70] Janey MacLaren's meetings with a certain young captain filled more than one letter. As a business enterprise, a means of travel and a carrier of letters, the railway had pulled the old country closer to Hamilton.

The urban lower orders formulated some distinctly different points of view from the ones held by those above them. Artisans, mechanics, carpenters and many others lived in a cultural world apart from merchants, speculators and manufacturers. The cultural orientations of the bulk of the city's residents were diverse, difficult to pin down. The folklore of Irish tenant farmers, the independence of Scottish handloom operators, the wit and worldly knowledge of American mechanics and many more categories of popular culture filled workplaces and saloons.

There were activities which attracted the working class: "baseball games, mechanics' festivals, union balls, commemorative suppers, picnics, and parades." The abundant saloons and sporting establishments were places of easy conviviality. Of course, not every skilled tradesman or unskilled labourer frequented the bars, and the more highbrow tone of the Mechanics Institute did not discourage all workingmen. Nonetheless, the casual establishments were well patronized. Dan Black's club house and bowling green, for example, was the virtual centre of working-class recreation and discussion by the early 1870s, for it was here that labour leaders held early talks to organize the nine-hours movement.[71]

Winter sports and spills on Burlington Bay during the continuance of good ice. Hamiltonians enjoyed their varied natural environment.

As an outpost of United Kingdom culture in North America, Hamilton had to adapt its celebration of the Prince of Wales's wedding to its locale and climate. The last ice race of the 1863 season was scheduled for the wedding day.

Workingmen often met in homogeneous bodies, but Hamilton offered a potpourri of public entertainments acceptable to most classes: horse races, boxing matches, parades, band concerts by the Thirteenth Battalion band, plays by amateur and travelling companies, excursions on the bay and train outings. The affection for display at outdoor events touched all classes. Uniforms, bands, banners and Sunday finery decorated public occasions.[72] There was a common body of culture, although the classes of Hamilton could and did borrow from it to make demonstrations that stated division and friction. One point of occasional convergence pertained to the city itself and its industrial base. There were frequent agreements between business leaders and workingmen in relation to the protective tariff as an instrument of local prosperity. The coexistence of barriers and contacts accents a dilemma to be raised in later chapters as well. What were the relative strengths of cultural activities that bound city residents together and the social cleavages that set them in opposition and encouraged separate cultural activities? At the extreme, the exclusive ways of the elite and features of working-class culture impeded meaningful exchanges between the two groups. Furthermore, as a test of contrasts, the experience of economic failure shared by all classes during the railway city's crisis was handled in special ways by the elite, especially through political favours and credit arrangements. It remains an unresolved question as to whether religion, political allegiances, British imperial sentiment and certain forms of open entertainment bridged the very evident spheres of class.

The richness of recreation began to encompass the formal aspects of arts and letters during the railway-city era. Founded in 1858, the Hamilton Philharmonic Society — assisted by artists who came by rail from Buffalo — staged Haydn's *Creation*. Again with Buffalo talent, the society arranged performances of a Mozart mass and part of Handel's *Messiah* in 1861. The society was the ancestor of the city's classical-music endeavours. Theatre groups had been present since the 1830s. In the late 1860s amateur thespians flourished and established the Hamilton Dramatic Society (later the Garrick Club). The Hamilton Association for the Advancement of Literature, Science and Art charted an enduring course following its formation in 1857. It was a local expression of the Victorian passion for natural history. On Sunday excursions around Burlington Bay in the summertime,

members collected plants and rocks and observed the birds on one of the major flyways of eastern North America.

In view of the prominence of the Scottish mercantile community and the usual interest in education among Scots, it is to be expected that they had a major role in the association's early years. The first president, Dr. W. Ormiston, was a clergyman from Scotland; the second president, John Rae, was born in the Orkney Islands, worked for the Hudson's Bay Company and was made a Fellow of the Royal Geographical Society for his Arctic expeditions. The ever-active Dr. Craigie served as recording secretary. That Buffalo and Scotland should amplify the formal culture of Hamilton underscores the American and United Kingdom connections which invigorated so many other fields of endeavour.[73]

CONCLUSION

The railway had introduced the city to significant strike action. It also had engendered a crushing fiscal crisis. The prospects of economic triumph produced architectural expressions of civic pride which enriched the cityscape for generations. Poems, paintings and even a cemetery marker depicted the locomotive. What is less obvious, but especially striking from the perspective of subsequent development in the urban economy and society, is that the railway, in its operations after construction, functioned as a forerunner of modern corporations, having a chain of command, strict rules, attention to time, and the prospect of promotion within the organization. These characteristics were to spread during a period of concern about efficiency in business and municipal affairs that commenced in earnest after 1900. Even aspects of urban crime were influenced by the railway. A gang of pickpockets who worked the GWR and American trains settled in Hamilton on account of its proximity to major urban communities on both sides of the boundary.[74] The point is that being an integral part of a maturing North American urban network had many implications. The railway cannot be blamed for crime any more than the GWR alone explains labour strife, ethnic diversity or the advent of modern corporate practices, but in each instance it was a likely catalyst, a pioneer at the very least. A mercurial and transient community — but one with a developing set of urban services — the railway city came as a transitional phase between the frontier boom town and the truly industrial city.

The ungainly vehicle produced by National Steel Car signified dramatic urban changes and local frustration; heavy industry and the internal-combustion engine had arrived, but Hamilton could not retain an enduring automotive industry.

Chapter Three

Hamilton, Ontario: The Industrial City Triumphant, 1870 – 1920

The industrial city created distinctive streetscapes. Large-scale industrial plants and working-class neighbourhoods can be detected easily in the contemporary city. Indeed, intermittent industrial construction and real-estate booms from 1900 to 1913 were responsible for most of the city's expansion to the east until housing demands after the Second World War forced new subdivision of rural land. Not every trait in the industrial stage of Hamilton's history came in tangible forms. Invisible economic and social developments are essential to the period: a transition in industrial management from local partnerships to integrated corporations, an influx of American branch plants, a gradual involvement of the provincial and federal governments in regulating industry, the decline of craft unionism, episodes in urban reform, and a broad advance in the regulation of the average urban dweller's life.

Selected careers chart the economic evolution. Senator James Turner (1826–1889), proprietor of an extensive grocery wholesaling firm, director of local railways, a director of the Bank of Hamilton and an early promoter of Hamilton business ties with Manitoba, embodies the city's commercial life at its most energetic. Turner had visited the North West Territories with Joseph Howe in 1869 and went down the Saskatchewan River from Edmonton to Winnipeg in 1882. Senator Donald MacInnes (1826–1900), a businessman of general mercantile background, had similar western interests as a director of the CPR and president of the South Saskatchewan Valley Railway Company. Both filled the shoes of Colin Ferrie and Isaac Buchanan. Younger men like John Moodie (1866–1919) and John Gibson (1842–1929) proclaimed a different era. Their promotion of electric power and traction, new industries and real estate helped to remake Hamilton between 1895 and 1920. The shift of banking and insurance from Hamilton to Toronto accentuated the industrial focus. The industrial city was also the home of a Yale University graduate originally from the iron and steel region of Ohio, Charles Wilcox (1856–1938), who became the first president of the Steel Company of Canada. Alan Studholme (1846–1919), representing East Hamilton's labourers at Queen's Park from 1906 to 1919, was as much a builder as any industrialist. All were protagonists in an industrial order. Other industrial-city features are quite concrete but meld so perfectly with the contemporary city that their point of origin is readily forgotten. Included in this category are electrification, mass transit and large-scale suburban tracts.

Nothing intrinsic to the industrial city allows for the patriotic intensity, emotional crises and social repercussions imposed by the First World War. War was obviously not part of an exclusively urban-history sequence. It was one of the profound shocks in the city's evolution. War affected housing, health, industrial expansion, labour relations, politics and culture. Another problem with an emphasis on structural change relates to the persistence of earlier themes. Railway or commercial ambitions lingered; old railway charters were renewed and new ones secured. Within southern Ontario, Hamilton successfully clung to an historic function as a wholesale distribution centre for groceries, dry goods and hardware. It retained financial institutions. What is more, the Bank of Hamilton (1872-1923) extended into the West. The Canadian urban system remained small enough so that a middle-rank city like Hamilton could claim a metropolitan influence. Finally, designating the years from roughly 1870 to 1920 as comprising an industrial stage begs a question.

What is industry? An overworked term, it has a complex explanation. At the beginning of the period there had emerged, in convincing fashion, industries with steam power. The complicating factor, also noted in the last chapter, was that shop-floor tasks demonstrated limits to a mechanized factory system; manual labour and craft trades abounded alongside steam-powered shafts and belts. At the other end of these decades, five developments — electric power, advances in iron and steel manufacture, radical designs for new factories, corporate mergers, and challenges to craft unionism — indicate the crossing of a second industrial threshold.

THE INDUSTRIAL ECONOMY

Railway ambitions endured despite the GWR problems. Scheming for commercial empires prodded railway ventures to life after the depression of the late 1850s and early 1860s. Earlier hopes for locally controlled steamship lines were reestablished; by the turn of the century there were three companies, one of which, the Hamilton and Fort William Navigation Company, delineated Hamilton's maturing bonds with the West. Formation of a Hamilton Provident and Loan Society (1871) and a Bank of Hamilton (1872) do more than confirm the economic recovery of the early 1870s — they establish that a handful of business leaders could sustain mercantile and financial ambitions even though Toronto had regional primacy.[1]

Hamilton changed to an industrializing city, but not without entrepreneurial action along former lines, a burst ill-fated with respect to railways. A revival in this sector commenced with the reorganization of the Hamilton and Port Dover line as the Hamilton and Lake Erie (1869). Construction proceeded from 1872 to 1875. More in common with the goals of the GWR was a scheme projected by a local syndicate promoting the Hamilton and North Western (HNWR). Even before the Canadian government had settled upon whether Toronto or Montreal capitalists should undertake a transcontinental line, a syndicate had organized "to connect Hamilton with the North Western Provinces." This proposal involved a line to Lake Huron and eventually tracks to connect with a railway to the Pacific. In 1875, with a bonus from Simcoe County, which hoped to spring free of Toronto's trade sphere, and resorting to a shaky arrangement with the contractor, the company placed tracks across Burlington Beach. The line edged toward Georgetown (1877), Barrie (1878) and ultimately Collingwood (1879). The leasing of a 100,000-bushel grain elevator in Hamilton expressed intentions about reviving the city as a grain port handling American and eventu-

ally Manitoban wheat. Nonetheless, the engineer's report for 1876 could not disguise cheap construction; locomotives rattled along at twelve miles per hour. In June, 1879, the HNWR announced an agreement with its Toronto rival, the Toronto and Northern. The Hamilton line surrendered autonomy and its aspiration for a connection with the CPR.[2]

The one railway to retain identity as a Hamilton institution, although control resided elsewhere, came into being for reasons quite apart from the former goals of linking the city to a settlement frontier. The Toronto, Hamilton and Buffalo Railway, eventually an industrial service company, originated in response to a lack of freight competition after the GTR had absorbed the GWR in 1882. A charter was granted first in 1884, but undercapitalized promoters and depression delayed construction. The line finally was carried into operation by an agreement involving the CPR, the Canada Southern, the New York Central and the Michigan Central. These systems valued the TH and B since it would connect the Michigan Central interests on the Niagara peninsula with the CPR. This modest function and external control confirmed Hamilton's last railway as a symbol for the city's real position in the North American urban system. The service given by the TH and B line showed Hamilton to be an industrial city with residual metropolitan institutions. Hinterlands were not contested in expansion of trackage, for despite considerable through-freight and passenger traffic, it was the industrial belt line, constructed in 1899, and subsequent factory loops that became mainstays. Volume on the belt line increased tenfold between 1901 and 1917, a measure of industrial activity and war orders.[3]

If railways failed to bring renown to Hamilton by the 1890s, then it is certain that iron did identify the city. Early product lines and technology are both inherently interesting and central to the city's evolving character. Additionally, it is important to explain how Hamilton eventually gained an ascendency over the resource-based Nova Scotia iron and steel industry.

The concentration of iron and steel manufacture in Hamilton is partly due to an advantageous location. The proximity to metallurgical coal in Pennsylvania and West Virginia, the availability of Lake Superior iron ore and a compact Ontario market provided advantages. Tariff policies which protected native manufacturers or induced Americans to move behind the tariff

The Toronto, Hamilton and Buffalo Railway's "gingerbread castle" at the corner of James and Hunter streets, here seen in the 1890s, initially served a dozen passenger trains a day.

barrier helped Hamilton in the late nineteenth century. In the early twentieth century, the tariff reductions on bituminous coal eliminated one of the props that had assisted the iron and steel industry in the Maritimes. In a way that cannot be measured, Hamilton had gained from a reduced tariff on raw materials and the protection of manufactured goods. Industrial bonuses do far less to explain Hamilton's industrial surge, for Hamilton was hardly unique in subsidizing free enterprise with cash grants or preferential tax and service charges. In seeking first causes, it is important to stress immigration and the evolution of the iron-goods manufacturers from the late 1830s and early 1840s. Iron merchants, founders and hardware jobbers formed a specialized talent pool alert to technical and marketing innovation, not to mention lobbying. Behind the accumulation of knowledge was the vital ingredient of immigration. Lacking in natural resources, Hamilton had accrued depth in human ones — marketing and entrepreneurial skill — before the Nova Scotia industries commenced. This critical distinction was one result of the enormous immigration (1830–1850) that bypassed Nova Scotia and moved into the Great Lakes region, forming markets for iron goods.[4]

Manufacturers filled the demands for stoves and farm implements, but iron merchants were an integral part of Hamilton's accumulation of special skills. Iron for moulders came from outside the city until the first furnace went into blast in 1896. Fragments of business correspondence and technical considerations indicate that Glasgow was an important — perhaps the most important — source of the essential pig iron from the 1840s to the 1870s. Hamilton iron merchants Daniel MacNab, Adam Hope and Matthew Leggat imported Glasgow iron because several — MacNab and Hope for certain — had contacts with Glasgow through prior experience in general wholesaling. What is more, Glasgow had secured primacy in the international iron trade by the mid-1840s with introduction of an exchange and warehousing system. In addition, Scottish pig iron was acclaimed by stove manufacturers on account of a fluidity which made well-defined casts, a desired characteristic in what was both an ornamental and functional household item. American iron was imported too and, once Nova Scotia supplies became available in about 1890, the United Kingdom became a less favoured source. The local iron men knew their material and the marginal economies of exchanging producers.[5]

Moulders and iron merchants placed Hamilton in a singular position as a manufacturing centre in the 1880s. It had an unusual concentration of stove foundries. Fortunately, the railway era had introduced additional metal-related industries because, in the long term, low levels of technological need and lack of incentives for innovation in stove production spelled weakness. Since the process of manufacture retained traditional simplicity and since patent control was weak, production stayed dispersed among a number of partnerships. Never did this older trade consolidate like the heavily capitalized rolling mills and forges. Toward the last quarter of the nineteenth century, modest technical changes in heating were taken in stride; old heating and cooking stoves were being replaced by furnaces, steam and hot-water heating. The ornamental character of the stove remained and adaptation was easy.[6]

The industry had growth periods attributable to new settlement in Canada. As early as 1873, John Stewart, a Hamiltonian who was a member of the unsuccessful Toronto CPR syndicate, had shipped stoves to Winnipeg. In 1882 the consul for the United States in Hamilton reported that:

> The manufacture of Stoves is the leading industry of Hamilton. From careful estimates, I learn that $900,000 of capital is employed in the business — constant employment is given to from 600 to 700 men. Nine thousand tons of iron were used in the business during the past year and nearly 25,000 stoves were manufactured — which were sent to every part of the Dominion including Manitoba and British Columbia.[7]

Later, price wars in the United States forced market competition on the Canadian prairies and moderated the potential benefits to Hamilton producers of the settlement of the West from 1900 to 1913. Gas and electric ranges in the 1920s used sheet metal and terminated old ways and partnerships. Yet it was in large measure on account of iron consumption by stove founders that a Hamilton blast furnace could have been thought economically feasible.

During the ascendancy of the stove industry a variety of other iron products were made locally: wagon and farm-implement parts, scales, wire, spikes and nails. To understand how Hamilton took advantage of national expansion, the iron mer-

Gore Park and King Street in the early 1900s, looking east.

The Hamilton Boys' Home, built in 1876 and designed by Hamilton architect James Balfour. Balfour also worked on the Canada Life Assurance Company Building (1883), renamed the Henry Birks and Sons Building in 1929.

The Hamilton General Hospital as it appeared soon after opening in 1882.

The Romanesque-style city hall to which James Balfour had contributed was an example, like the Hamilton Boys' Home and the Hamilton General Hospital, of institutional construction in a relatively prosperous city. It is seen here soon after it opened in 1889.

Built to serve as a station for the radial-streetcar network that reached into Hamilton's hinterland, the Terminal Building (seen here around 1912) contained the Temple Theatre and offices.

chant reenters the picture as hardware jobber. Usually the same firms which imported iron for industry also promoted sales of finished works. The iron merchants were nerve centres for the manufacturing community and, as a February, 1913, banquet testified, the merchants were part of a manufacturing fraternity. At this first banquet of the Canadian Hardware Manufacturers Association, held in Hamilton's Alexandra Rink, 600 members honoured iron merchant William Vallance, who had entered the trade in 1853. He had joined the firm of Wood and Leggat as a salesman, worked his way up to a buyer and then moved into partnership with Senator Alexander Wood. Their firm branched into the Canadian West in the infancy of prairie urban expansion. One is repeatedly struck by the western interests of Hamilton's business leaders. By 1894, the partners had forwarded their first carloads of assorted goods to Calgary. In 1896 they had placed a salesman in the Kootenay district of British Columbia, servicing the mining frontier. It was commonplace for Wood Vallance to order 10,000 kegs of nails from the Ontario Rolling Mill Company for the construction season which ran from April to December. Likewise, large orders were placed with Greening Wire and the Canada Screw Company. Such mundane transactions, multiplied many times over, were central to the health of a large portion of the city's manufacturers.[8]

Some products that jobbers moved west used wrought iron or steel. Sewing-machine manufacturers, wire drawers and farm-implements producers utilized more advanced and varied metallurgical supplies than did the stove founders. This required the importation of wrought iron and steel. It is probable that some wrought iron was produced locally by the 1880s since its production merely involved melting pig iron so that it could be worked manually with stirring poles. Steel was another matter. Its manufacture also involved reheated iron that had been produced in a blast furnace, but after that there were two techniques that could give the iron the desired hardness or tensile strength that characterized steels. The Bessemer method blew air through the molten iron, causing a sudden and violent transformation. The open-hearth technique, the method adopted by Hamilton producers, mixed iron and scrap metal in a slow process of heating that allowed testing to control quality or to permit production of specialized metals. Steel had variations in composition, so that in the 1880s and 1890s the Hamilton toolmakers and machinists

never seriously considered American imports, let alone a home-town producer. They insisted that the iron merchants supply them with steel from Thomas Firth and Sons of Sheffield, suppliers of ordnance steel to the British government.

Clearly, marketing and technical knowledge permeated Hamilton's metal trades. When iron and steel making were finally introduced, there were men who knew how to use the metals and, in a reciprocity of experience and knowledge, users of iron and steel along with a local producer worked out specifications suited to a diverse market. Such natural integration, enormously expanded with the presence of new iron and steel-using industries after 1910, gave Hamilton trump strength. Unlike Nova Scotia's iron and steel producers who had a sparce local market, Hamilton's producers moved in step with an impressive market for commonplace but necessary articles.[9]

Among experienced purchasers of iron and steel, three concerns warrant special attention, both as examples of the rich product lines made in Hamilton and as parties to the 1910 mergers that created the Steel Company of Canada. Most important was the Ontario Rolling Mill Company, organized by Cleveland and Youngstown iron specialists in April, 1879. They came to Canada because of a protective tariff, part of the Conservative National Policy, which would have jeopardized American shipments to Canada. At the same time, Hamilton attracted their interest because a rolling mill once run by the GWR had stood unused since 1872. The new mill company soon was rolling and forging parts for carriages, farm machinery, sleighs, sewing machines and items for hardware jobbers. Highly profitable, the company invested in more facilities and subsidiaries. In 1892, its Hamilton plants employed 550 men, used fourteen steam engines and several steam hammers.

The second firm, the Ontario Tack Company, opened in 1885 and introduced the latest American technology to local nail manufacture. Formerly nail producers like Richard Juson, who had supplied spikes for GWR construction in the 1850s, had slit iron plates to form square nails. By the 1880s, the tack company's process, using American machinery and local wire stock, had started to supplant the square nails with wire ones. At the turn of the century, the company processed twenty-five tons of steel bar daily.

The third enterprise, the Canada Screw Company, was founded

A vital part of Hamilton life, the farmers' market was roughly seventy years old when this picture was taken about 1905.

by a Dundas farm-tool and sewing-machine partnership which had experimented with the manufacture of wood screws in 1866. Three years later a reorganized firm with stove-founder Edward Gurney at the head took charge of a shop with forty employees. It moved to Hamilton in 1887 for access to the improved freight yards of the GTR. A decade later, 300 employees manufactured 2,000 gross of screws per day.[10]

Significantly, in view of prior references to links between stove and other iron industries, stove-founders John Tilden and John Milne and iron merchant Alexander Wood promoted the Hamilton Blast Furnace Company, the corporate entity which rounded out Hamilton's nineteenth-century iron industry. Capital shortages in the depression of the mid-1890s delayed completion. Then, on 31 December 1895, 500 city residents were taken by train to observe "the blowing in of the furnace." Once initial production problems were reduced, the blast furnace became an attractive purchase for the Ontario Rolling Mill. That was in 1899 and the resulting new corporation, the Hamilton Steel and Iron Company, soon had an open-hearth facility and an extensive product line: iron angles, plates and rivets; pin iron for the nail and tack plants; structural steel, soft steel, medium steel, firebox steel, boiler steel, and other grades defined by properties of shape, flexibility and strength.[11]

The mid-1890s brought major undertakings. The blast furnace was one project; the completion of the Hunter Street tunnel for the TH and B a month later was another. But a third entailed much more than an application of well-known technology; it was virtually experimental. Conceivably more than any other element, it sped local adaption to a second industrial revolution. Nestled below the DeCew Falls, about thirty-five miles from the city, the Cataract Power Company had assembled a hydro-electric generating plant. The year was 1898 and sceptics ridiculed the ambition of transmitting electricity on what was considered an exceptionally long transmission line. The system functioned well, bringing power to industrial users, to the city for its street lighting, and to the electrified streetcar system.[12]

No immediate change in factory architecture or layout accompanied the earliest applications of electricity, but it was proven cheaper than steam power. As well, it was less expensive than the thermal electricity generated in Toronto. Thus firms like Westinghouse and Frost Wire preferred Hamilton's power option.

Ultimately, electricity afforded a leap in adaptability since it made possible the application of energy in measured quantities whenever it was needed, a boon denied to steam-powered plants with cumbersome pulleys, shafts and belts. Within a decade, the elimination of the shafts and belts allowed new factories to be designed on a single- rather than three-storey plan; skylights then could be used to improve visibility and ventilation on shop floors.

Among the first Cataract clients were the Canadian Coloured Cotton Mills and the Imperial Cotton Company. The latter firm, incorporated in 1900, was a child of Cataract, because all common stock went to the electric company "for services." The textile industry had more recent origins in Hamilton than the iron trades, although there had been a few water-powered mills in the region since midcentury when Hamilton merchant John Young received this 1861 report on the textile industries in the Hamilton hinterland: "Already an English Company have commenced spinning and weaving dry goods in the large factory building at the bridge in Dundas, others are building or about to be, at St. Catharines, Hespeler, Indiana, Pt. Dover." Young took control of a Dundas mill in 1866. His family opened their Hamilton Cotton Company mill in 1880.

A second firm, the Ontario Cotton Mills Company, was established the next year. As a preelectric steam-powered mill, this latter plant had the classic forms and serves as a contrasting reference for later industrial designs. The main structure was three-storey brick and 365-by-50 feet. Raw cotton was taken in at the top level and moved down through its various stages of manufacture. A fifty-horsepower steam engine, manufactured in Providence, Rhode Island, ran a main shaft to which machinery on each floor was attached by a maze of belts. In 1885 this single power source ran 12,000 spindles and 362 power looms. All but fifty looms were of American manufacture, one of many examples of American industrial influence on Hamilton manufacturing.[13]

The first knit-goods producers in the region, Penman's of Paris and Forbes of Hespeler, commenced operations in 1868. Not long afterward, small knitting establishments settled in Ancaster, Dundas and Hamilton. Of all forms of late nineteenth-century manufacturing, knitting employed the most intricate machinery. Fabric made on knitting frames came out unshaped or partly shaped and was cut to pattern and pieced together on a sewing machine. This connection between textile manufacture and garment making explains why Hamilton's initial entrepreneurs in knitware included a fancy-goods retailer and a merchant tailor. The former, retailer John Moodie, also was a founder of Cataract Power; by 1901 he controlled the Eagle Spinning Company, the Eagle Knitting Company (founded 1888) and the Peerless Underwear Company. Altogether these mills in 1901 employed 700. Zimmerman, the tailor, founded Zimmer Knit; in 1901 this firm employed 250. Chipman-Holton had 110 employees. But it was Moodie who remained synonymous with knitting — particularly when in 1913 he opened Mercury Mills, capable of employing 850.[14]

Acquisition of electric-power and iron-production capacity tied into the long-appreciated harbour and the national economic booms of 1896–1907 and 1909–1913. Only during the 1830s and 1850s had local and international events fused so propitiously from the perspective of urban growth. Between 1900 and 1905, the city-wide increase in manufacturing employees was 24.2 per cent, but from 1905 to 1910 it rose by 67.0 per cent. The rise was 22.6 per cent between 1910 and 1915. It is no exaggeration to associate the initiation of this concentrated boom with one firm — International Harvester. It was not the city's first farm-implements manufacturer, but Sawyer-Massey had not expanded significantly.[15] It acquired the rights for Canadian production of American machinery.

Harvester was more ambitious and it heralded trends in the second phase of industrial organization. First, the company was the product of combinations. Five principal firms making harvesters and mowers in the United States had merged to control markets and to promote sales abroad. Second, when Harvester expanded its Hamilton plant in 1911, it employed an innovative layout with specialized departments in separate structures, many with sawtooth roofs for improved lighting and ventilation. Though the company was self-consciously modern in all corporate regards, the work process involved a synthesis of forms in which traces of old technology and traditions abided on new shop floors. Of course, the situation was fluid and an industry leader like Harvester continually applied mechanization, but even after the introduction of moulding machines the skills of manual moulders were needed to produce intricate pieces. Heat and blue haze from the puddling made work uncomfortable and unhealthy. In the

forge department, hearing was impeded by the racket from a hundred or so immense hammers. On the other hand, moulding machines, electrically powered blowers on casting cupolas, electric grinding wheels and power sheers to cut metal rods and sheets defined Harvester and many other plants as beneficiaries of the second industrial revolution. Aside from the quest for technical innovations, there was a reorganization of shop floors to realize greater efficiency.[16] A 1905 description of Canadian Westinghouse conveyed the orderly pressure of efficiency studies; it is likely that Harvester and other plants were alert to the same organizational economies.

> The thing that strikes the notice of observer before all else is the manner in which everything is planned out so that everything that is being made makes a direct progression through the works. Economy is seen everywhere.... And the machines are situated so that each piece passes right down the line to where the parts are assembled and put together for testing and shipping. Nothing is handled twice.... Everything works like clock-work, and all are truly 'parts of one stupendous whole.'[17]

Harvester's decision to locate and to expand in Hamilton revives the question of industrial location and Hamilton's attractions. Harvester wanted a Canadian plant so that it could exploit the expansion of farm settlement on the prairies and save the 20 per cent import duty on mowers and binders. The company assessed a number of Canadian sites, but according to Harvester president Cyrus McCormick, Hamilton won because it had waterside property that enabled the firm to control its own docks. There were good railway connections. Cataract Power supplied cheap energy. Proximity to the Hamilton Iron and Steel Company was an added benefit. McCormick failed to mention a municipal-bonus controversy. It is not likely to have been a necessary inducement, but no well-known company of the era was likely to forego an opportunity to trade on its name to squeeze supplicant municipalities. In this instance, Harvester had requested a $50,000 bonus. After a campaign against the bonus by organized labour, which detested the company's labour record, voters defeated a bonus bylaw. Council then adopted a novel strategy in 1903 by annexing part of Barton Township and offering to fix tax assessments at a rural rate on industrial sites in the annex. As a further concession, the city turned over a section of the Sherman Avenue right of way.[18]

The Chicago head office sent a superintendent "to get production rolling — quickly." Men were ordered to work at top speed to meet shipping schedules. Accidents rose to appalling levels. Pressure for rush production had come because of a drive to meet western orders. Between 1898 and 1911 an estimated 250,000 Americans had settled in Canada and many brought capital. It was natural for them to apply assets from sales of their United States property to purchase implements from the proven midwestern manufacturers who comprised International Harvester. So swiftly did the West open that Harvester consigned carloads of machinery to the end of the new rail lines and construction trains on branch lines hauled them to farm-service towns. The Bank of Hamilton with nearly eighty offices west of Ontario (1911) — it had none east of Montreal — put an additional business foothold on the prairies and aided the merchandising of Hamilton articles.[19]

In early 1910, Harvester announced a massive expansion to create a compound of shops expected to employ 2,000. No sooner had this news enlivened real-estate speculation than the Oliver Chilled Plow Company of South Bend, Indiana, announced that it would construct a set of warehouses, foundries, forges and related shops. Employment for another 2,000 was forecast. The Oliver people introduced their engineering and architectural firm, Prack and Perrine, to Hamilton where it retained an office that planned structures for most major industries. The opportunities for industrial engineering and construction proved rich. Prack and Perrine had considerable involvement with the plant construction boom and, appropriately, they designed the exclusive Tamahaac Club, a businessman's retreat situated near Ancaster, well above industrial clamour and smoke. By turn of fate, the industrial elite could escape noise and fumes on a tranquil hill close to where manufacturing actually had begun over 100 years earlier.[20]

The extraordinary industrial construction of 1910 to 1912 had been possible because of major international events. The scale of growth did not flow as a simple consequence of Hamilton bonuses, tax concessions and hiring of an industrial commissioner. Assorted considerations taken together explain the industrial boom. As injections of American capital, managerial drive and

architectural resources made clear, the city was not arbiter of its economy. A dependent condition had been the case during the frontier town and railway-city stages, when international circumstances cast up opportunities and just as swiftly cancelled them. The familiar sequence came again when a serious international depression struck hard at all Canadian cities. It afflicted Hamilton from the winter of 1913-1914 to the spring of 1915.

The tightening of international credit that commenced in 1913 precipitated a fall in railway and urban construction. Prairie settlement slowed. Hamilton hardware producers and farm-implements manufacturers reacted to tumbling orders by closing plants or putting men on short time. Hundreds of moulders were out of work. At one point during the winter of 1913-14, an estimated 2,500 men were unemployed. Perhaps as many as 20 to 25 per cent of the city's families were affected. Thousands of workers clung to short-time positions; many precariously employed individuals received wages for only several days' work a week which was, as a local correspondent for the Dominion Department of Labour suggested, "insufficient for a man with a family to exist upon." The presence of more than one wage earner in a family moderated distress for some households, but families with young children suffered greatly.[21]

By the spring of 1915, war orders and enlistments had cut into unemployment and underemployment. In May, the United Relief Association, formed to coordinate civic welfare, could close its files. The industries with shell contracts operated day and night shifts after the government announced it would take all that could be produced. Across Ontario, between January and December, 1915, employment in iron and steel trades rose from 4,300 to 9,400; in the foundries and machine shops the increase was 9,000 to 13,000. Military recruitment stayed brisk for a while longer. A 1914 federal announcement that wives of volunteers would receive twenty dollars monthly coupled with the efforts of civic welfare officials to discourage able young men from receiving relief gave patriotism a practical boost. During September, the Dominion Immigration Agent in Hamilton placed newcomers in industries and believed that demand for labour was the highest since 1911. The Ontario government opened a Public Employment Bureau in the city in January, 1917, and, among other duties, assisted in placing women with munitions manufacturers. Many women left domestic service.[22]

The stove industry included a half dozen foundries by the 1890s and helped to launch Hamilton as an iron and later a steel centre.

Proximity to the Niagara fruit belt gave rise in Hamilton to a food-processing industry. The cases of jam seen in this 1910 picture are headed for the United Kingdom market. Eventually Canada Canners took control of this and many other firms.

Foundries and machine shops adapted readily to shell manufacture; the American Can Company turned out mess articles; National Steel Car produced field kitchens. War quickly restored full employment. However, a wartime economy also cut into real wages by intensifying inflation. An escalating cost of living and industrial accidents came as social costs. The winners were industrial corporations. Records of the Business Profits War Tax disclose high declared returns in virtually all industries with war contracts. International Harvester claimed a loss of $11,000 in 1914; the 1918 balance sheet reported a profit of $1,770,000. The Steel Company of Canada had done well in 1914 with profits of $1.25 million, but the 1917 figure was nearly $3.5 million. Amidst all of the war-industry success stories came the exception that proved the rule. National Steel Car, founded with American capital in 1913, had a small 1914 loss, but in 1916 and 1917, within a fourteen-month period, its losses were roughly $780,000. In 1915 it had jumped at a French tender to build 4,000 railway carriages for mounting artillery. The Hamilton-produced parts went to France for assembly, but only 3,721 carriages could be finished. The French government refused payments on grounds of the shortfall; the company alleged that the missing parts had been pilfered on the French docks.[23]

The real level of the benefit of war to several local industries went beyond declared profits. One long-term gain was an increased cash flow enabling plant expansion. At war's end corporate assets had risen appreciably, though none so much as those of the Steel Company of Canada, which was confirmed as the city's industrial giant during the conflict. It found that increased calls for steel and its new steel ovens required more basic iron than the two existing blast furnaces could provide. Thus part of the company's wartime revenue went into increased iron-making facilities and was exempt from the business-profits war tax. At the outset of war production, the Steel Company's assets were at $31 million; in 1918 they were worth between $45 and $50 million. The postwar recession, a return to the slump of 1913–15, meant considerable layoffs and falling profits, but the war orders had enhanced the physical plants of several of the successfully managed larger companies.[24]

The war was an appalling exercise in prolonged carnage. On the home front the repercussions obviously were not of comparable brutality, but if "brutal" is not an apt description then "callous" applies. In the name of victory and in pursuit of profits, the industrial pace was set recklessly and the hours too long for reasonable safety. During 1916, National Steel Car reported 130 industrial accidents and the Steel Company 450. The Ontario factory-inspectors' reports for 1917 failed to arranged the accidents on an industry-by-industry basis, conceivably to avoid specifics that would aggravate labour discontent or rattle morale. In any case, there were 3,925 Hamilton industrial accidents reported that year, as opposed to about 1,600 in 1914. Emphasis on plant expansion rather than on safety or employment security was a fact of corporate management. Managers knew how to plan facilities but evinced no will to comprehend the social problems of a return to peace. Veterans and wartime labourers were hit with layoffs during a recession in a transition to the peacetime economy. War profits had been paid out in dividends or plowed back into increased plant capacity without provision for the future of personnel.

From the 1870s to the 1890s, in order to reduce competition, Canadian manufacturers of twine, wire, nails and assorted iron products formed price-fixing pools. Price-fixing combines usually fell apart due to renegade producers willing to "kick over the traces." Corporate mergers closed this possibility and had the added effect of driving smaller producers out of business or discouraging new competition from entering. From the turn of the century until the war, Hamilton was rife with mergers and take-overs. International Harvester's interest in the city came about when the Chicago conglomerate absorbed Deering Harvester, which had a Hamilton plant. Later Harvester purchased its neighbour, Oliver Chilled Plow (1919). Otis Elevator, which had opened a Hamilton factory in 1901, dominated the North American elevator industry by 1918 after mergers which had involved roughly fifty manufacturers, including several Canadian firms. Dominion Canners, its head office in Hamilton, controlled forty-seven canning factories across Ontario in 1911.

The consolidation trend spread to retailing and banking. City grocer William Carroll organized one of Canada's first chains. Owning 1 store in 1898, Carroll had acquired 7 by 1911, 19 by 1920, and 113 by 1934. The chain pioneered cash-and-carry purchase practices in Canada. The Bank of Hamilton, the object of a takeover bid by the Royal Bank in 1915, merged with the Bank of Commerce in late 1923, ending the contact that the city's elite had with running a major financial institution and conceding financial power to Toronto or Montreal.[25]

Another principal consolidation involved formation of the Steel Company of Canada. The 1899 creation of the Hamilton Iron and Steel Company by merger has been recounted; in 1907 the Canada Screw Company integrated its operations with the Ontario Tack Company. In turn, the new combinations were Hamilton parties to the 1910 merger that created the Steel Company. Hamilton's involvement was passive. Montreal financier Max Aitken acted as catalyst in drawing together the holdings of many firms.[26]

The concentration of financial institutions in Toronto, Aitken's Montreal base and the American branch plants diluted the number of major concerns operated by local businessmen. Would the international or domestic companies with out-of-town directors take an interest in the city? To their credit, the corporations would make philanthropic gifts and patronize the arts; they would keep themselves competitive and contribute tremendously to the flow of capital through the city. But they also extracted concessions from the city in the areas of tax assessments and urban services. If advantages were evident elsewhere, corporations could decide to close local plants despite years of civic aid. Rather than attributing these cynical calculations merely to a particular corporate structure, let us recall the ambiguous relations that the city had had with its own sons. The city's railway promoters in the 1850s had not been entirely dedicated to community welfare. During the early industrial age, local prodigies W.E. Sanford and George Tuckett threatened to move elsewhere if they were denied tax concessions. Industrial capitalism lacked sentiment whatever its leadership origins. If a real distinction between local industrialists and the corporate decision-makers existed, it was in their relative magnitude and accounting expertise. The consolidated corporation was better poised to assess the costs or benefits of leaving, staying or expanding. With plants in different centres, it held greater potential for a threatened or real withdrawal from the city. [27]

A GROWING AND VARIED POPULATION

An understanding of social relationships requires a solid foundation of demographic information. When and how quickly the city grew can have implications for housing, sanitation and labour relations. The origins of the additions to the city's population have a bearing on culture. Unfortunately, information on an urban population is exceedingly difficult to codify.

It is not until the turn of the century that a precise historical reconstruction of population growth is feasible for Hamilton. After all, the urban population enlarged in three ways: the natural increase of births over deaths, the volume of immigration and migration that is in excess of the numbers of people who are leaving the city and the annexation of neighbouring municipalities. The series of data on any one or all of these variables can be fragmentary and upset description of population trends. Moreover, annual population estimates for Hamilton compiled during the yearly assessment of property tended to be inflated. The practice of submitting a high population estimate reduced the per capita debt statements; it also enhanced civic prestige. Consequently, the components of growth cannot be isolated with precision. For the moment, however, the crude growth rate will be examined in relation to the economy across the decades of the industrial city. Only the critical boom years 1909 to 1913 present peculiar problems that call for detailed argument.

What emerges from weak data is that Hamilton stove industries, rolling mills and textile operations had furnished a base for supporting steady increments of population from 1871 (26,900) to 1901 (52,700). There were no stunning years of rapid increase. The annual increase typically hovered between 500 and 1,500. The flourishing metal trades in the early 1870s attracted more than the usual flow of newcomers, but the generally depressed state of the mid-1870s actually precipitated a loss of several hundred residents between 1875 and 1876. The 1880s contained fluctuations. Natural increase probably accounted for no more than a quarter of the new population of the 1880s. The 1880s constituted a major period of immigration. A rough sense of what that era of immigration, almost entirely from the United Kingdom, meant to Hamilton was presented in the 1901 census. Of 6,800 immigrants residing in Hamilton in that year, the breakdown of their arrival in Canada was as follows: 32 per cent in the 1870s, 46 per cent in the 1880s, 22 per cent in the 1890s.[28]

The second industrial revolution and corporate decisions for expansion gave a dynamic stimulation to population growth. Since reasonably accurate statistics for births and deaths exist after

1896, natural increase can be weighed as a factor and then discounted. In the few slow-growth years between 1900 (51,500) and 1913 (100,000) it accounted for one-quarter of the annual increase; in the wildly expansionist years it brought about one-tenth of the gain. These latter years threw impossible obstacles in the way of determining the actual population of Hamilton. There were the city's swollen population reports. The registrar general of Ontario also kept a tally. The two do not coincide.

In the fall of 1909, the city annexed 1,200 acres of Barton. No reports declared the numbers of residents involved and whether the additional population was first worked into the 1909, 1910 or 1911 estimates. Yet it is vital to make a reasoned guess at the actual increases by immigration and annexation as a complement to discussions about housing conditions, the real-estate boom and health. Sorting out population growth also affords a necessary background to discussions about labour, reform and culture. In the civic statistics, the Barton annexation shows up as a slight abnormal increase from 1909 (67,000) to 1910 (70,200). This leaves far more extraordinary rises to be interpreted: 1911 (73,500) to 1912 (82,100), 1912 to 1913 (89,000) and 1913 to 1914 (100,000).

Perhaps portions of these increases can be explained away by inefficient or confused data collection, which meant that corners of the newly annexed tract had been missed until well after 1909. However, the bulk surely describes a real influx from the United Kingdom, the United States, continental Europe and other regions of Canada. Taken together, the new employment requirements of International Harvester and Oliver Chilled Plow meant 4,000 jobs. Including families (although assuming that many men came alone), the number of arrivals drawn by just these two firms could have been 10,000 to 15,000. Other new plants, expansion of linked industries like the Steel Company and the boom in the construction trades attracted thousands more. Census data corroborate the claim that immigration produced the extreme jumps of 1911, 1912 and 1913 because they suggest that over 20,000 immigrants arrived in Hamilton between 1911 and 1920 and an estimated 14,500 of these came before the war.[29]

One outstanding feature of the industrial city's population boom was the first significant wave of immigrants who came from southern and eastern Europe. Immigration from the United Kingdom continued to be the largest source, supplying about two-thirds of immigrants, but these immigrants were accompanied after 1900 by what the press and civic officals referred to as "foreigners." The single male labourer, typical of this sojourning stage of immigration, was highly mobile and laboured long hours. The possibility of being missed by an enumerator was greater than was the case for native-born residents with families. But the anonymity of non-British newcomers also was institutionalized in chilling ways. The city directories frequently inserted "an Italian" at an address rather than the name of the occupant. A few employers kept neither names nor addresses for foreign labourers, recording time worked by a number. They were all called "Joe." One "Joe," injured by a falling steel beam, died unidentified until his wife inquired about his failure to return from work. "He was timed by number, paid by number, and was lost in the great plant like one of the numbered pieces of machinery."[30]

Indifference or contempt for foreign labourers abounded. In the summer and fall of 1913 it was a sport of "dirty and thoughtless men" who rode the streetcars to spit tobacco juice at Italian labourers digging trenches. Hostile baiting, the occasional fracas about immigrants stealing jobs from British subjects, and inspections by the health department intensified suspicion. Deceit or avoidance were understandable responses to the probes of census enumerators. For all of these reasons — of interest as social indicators in themselves — the 1911 census recorded that only about 5 per cent of the city's population was of continental European origin. It was thought that 91 per cent of Hamilton's population was composed of British subjects, a figure similar to that for Toronto. In all likelihood, the number of Italians residing in Hamilton by the First World War was 5,000, or triple the 1911 census estimate. There may have been a comparable number of eastern Europeans.[31]

Only a handful of southern and eastern Europeans had resided in Hamilton before 1900. The practice of bringing in labour crews composed of foreigners was adopted by the TH and B in the mid-1890s. However, these crews apparently were employed on construction works outside Hamilton. The true innovator was again International Harvester. It had introduced a considerable number of European labourers to its Hamilton operation as early as 1904. A number came from the company's American plants. The American consul in Hamilton handled applications from city residents who had immigrated to the United States and later were

The Paareburg Chapter of the IODE, Hospital Committee, 1915. A stronghold of British patriotism during the Boer War, Hamilton was where the Imperial Order, Daughters of the Empire originated.

In 1897, Adelaide Hoodless of Stoney Creek started the movement that led to the formation of the Women's Institute. Seen here around 1910 are students in a home economics course — also part of the domestic revolution to upgrade household health and comfort.

An immigrant family mourns the death of a child during the influenza epidemic, November, 1918.

There were many responses to the swelling number of newcomers. The Methodist Church on Barton Street went to the streets in an attempt to attract the numerous United Kingdom arrivals.

sent by Harvester to Hamilton. The consul estimated that the American colony in Hamilton during the war numbered 4,000; a good many of these had been born in England, Sweden and Italy. As mechanization minimized the importance of craftsmen in the metal industries and as the scale of the blast-furnace and open-hearth facilities increased, the demand for common labour grew apace. The Hamilton Iron and Steel Company, for example, employed at least 150 foreign labourers in 1907 and many more in 1910, when 700 men went on strike to protest against foreign foremen who were extorting money from some of the foreign labourers. Factory construction and the extension of urban services provided additional employment opportunities.[32]

Boarding-house areas with a concentration of immigrant occupants sprouted around the industrial annex, especially the north Sherman Avenue area. Boarders in some establishments returned from their shift to occupy the vacated beds of men who had just departed for the next shift. The abundance of labouring men with common origins living in the same dwelling created a distinct boarding-house society. Lacking accounts of life in these labourers' barracks from the occupants, we can for some evidence quote the medical health officer (MHO). "They live," he reported, "a form of a club life and throw a lot of money in a pot in some instances to have booze on the premises."[33] He caught an element of the social life; the police raids on Saturday nights produced abundant evidence of boarding houses doubling as illegal drinking establishments. A few immigrants — Paul Gravetz was one — turned the boarding situation to advantage. Arriving in 1907, he boarded with forty-five other men and earned a dollar a day. Eventually he saved enough to send for his family; he rented a house and went into the boarding-house business, which his wife managed while he worked.[34]

There is no means by which an outsider such as the MHO or the reporter who extracted the Gravetz story could have acquired a feeling for the talk about home, labour conditions, bully foremen and the absence of women. Life in the boarding camps did not conform to middle-class standards of order. Concerned about moral and spiritual needs, Bishop T.J. Dowling called upon Father J.F. Bonomi to come from Boston. Bonomi was a Scalabrini Father, a member of an order devoted to missionary work among Italian immigrants and pledged to assist them in holding in high esteem their culture and religion. In 1910, an Italian chapel was opened at St. Ann's School on Sherman Avenue, close to the concentration of Italians living in the east end of the city. This was followed by St. Anthony's Church in 1912. In the meantime, a cluster of Italians had located in north-central Hamilton. Evidently this group included a large contingent from the Sicilian village of Racalmuto, because on 1 June 1913 they held the first annual celebration of the village feast day. One purpose of the occasion was to formulate plans and raise funds for the erection of a second Italian church. Ten years later, All Souls' Church on Barton Street was formally opened. The Polish population followed a similar course, with Father Tarasiuk arriving from Chicago in 1911. Upon his arrival construction commenced on St. Stanislaus. These churches would be the stable base of growing ethnic communities for over fifty years, until movement to the suburbs brought about decentralization.[35]

THE INDUSTRIAL ENVIRONMENT

Large-scale industrial organizations forced Hamilton into new spatial arrangements and created a district of architectural leviathans. Between 1896 and 1913, with concentrated activity during the last years of that period, the city attained much of its contemporary cadastral and land-use form. Factories were suddenly so apparent to downtown businesses and central-city residents that they had to strain to comprehend what had transpired in the east end. To enable them to grasp the change, the Board of Trade organized a tour for bankers, brokers, store-keepers and grocers. In a May, 1911, outing, automobiles and special streetcars conveyed between 300 and 400 businessmen eastward to the manufacturing district. The central core had changed, but the industries, working-class neighbourhoods and new commercial districts along Barton Street East and Ottawa Street actually had revolutionized the city. The old John Street South business district had fallen into visible decline. Around Gore Park and along James Street a few retailers had improved old buildings, but the changing skylines that advertised growth in Montreal, Toronto and Vancouver had a restrained counterpart in Hamilton.

The availability of office space in Toronto, a locale for corporate headquarters, detracted from Hamilton's architectural maturation in the era of the office tower. The Federal Life Building and

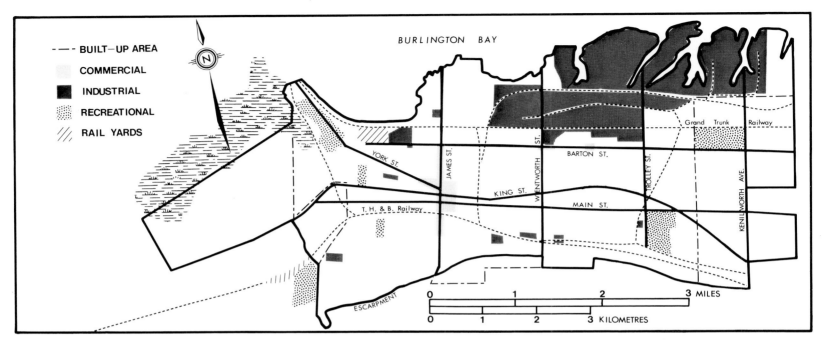

5 Land Use and Railways in Hamilton, c. 1914.

the Bank of Hamilton head office, both just under ten storeys, occupied the same side of James Street between Main and King. Slightly larger was the Royal Connaught Hotel. Called for by the Board of Trade to prevent visiting businessmen from having to seek accommodations in Toronto, the hotel was constructed between 1914 and 1916. The massive east-end developments captured more attention than these modest additions, for the industrial expansion had generated a second city segregated from the core by distance, economic function and social composition.[36]

Whereas earlier manufacturing had settled into pockets around the core of the city, establishing proximity to the labour force, the enormous plants of the second industrial revolution required extensive acreage for sprawling shops and rail facilities. Horizontal expansion and locational decisions that took water and rail transportation into account carried expansion along the bayshore. Significantly, the historic name of Burlington Bay was changed officially to Hamilton Harbour in 1919. Old landmarks vanished

with the name, as landfill projects obliterated inlets. The 1860 pumphouse had to share status as an industrial emblem at the city's eastern approaches with a greater, if less elegant, mass in the form of the blast furnace.[37]

The expanded Harvester plant of 1912 furnished an added measure of the scale of industrial architecture. A gray iron foundry measured 84 by 861 feet; attached to it were sheds for the skilled moulders and coremakers. There was a comparable malleable iron foundry. The forge shop was 84 by 702 feet. Separate buildings housed the woodworking shop, paint shop, drafting department and business offices. Warehouses, dock facilities and spur trackage completed a complex with over thirty acres of floor space.[38]

The physical developments in housing also were impressive. The city's housing stock nearly tripled between 1901 and 1921. The peak year for housing construction in the industrial-city era was 1912, when the city issued 1,476 building permits for new

By the First World War, industry had encroached slightly onto the indented waterfront around Gage Inlet. More drastic changes were to come as landfill projects effaced the original shoreline over many decades.

dwellings, ten times the number issued in 1900. In addition, social attributes accompanied the increase in dwellings in the industrial-city era. First, between 1871 and 1921, the proportion of dwellings that were owner-occupied increased from roughly 25 to 50 per cent. The introduction of instalment payments may have been a factor, but this increase in home ownership likely involved the growth of a clerical and managerial middle class. Second, the expanse of new industries, a street railway system (incorporated in 1873 and electrified in 1892) and two inclined railways up the escarpment placed substantial numbers of workers on streets outside the neighbourhoods of their work. Particularly the white-collar and high-skilled employees in the industrial groupings chose a modern pattern of living at a remove from their plant.

The industrial city carried forward the trend toward income and ethnic segregation. The environmentally obnoxious traits of the manufacturing boom — plant size, noise, fumes, rail traffic — deterred men of means from dwelling close to their place of employment. Some classes were protected from the industrial environment but others were made vulnerable. A vivid expression of class distinctions and corporate decree in the destruction of neighbourhoods accompanied the entrance of the TH and B. East of James Street, it slashed through Corktown, an act hailed for eradicating "the old rookeries which have stood for years as impediments to the onward march of Hamilton's prosperity." West of James Street, the railway had to enter by a tunnel through the "hogsback," shielding most of the adjacent elite neighbour-hood. In a later episode (1913), the benefits of zoning as a pro-tective device were seized upon by the affluent who lived along Duke, Markland, Forest, and the southern portions of Bay, James and John, when they petitioned for a bylaw making their district exclusively residential. Hamilton civic officials abetted segregated land use when they annexed over 650 acres of Barton Township in 1903, for they designated this tract an industrial annex with a special tax rate. Private land developers, a few of whom had been the very same civic officials who had arranged the annexation, marketed the property to manufacturers. The city's actions to secure industries were part and parcel of the private real-estate manipulation which had engaged Hamilton from its founding. Now, however, the scale of land assembly and the levels of industrial nuisance split the city into social fragments.[39]

The developers who read these factors and then acted to profit from the movement of people into suitable neighbourhood niches plunged into real estate on a scale that suggests a parallel with the consolidations in manufacturing. Many individuals speculated in city lots, but only a handful dominated the property industry. Most major operators had entered through a kindred enterprise: J. Walter Gage from fruit growing and rural real estate; Alex Metherell from stock brokerage in the United Kingdom; George Armstrong and Alex Dickson from insurance agencies; W.D. Flatt from lumber and building supplies.

The real-estate action came to resemble that of 1851-1856 except that the number and scale of surveys had risen. From the surviving registered plans of 1851-1856, the average survey had about 100 lots; the average from 1860 to 1880 was about 50 lots, conveying the caution of the 1870s and 1880s. In 1911, the city's developers registered forty surveys with an average of more than 100 lots. Gage's Eastholme contained 500 and he maintained sales offices in Montreal, Rochester and Buffalo. The thirty-seven surveys of 1913 averaged nearly 200 lots. These surveys packed narrow-frontage lots onto a grid street plan. Most were promoted to attract wage earners from the new industries. Gage, for example, assembled the workingmen's districts of Normanhurst, Fairfield and Kensington. Altogether he registered fourteen sub-divisions between 1904 and 1911. The real-estate developers' concentration of workingmen's surveys around the industrial region was likely a consequence of several considerations. First, the mountain imposed limits; the inclined railway fares were a barrier. Second, the smoke and noise around plants and the rail-ways depressed adjacent land values and inflated the values of more remote and healthful properties. Finally, the streetcar was a reasonable mode of transit, but the cost may have combined with the expense of land outside the industrial sector to weigh against a labourer's residing at a distance from his place of employment.[40]

The property industry also tailored an array of middle-class and elite neighbourhoods to accommodate the foremen, clerks, engineers and sales personnel associated with the industrial boom. Flatt arranged his Beulah, Westmount and Chedoke Park surveys in the southwest for this clientele. On the west mountain above the Chedoke Ravine, the Home and Investment Realty Company promoted a 132-acre tract with building restrictions. Members of the business elite, not the run-of-the-mill land developers, laid out the posh Ravenscliffe district whose dead-end street, 100-foot

The Hunter Street tunnel of the Toronto, Hamilton and Buffalo Railway protected an elite 1890s neighbourhood against some of the disturbances caused by trains.

Modest homes like these were exposed to the disruptions of streetcars and railway traffic. The towers in the upper right hand of this 1917 picture are level-crossing observation boxes.

The Toronto, Hamilton and Buffalo Railway freight yard at Walnut Street cut a path through the neighbourhood of old Corktown in the 1890s.

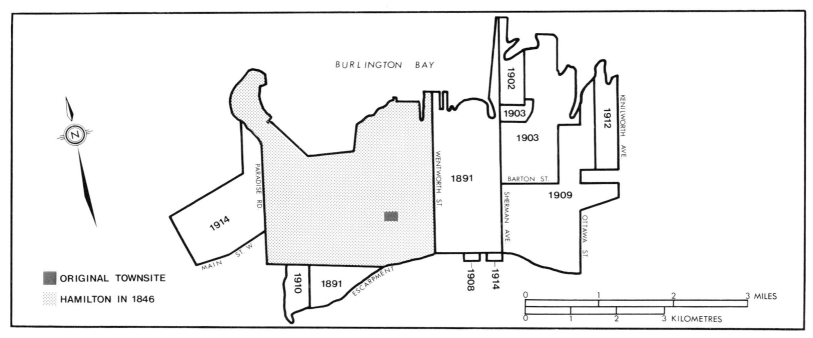

The map shows the following labels:

BURLINGTON BAY

1902
1903
1903
KENILWORTH AVE
1912
PARADISE RD.
WENTWORTH ST.
1891
BARTON ST.
SHERMAN AVE.
1909
1914
OTTAWA ST.
MAIN ST. W.
1910
1891
ESCARPMENT
1908
1914

ORIGINAL TOWNSITE
HAMILTON IN 1846

0   1   2   3 MILES
0   1   2   3 KILOMETRES

6 Hamilton's Boundary Extensions, 1846-1914.

frontages and physically attractive setting at the face of escarpment contrasted with monotonous workingman's surveys. There were further contrasts because of the willy-nilly promotion of east-end surveys by land developers. A few surveys were products of true developers who graded streets and constructed sidewalks. Others were thrown onto the market by men drawn to quick profits.

In June, 1912, the city had to threaten legal action against owners of several eastern surveys to carry out promises to grade all thoroughfares to the city's satisfaction. The march of surveys eastward outstripped the city's ability to install sewer lines. The real-estate people and civic authorities blasted recriminations at one another, but they could unite with industries and labourers in an assault on the Hamilton Street Railway for being caught without the cars and trackage to handle the jump in traffic between plants and suburbs. In the east end, the uncontrolled private promotion of residential space had created difficult situa-

tions for residents and the public or private utilities. The attractive features of the east-end neighbourhoods would owe much to the pride of home-owners, expressed through gardens and handiwork; they would owe little to the land developers. The creativity of developers — for that matter the achievements of authorities who planned the parks network — was confined to middle-class areas in the south or the west.[41]

The property industry was alert to the advantages of consolidation. However, the fulfilment of the process was to occur several decades behind consolidation in manufacturing. Just as certain manufacturers had formed price-fixing pools, the real-estate men agreed to behind-the-scenes manipulation. When a disgruntled party to a price-fixing scheme threatened to present the story to the *Hamilton Herald*, he was cautioned by *Spectator* owner and real-estate investor W.A. Southam that "we should help each other along instead of trying to let the public into our interesting methods of promotion, purchase and sale."[42]

Besides the backroom approach, realtors followed the lead of local manufacturers who had established a Hamilton branch of the Canadian Manufacturers Association in 1909. A real-estate board was planned in 1914. Formation of what became known as the McKittrick Syndicate attests even more convincingly to parallels between property and industrial business consolidations. Like a well-conceived industrial corporation, this land syndicate collected executives with specialized talents. By 1920, it had a general manager, sales staff and consulting reports.

The level of private planning was impressive. Many streets broke away from the grid pattern. The central shopping district, parks, schools and a dozen surveys catering to different income levels bear continuing witness to an enterprise that operated at the advanced level of the property industry. Yet the syndicate had profits, not service, in mind and, like a consolidated manufacturing concern, it wielded power to serve its own ends at nearly any cost. It repeatedly manoeuvred to receive tax assessment benefits. It imposed restrictive covenants on the deeds to lots. The Westdale covenants forbade sales to "Negroes, Asiatics, Bulgarians, Austrians, Russians, Serbs, Rumanians, Turks, Armenians... or foreign born Italians, Greeks or Jews." Only toward the end of the Second World War and into the 1950s did the courts destroy legal segregation by nationality or religion.[43]

The large land developers, including the makers of Westdale, failed to consolidate all dimensions of the shelter industry. The integration of land development and construction phases became a firm trait of city building processes only after the Second World War. Typically, the contractors in the industrial-city stage acquired lots from the developer and assumed responsibility for the sale of houses. Contracting remained highly decentralized; family or partnership arrangements accounted for all but several of the forty or more contractors active in 1911. Usually contractors hired carpenters and other tradesmen through craft unions, which set wages and working conditions. Compared with upheavals in other sectors of the economy, home construction remained comparatively undisturbed. Craftsmen retained a respected and significant position, and they were not exposed to sweeping technological changes that deteriorated the status of craft unions in manufacturing. The only change of note was in the increased use of brick in home construction.[44]

The built environment of segregated land uses — commercial core, industrial district, working-class neighbourhoods and middle-class tracts — overlapped with a social landscape that pertained to more than occupational or class configurations. The household composition and health of certain districts contrasted with others. Additions to the city's housing stock extended the distance between the affluent and poor, between the culture and health of the middle class and that of the industrial labouring class. In the early 1900s, Ward Two in the south-central portion of the city retained streets with exclusive airs which had been implanted in the 1850s. Wards Six, Seven and Eight in the east end had the city's lowest property values, about one-third the average value of property in elite Ward Two. The crush of industrial labourers into these former wards produced 16,000 people per square mile. The built-upon section of Ward Eight likely had a comparable concentration. Wards One and Two supported the city's lowest densities at 4,000 and 5,000 respectively.

The most densely occupied wards registered the highest crude death rates in 1911. Experts are divided as to whether overcrowding, poor sanitary facilities or poor dietary conditions enforced by limited budgets had the most determining role in urban mortality. In any case, the industrial-shelter wards encountered all of these disadvantages. Infant mortality was higher in the working-class Wards Six and Eight, although the incidence of *cholera infantum* appears to have been higher in the affluent areas. This latter peculiarity is significant for it indicates a geographic and social pattern in childrearing. The high incidence of *cholera infantum* in Ward Two indicates a peculiar quirk in neighbourhood character. It seems that middle-class mothers had begun to abandon breastfeeding in favour of the less hygienic bottle. This concentration of *cholera infantum* may help to explain the clean-milk campaign and Babies' Dispensary Guild; both were advanced by largely middle-class women.[45]

Environmental reform swept the continent in the early twentieth century and Hamilton was heavily involved. The dedicated medical health officer, James Roberts, stands out as the foremost reform figure in the city. By no means perfect, he got above the stubborn bigotry that too frequently tainted progressive rhetoric on sanitary and housing reform. His participation in the international public-health movement was recognized by peers who elected him as vice-president of the American Public Health Association in 1912. A Hamilton Board of Health had been formed on a permanent basis in 1884 and had functioned primarily as an office handling complaints about privy pits and industrial odours.

The hiring of Roberts in 1905 coincided with the immigrant labour arrivals and lags in the completion of sewer lines. Roberts struggled against a relaxed standard of food and milk inspection and municipal government bodies intent on penny-pinching where health services were concerned. The city council had cut corners on a sewage disposal plant; it dragged its feet on financing proper milk-inspection equipment; it bucked Roberts's efforts to hire a larger residential inspection staff.[46]

A 1912 provincial act coerced reluctant municipalities like Hamilton to dedicate more time and resources to public-health planning. It specified that a provincial board of health had to approve municipal water and sewer plans. This same board could force improvements without the consent of ratepayers. Medical health officers were empowered to close any premises deemed unfit for habitation. There had been no house-to-house sanitary inspection since 1895; Roberts renewed the practice in 1910. He ordered roughly 1,500 sewer connections in the older parts of the city from 1911 to 1913 and virtually eliminated outdoor vaults in these regions. There were school closings and quarantines meant to arrest smallpox, scarlet fever and measles, all of which occasionally had reached epidemic levels during the industrial boom before the war. In Hamilton as elsewhere in urban North America, the sanitary reform movement had succeeded in placing ordinary men, women and children under an unprecedented degree of supervision. Not only were residents and schoolchildren under scrutiny, but slum landlords and industries that polluted the bay also heard from Roberts. Unfortunately the mortality statistics fail to confirm immediate benefits, although one suspects that matters might have deteriorated without his tenacious campaigns. The dreadful effects of the great influenza epidemic in the winter of 1918–1919 could scarcely have been countered by Roberts, although he took steps to reduce public gatherings. Well over 500 died in Hamilton as a result of the influenza or its resulting complications.[47]

Parks and recreation formed a significant wing of the progressive reform assault on environmental conditions. If we take an analogy from the period, playgrounds and parks formed the lungs of the industrial city. Advocates of green spaces chalked up extensive achievements. This is not to say, however, that they strove with idealistic commitment alone, for they expressed many purposes. Civic boosterism and the enhancement of real-estate

values were mixed into parks policy. In the instance of playgrounds, there was the added objective of assimilating foreign-born children. From sportsman Tasker Steele, president of the Hamilton Playgrounds Association, Hamiltonians had this explanation.

> Playgrounds were a necessity in all modern cities and they were as necessary in a community as churches and schools. It was compulsory with large numbers of foreign children pouring into the city to do something to educate them along the same lines as native children, so they could assimilate Canadian ideas and customs.[48]

To that end, the children had to arrive scrubbed for inspection; they had to listen to fables with proper morals. Begun in 1909 by women who worried about the rectitude of the city's youth and blanched within earshot of street play, the association at first relied on volunteer work and borrowed a school playground. In 1918, it began to hire instructors from the YMCA college in Springfield, Massachusetts, and, by the time that it evolved into the Hamilton Playground Commission in 1931, it had accumulated seventeen playgrounds. There were thankful mothers, relieved that their children could find a place to play off "the dusty, dusty street."[49]

In the meantime, quite a different group worked to introduce the aesthetic ideals of an international city-beautiful movement. From the 1890s to the war, most North American cities commissioned plans for union stations, boulevards, zoological gardens and botanical parks. From 1917 to 1920, Hamilton toyed with ambitious schemes concocted by Ottawa urban planner Noulan Cauchon. His proposals for a union station, a grand boulevard honouring the war dead, a traffic circle with a "Monument of Humanity" and an "Altar of Human Sacrifice" to commemorate man's quest for freedom and a mountainside stadium were not adopted.[50] That too was typical of experiences in other Canadian cities.

More successfully, the city started to assemble land in 1912 for a park to run along the face of the escarpment. The scheme had flaws. First, the properties were in the hands of known speculators and the land had limited residential value, being hazard land prone to rock slides. Therefore the prices paid were likely to have been

Dr. Algernon Woolverton's house on James Street North was typical of the substantial dwellings being constructed for the city's more affluent professionals in the 1880s.

The grand style of housing depicted here around 1890 remained concentrated in an area of the city near the James Street mountain access as it had been in the 1850s. "Ballinahinch" had been designed by William Thomas, the architect for St. Andrew's (St. Paul's) Church. Scottish-born dry-goods merchant Aeneas Sage Kennedy was the first occupant.

exorbitant. Second, parkland ran close to middle-class streets and was comparatively remote from heavily populated working-class areas. This also was the case with the sixty-four acres of the Gage homestead purchased for what became Gage Park in 1917. Gage Park came as a rare civic commitment to beautification in the east end, but it was in the southern reaches and not next to working-class streets. It was feasible for working-class families to visit park facilities, but it was not their neighbourhoods that benefited from civic enhancement. The inequitable concentration of parks was policy, for concurrent with purchases of parkland the city sacrificed public access to the waterfront by encouraging industrial concentration. The most blatant incident happened in 1911 when the American-owned Grasselli Chemical Company, later CIL, demanded land set aside for a park in the beach area. The city made the transfer.[51] Industrial progress was the byword.

LABOUR AND PROGRESSIVE REFORM

If success were defined by the achievement of expectations, then many labourers could have been counted as successful. Crowded into boarding houses to increase the portion of the pay envelope saved, they extracted gains through long hours, hard labour and self-denial. Among the Italians, there were those who came without family and returned home. By sacrifice, they had secured the savings that had enticed them. However, we must not ignore the toll of industrial accidents and the discontent over wages that touched immigrant lives.

Conceivably the expectations of native-born or United Kingdom workingmen were somewhat different from those of foreign labourers when they arrived on the Hamilton labour market. Generally what were considered "British workingmen" had their families with them in the city. Perhaps, too, their aspiration for home ownership was stronger. All such speculation introduces the problem of evaluating living conditions during the early twentieth century when civic boosters generously described Hamilton as a remarkably prosperous city with a contented labour force. An exceedingly crude — but not wholly misleading — summary of circumstances for workingmen of all origins puts a fine point on hard truths: the industrial boom failed to increase the real wages of workingmen, and it is likely that during the war the quality of life declined.

There was an increase in real wages from 1900 to 1905. From 1905 to 1914, there was a stabilization of real wages. Then wartime inflation brought a deterioration. Conditions seem to have improved in 1920. The problem with this account is that the wage-index component rose unduly because it was "preponderantly composed of skilled or abnormally affected classes." Also, hourly wages in various occupations were not equivalent to income because the number of hours of work per week declined from 1900 to 1913 and again from 1918 to 1920. The crises of layoffs and short-term employment have been recounted already in the discussion of the 1913-1915 depression.

Accommodation costs were a major feature in the loss of real wages. Rents between 1900 and 1913 increased by 60 per cent. Home ownership increased in the same years, but this progress was of a special kind that benefited the growing numbers of white-collar workers. Even so, home-ownership increases faltered by 1913 as lot prices became inflated. If some middle-income families became home-owners, the city's poorer labouring families faced a crisis. Rental accommodations became scarce. A qualitative measure of the shortage was the concern of some industries that a spiralling cost of housing would intensify wage demands or tarnish Hamilton's reputation. Several companies prepared home-ownership assistance plans.

On a broader front, the Hamilton Board of Trade, supported by the Canadian Manufacturers Association, initiated meetings with the city during 1912 and 1913 with the goal of creating a limited-dividend housing company. The proposal, common enough in urban reform circles, called for the incorporation of a firm which would build and let quality housing for labouring tenants. Rather than gouge tenants, its sponsors would limit themselves to 5 or 6 per cent return on company bonds. To sweeten the investment, risk would be removed by having a municipal government guarantee the 5 or 6 per cent interest payments; in Hamilton 8 per cent was mentioned. The model-village advocates' first setback was the discovery that speculators held the land along streetcar routes and cheap land was "tainted by industrial gases." The depression of 1913-1915 weakened the city's interest and that killed the project. The episode illustrated the extreme difficulty of finding decent low-cost housing.[52]

The gloomy depiction of living conditions during an industrial boom underscores a crisis in organized labour and a reversal from

Construction of the Hunter Street tunnel was rushed because the Toronto, Hamilton and Buffalo Railway tried to finish in time to collect a bonus from the city. Among the hazards workers faced on the project were mudslides caused by rainfall.

the more flourishing condition of labour in the mid-to-late 1880s. Beginning in the mid-1880s, the Knights of Labor realized a direct and indirect influence on the outlook of the city's labour force. The enthusiastic movement enrolled perhaps as many as a third of the hands employed in Hamilton manufacturing. The growth of the Knights in the midst of a buoyant economy, led by the foundries and urban construction, made the late 1880s an especially prosperous and optimistic time for workingmen. The attendant strength of organized labour definitely unsettled the Hamilton elite. George H. Mills, lawyer and landlord, confided in his diary that capitalists faced bleak prospects if the trend continued. His forecast was prepared in April, 1887, just as the Knights' movement crested.

> I see before me, and not in the very remote future, great social and political disturbances. The working classes and the unemployed, assisted by adventurers, are everywhere organizing and clammoring [sic] for what they call their rights, but it is not only their rights they are after, but far beyond this they seek, and the logic of their actions will be to destroy vested interests, to seize upon and appropriate property not their own, not to share equally the profits of the world, but to make themselves rich, and the rich beggars. To totally destroy existing rule, and assume the direction of public affairs themselves, in a word it is labor against capital . . . They as yet are not sufficiently strong in numbers and intelligence to attempt an overthrow of the ruling powers.[53]

Another source of discontent in Hamilton and southwestern Ontario during the late 1880s likewise disturbed the civic elite, for it also posited an alternate vision of Canadian development. The commercial-union movement that proposed a North American free-trade area had supporters in Hamilton. The dissent that was being expressed through talk about commercial union was a consumers' protest. Local tax rates, interest on mortgages and consumer goods tended to be higher in Canada. In a period when Hamilton industry seemed on a strong footing, it was natural for a number of residents to question the value of a protective tariff. Together the challenges of the Knights of Labor and of the commercial-union movement could be seen as a crisis in loyalty; radical American attitudes, it seemed, threatened the established patterns of loyalty. That certainly describes the in-

terpretation of contemporary events favoured by George Mills, who founded the Wentworth Historical Society (1889) in the hope that its influence would "check the progress of discontent and elemental sedition of those who feel little interest in the country which the pluck and patriotism of the early pioneers preserved against great odds." History was not the sole art to be put in the service of patriotism and social stability, because in June, 1887, the civic elite arranged an extravaganza to celebrate Queen Victoria's Jubilee. Patriotic music and oratories entertained and instructed the public. But really it was not on the cultural front that the Knights and commercial unions lost ground. The depression of the 1890s caused workingmen to retreat into the doctrine of protective tariffs. Prosperous years had supported the luxury of social and economic criticism. The 1880s represented an exceptional period of confidence from which it seemed safe to question the economic and historic foundations of the civic establishment.[54]

After the turn of the century, craft-union strength slipped in consequence of technology and management-efficiency campaigns. These gave employers at heavily capitalized plants power to enforce their conception of wages: wages were determined by the labour market and not swings in productivity. When the skills of craft-union members had been a commodity valued by the city's early industries, employers could not entirely enforce this conception of labour. Craftsmen—carpenters, joiners, moulders and others—tied their earnings to productivity. By hand, eye and deftness born of experience they determined the outcome of work, and some preferred to be paid on a piecework basis that reflected this. Unskilled labourers had much less to barter. Moreover, craftsmen had associations practised in enforcing shop rules that defined work and wage rates. The superior leverage of craftsmen and their suspicion of unskilled labour's encroachment often made them a distinct group. Another fifty years were required —years during which the craft unions were burned by technology—before industrial unionism was realized. However, the Knights, with their radical purpose of harmonizing working-class struggles, had an influence. The movement politicized a number of craftsmen, including the future labour statesman Alan Studholme, who was a member of both a Knights local and their political association in the early 1880s.

The second industrial revolution created adverse conditions among some skilled crafts. A federal inquiry into the cost of living in 1913 mentioned that "in the larger manufacturing establishments (the growth of which has been marked during the past decade) a relatively greater proportion of low skilled or merely dextrous workmen is noticeable."[55] The jolts which upset the crafts can be witnessed in the mechanization which vastly augmented production and divorced industrial output from labourers' hands. For example, the manual puddling of wrought iron with all the care that the process entailed was a procedure that related wages to production. The switch from wrought iron to steel with its enormous production facilities made a devastating point. Industrial output, it appeared manifest, came from huge capital expenditures and not from direct human exertion. Precisely this principle of industrial management had guided the Steel Company's investment of its wartime capital flow. There was cold realism in the position taken by industrialists; technology gave that realism a powerful logic.

Unquestionably, the early twentieth century introduced an interlude when corporations sapped the potency of craft unions. Managers of certain plants enforced campaigns for discipline and speed to exact greater efficiency and productivity. In the course of introducing new technology, speed-up practices and efficiency studies, the corporations contested with and weakened unions in a struggle for control of shop floors. There were exceptions to the defeat of craft unions generally. First, where mechanization and large-scale enterprises could not alter conditions at work — for example, in the residential construction industry — craft unionism had strength. Second, during the 1900-1920 period, there were episodes when short-term gains were made by the unskilled or semi-skilled — streetcar employees, civic workers and men and women in the garment industry. Third, any impression of absolute defeat would be incorrect. Experiences, admittedly unhappy ones for the craft unions, were recalled in future disputes. The sheer possibility of renewed union organization or spontaneous turbulence forced a calculated level of corporate paternalism. Finally, the city's labourers may have lost on the union front, but in civic and provincial elections they scored a few triumphs.

The undulating fortunes and demise of moulders best opens an account of craft unionism under stress. From the 1860s to 1880s, employers had attempted to crush early craft unionism. Sometimes antiunion campaigns succeeded, but moulders would persist and reorganize. After a particularly severe weakening of union strength in the early 1890s, the moulders' union revived and extracted an 1899 contract from owners that gave a 15 per cent wage increase and other concessions which bolstered workers' control over shop practices. There were additional gains until the recession years of 1907-1909. The tide ran the other way during the economic slump, since founders had little incentive to avoid a strike. After a demand for a 20 per cent wage reduction was rejected by the union, a decade of workers' strength ended; the employers forced the men to accept terms or seek other employment. Eventually the obsolescence of the cast-iron stove killed the craft.

Meanwhile other foundry operations had accompanied the new industrialism and were able to exercise greater control over the workplace and employees than the stove manufacturers. New factories like those of International Harvester, Westinghouse and Oliver Chilled Plow contained departments with different functions. Usually the moulding department, because of hand skills, was a bottleneck; moulders came under management pressure to work up to the capacity of other departments. In the stove industries, the moulders had not had to coordinate with a variety of other departments in a mass-assembly process. The new industries experimented with production methods which undercut the position of craft unions. By the early 1900s, commercially viable moulding machines could impress simple shapes. By the end of the First World War, the city's major foundries had procured a number of processes using fractional-horsepower motors which saved space and permitted numerous innovations: sand mixers, conveyor belts and grinding devices for finishing castings. Formerly in a position of central importance, artisans were relegated to a corner of the shop where they handled a few complex pieces that could not be turned out by mechanized aids.[56]

Skilled machinists were undercut by metallurgical achievements rather than by mechanized processes. Before the innovation of alloy steels which could withstand intense friction and stress, lathe and press operators who cut metal shapes had to work diligently and slowly with fragile steel dies and bits. Weakness in the metal cutting tools dictated a measured pace to work and a level of skill which gave the artisan — through his union — considerable influence over the work practices at the machine shop. The technology of the first industrial revolution nurtured skilled machinists as well as their unions. High-speed steel shattered

Tuckett's Tobacco Factory, a major manufacturer of Canadian cigarettes, employed a number of boys as well as women. Handling the pungent tobacco was an uncomfortable chore, but the added family income was needed in many working-class households.

security. A number of steps were taken by management to push productivity as far as the new technology would permit. Machinists were pressured to run two machines at a time; this was one of Harvester's innovations in 1904. Piecework and bonus incentives were introduced. Semi-skilled labourers invaded the machine shops.

Wartime production demands exacerbated the speed-up campaigns until in April, 1916, the machinists' unions attempted to enforce a standard for wages, hours and working conditions. Worried about the impact of a crisis on shell production, the federal government appointed a commission to investigate machinists' grievances in Hamilton and Toronto. Its recommendations, generally favouring the unions' position, were ignored by employers. This precipitated a strike of 1,500 Hamilton machinists. The companies replaced many strikers; strikers also returned to work or went elsewhere for employment. Thus in 1919, when there were general strikes of metal workers in other centres, notably Winnipeg, the Hamilton unions were too weakened to join. The turbulent summer months of 1916 also witnessed militancy among garment workers who had been struggling against speed-ups for several years. As well, in the spring and summer of 1916, there had been strikes at the TH and B car shops, the Steel Company and Dominion Steel Foundries.[57]

The hiring of foreign labourers coincided with the introduction of radical processes that challenged skilled labour. The two phenomena were related at times, although the newcomers were heavily represented among nonindustrial occupations such as heavy construction, railway labour and the digging of water and sewer trenches. It would thus be erroneous to associate mechanization and European immigration in a direct relationship. On the other hand, factory managers made use of foreign workers to operate equipment that had been replacing skilled labour. The pattern was well enough known to appear in a contemporary Hamilton novel.

> "Who would run such machines?"
> "Dagos," smiled Brasmore. "You get them for a song. Wickens made his big mistake in hiring such an expensive class of labour."[58]

Occasionally construction superintendents and plant managers brought in a crew of newcomers as strikebreakers. During the summer of 1916, the Dominion Steel Foundry went so far as to ask the Immigration Department for permission to import 100 black labourers from the southern states.[59] Due to these instances and the connections between immigrants and semi-skilled positions in places like International Harvester, organized labour criticized the federal government's aid for the recruitment of European labour. It was "forcing keener competition among our mechanics and labourers in its already over crowded markets."

The widely held belief that immigrants accepted low pay, abuse by employers and strikebreaking jobs occasionally ran into contrary incidents of protests and strikes from the supposedly passive foreigners. Italian navvies struck against assorted contractors on streetcar lines and watermains. In the spring of 1907, for example, 150 Italian navvies struck the Hamilton and Brantford interurban line. When Austrian workers failed to join them "there was a lively free fight."[60] The foreign workers at the Hamilton blast furnace went on strike for pay increases and better working conditions in 1907 and 1910. It was a strike of 55 foreigners in 1916 that had provoked the Dominion Steel Foundry to try and recruit black labourers. The radical One Big Union movement had staunch local support from some unskilled Italian work crews in 1919. The fact that "foreigners" had been discriminated against by the city relief department during the 1914–1915 slump and by employers who laid them off before other labourers honed the workers' sense of justice. The newcomers and the changing techniques of manufacturing were more than discrete traits of an industrial city; they were connected phenomena, but the connections were complex and did not conform to stereotypes of either foreign troublemakers or foreign scabs.[61]

Management gains in the contest over control of work practices were to be secured, it was hoped by several corporations, through paternalism: profit-sharing schemes, improved facilities in the factory, accident-compensation plans, unemployment-insurance funds, housing assistance and company unions. Of course there were other practices such as the formation of employers' associations, which blacklisted troublesome labourers or attempted to set fixed wages so as to prevent men from moving about in search of better pay or to stem dissatisfaction because one employer paid more than another. International Harvester led the way with paternalism. The fact that its new 1911 plant incorporated improved ventilation and lighting was a reform of sorts. Local author Mabel Burkholder's first book, a 1911 novel about industrial relations, focussed on a mill described as "a gloomy old fashioned structure with dark walls and dingy windows." In this fantasy, the candour of a feisty mill girl swept the elderly proprietor into an act of benevolence. He bequeathed the mill to her and she reconstructed the building, adding large windows and a cafeteria.[62] Whether Burkholder really understood the women who worked at the mills and industrial labourers of her native Hamilton is dubious, although to her credit she understood sweatshop practices.

She definitely absorbed current corporate views about what would contribute to labour contentment, because a decade later, when advertising the modernity of its Hamilton knitted-goods factory built in 1916, the T. Eaton Company boasted of benevolence.

> Every detail of its construction and equipment is the most modern and practical, thereby not only increasing the output, but promoting the welfare of the workers, making the healthy, happy citizens which modern civic ideals demand. The building itself is well lighted, well ventilated, and in winter, well heated. Chilled water fountains are conveniently placed throughout the factory.[63]

Attractions included a week's holiday with pay, insurance for employees and a savings-bank scheme. Other firms had practised variations. Procter and Gamble had a profit-sharing plan and an unemployment-insurance fund built upon company and employee contributions. Frost Wire set up a profit-sharing program and lent funds to its men, assisting with their purchase of homes. Frost's president preferred corporate paternalism to government intervention in social measures because it kept the company's identity in the forefront; it was advertising.[64]

The International Harvester measures were the most comprehensive. The company recognized that industrial trusts like itself faced two adversaries — unions and public opinion. Therefore it turned to corporate welfarism and advertised its enlightenment. Accidents in the initial years had registered a black mark against the Hamilton plant. Consequently, when the new facility was opened, newspaper advertisements boasted about covered machinery, exhaust fans, a first-aid hospital and safety commit-

tees. A workman's-compensation scheme, an expensive pension plan and a profit-sharing program all contributed to a campaign for employee loyalty. The pension had an antistrike feature so that a man who could look forward to a pension at the end of a term of years might hesitate about jeopardizing that prospect by walking out. The 1916 Hamilton machinists' strike and parallel actions in the United States forced additional paternalism. In 1918–1919, Harvester formed a company union or works council which could act on petty grievances. However, on major questions like the eight-hour day, where the labour and management representatives reached a tie vote, the head office in Chicago cast the deciding vote. For a while, the council split labour. There were employees who accepted it as a bird in the hand; others ridiculed its impotence. The division ran roughly between the unskilled men and the skilled men with their craft-union notions. Many of the former wanted "to get out of the hole," and Harvester's benefits were more than they had known. Also, the council had whittled away the foreman's tyranny. "Under the old system the foreman was a little god, a little kaiser, in his own department, nobody dared to brook his authority."[65]

Motifs parallel to corporate efficiency campaigns and to labour's quest for a voice in industrial society penetrated civic affairs. Hamilton participated in the political uplift movement commonly described as progressivism. Reform waves commonly included sensational exposures of graft, reorganization of municipal government, efforts to eliminate waste, housing schemes, public ownership of utilities, and improvement of sanitary and recreational facilities. Hamilton's probe of civic corruption and malfeasance, undertaken by County Judge Colin Snider, was a caricature of weighty revelations in larger cities. Charged with investigating thefts and bribery in civic departments, Snider documented a score of incidents when civic small fry picked up small change. Snider had no authority to investigate conflicts of interest and land deals. Newspapers and ambitious politicians exploited the inquiry. Given the city's sanitary and housing problems as well as the prewar recession, the ensuing tempest was out of joint with real urban emergencies. Furthermore, it generated no significant reform. Usually muckraking investigations whipped up demands from within the middle class and the business community for urban government to be reorganized along the lines of a modern corporation. A stronger executive branch, improved

Dominion Foundries prospered during the First World War by taking contracts like those for shell forgings. Bursts of teamwork and heavy labour amidst heat, noise and furnace fumes carried the metal shapes through processing stages.

accounting procedures and professional advice on technical matters were goals of municipal government reform.

Hamilton already had dabbled with business-efficiency reforms. Presented with a choice of progressive constitutional forms — city government by commission, the city-manager system or a board of control — Hamilton had opted for the latter in 1910. A tame measure, it complicated municipal government without demonstrable advantages, but it retained the democratic form of an elected body. Not all constitutional options did that, and the powerful Hamilton Harbour Commission (1912) and the modest Burlington Beach Commission (1907) were examples of appointed agencies with territorial authority. The reform wisdom of the day maintained that commissions would act with greater efficiency and honesty than elected officials. It was a naïve expectation; politics permeated appointed commissions. By 1914, the city's hodgepodge of special boards and commissions included those already mentioned as well as a Board of Health, a Hydro-Electric Commission, and independent boards for schools, library, cemetery, hospital and parks. Membership selection varied.[66]

Public ownership of utilities, another progressive cause, had adherents but few victories. Both the Cataract Power Company and the Hamilton Street Railway were criticized for poor service. Industrial managers and labourers complained about HSR bottlenecks inconveniencing shift changes. Real-estate developers fumed about delays in construction of new lines. The electric utility was the object of a much greater working-class reform campaign than the streetcar system since there was a potential alternative at hand, namely Ontario Hydro. A few industrialists also supported the idea of having Ontario Hydro enter the city on the grounds that competition would improve rates and service. Even so, a more accurate generalization emphasizes labour's campaign against the locally owned utility monopoly and the business community's defence of its own brethren. In the crucial 1911 bylaw election to determine whether the city would distribute Ontario Hydro electricity, the Trades and Labour Council paid for 20 of the roughly 100 campaign workers supporting the measure. Only two of the eight wards backed the Cataract position and rejected the Hydro bylaw; these were the wards with a concentration of the business and managerial elite, "famous as Cataract monopoly wards." But the triumph of 1911 was unique. Until Ontario Hydro absorbed the Cataract operations in 1930,

Hamilton had power from both private and public-owned sources and a privately operated streetcar system.[67]

The participants in assorted campaigns to improve the industrial city were diverse in aims and class interests. Business groups had a definite role seeking, as they had on shop and office floors, a regulated efficiency. In addition, a labour political movement functioned as a civic force. Its reform ideals and moderate socialism were personified by Alan Studholme. Studholme represented Hamilton East at Queen's Park from late 1906 until the summer of 1919. When he died in that year, petitions circulated in the plants asking management for the afternoon off to allow the men to pay last respects. The funeral was one of Hamilton's largest. From Studholme's election in 1906 until 1921, labour candidates had considerable success in municipal and provincial contests.

The Independent Labor Party, founded in 1907, formed the real political opposition to the city's Conservative machine. The ILP cultivated its base of support with popular social functions and its service as a clearing house for local grievances. Its leaders were moderate socialists, although the party had a radical faction. A typical platform from the moderate leadership advocated the eight-hour day, free compulsory education, improved government factory inspection, minimum wages based on local conditions, public ownership of utilities, abolition of child labour (those under fourteen), exclusion of Asiatics, abolition of bonuses to steamship companies aiding European immigration, and old-age pensions. Before 1914, the platform would have included a call for workman's compensation. Candidates like Walter Rollo and George Halcrow put the Conservatives on notice that a strong opposition was in place. In a 1914 provincial by-election in Hamilton West, Rollo lost a two-way fight to the Conservative candidate by forty votes, an event that the *Times* reported was "the worst hammering" taken by "the Tory machine."[68] Running in the federal election of 1917 against a Unionist candidate and a powerful wartime campaign mounted by the government, Rollo again came second but had carried several wards. Finally, in 1919 he won Hamilton West provincially and Halcrow took Hamilton East. In the municipal election which followed, the ILP placed two men on the Board of Control and elected six aldermen. Rollo subsequently became the Minister of Labour in the Farmer-Labour government of E.C. Drury.

What had Hamilton acquired in the complicated arena of reform action? There were no immediate and sweeping changes. A few proposals died at the planning stage, including limited-dividend housing and civic beautification. Parks and playgrounds were secured but with underlying biases. Other efforts like the health movement are exceedingly difficult to evaluate in terms of instant results. The hydro-electric bylaw involved labour but also some business interests. Municipal government reform led to nondemocratic commissions, but the essence of civic politics was not discarded.

Given the mixed record, a vexing and fundamental question remains to be answered. If the economic burdens and employment hazards were so pervasive and harsh, why then did the working-class majority fail to make greater use of its latent political power to reshape the urban industrial society? The breakthrough of 1919–20 was another example of substantial social and political ferment coming at sharp but rare interludes in the city's history. Why was it only an interlude?

A series of circumstances explains the domination of civic, provincial and federal offices by the traditional parties, with the Conservatives in control. First, the rules of the political contests favoured the established parties and propertied interests. Not until 1920, during the first year of the Farmer-Labour administration at Toronto, was a property qualification for municipal office dropped. Electoral boundaries were arranged to dilute the working-class vote. The standard two-dollar bribe as well as tampered voters' lists helped affluent and experienced party machines. Second, the Liberals made occasional bids for alliances with labour leaders and thereby drew off some working-class voters. Finally, the Tories achieved an even greater success with workingmen because the party heartily embraced a series of emotionally popular issues. The Conservatives attacked the Liberals for their temperance views and, among a distinctly wet working class, this proved to be a popular position. The Tory glorification of Crown and Empire appealed to a population that included thousands of recent arrivals from the United Kingdom, where the Conservatives likewise had exploited the rhetoric and spirit of patriotism. The Tory articulation of these views was at its best during the relaxed "smokers" for men or "monster picnics" for families. The party also used civic patronage to reward its workers. During hard times, the Conservative advocacy of protective tariffs answered some of the anxieties held by working-

men about their vanishing jobs. For all of these reasons, there were limits to the political action of a fragmented working class. The Tories crushed labour's political action after 1920 and reasserted control of the civic machinery until the end of the Second World War.[69]

FIN DE SIECLE CULTURE IN AN INDUSTRIAL CITY

Labour disputes and urban-reform controversies focussed on new technologies and administrative practices. At the same time, the cultural aspect of organized labour and politics maintained some venerable traditions. Labour outings and party rallies continued, as in earlier times, to combine recreation and entertainment with political intent. Conservative identification with the robust character of civic culture had formed an essential part of the party's success. Most activities had a street setting and a colourful air. On 3 June 1890, Premier Oliver Mowat visited the city on a political campaign. Horsemen congregated in preparation along one street; the Bugle Band and Independent Fife and Drum Band assembled on the market square. Wagons, all aglow with Chinese lanterns and Roman candles, followed the musicians. As befitted an industrial city, Labour Day demonstrations like the one organized for 6 September 1897 were among the most entertaining interludes of the year. Again the bands played. Baseball games were held; children participated in field-day contests. The Watanabe Japanese Acrobatic Troupe was hired and performed various exhibitions including one on "Chinese Methods of Torturing War Captives." The crowds wanted to be titillated. The gala affairs of 1897 received some sponsorship from the city's businessmen. Indeed, it appears that collaborative activities involving labour and capital in festive affairs were commonplace expressions of civic pride. During the Summer Carnival of August 1889, the illuminated barges, fireworks and rowing regatta were complemented by a procession of the city's tradesmen organized by labour and civic boosters. During the city's premature celebration of its centennial in 1913 (the actual centennial should have been held in 1916), craft labourers organized a parade of decorated floats and a building contractor with support from the construction trades erected a house in one day.[70]

There had been scores of other celebrations: lodge parades, regattas and a multitude of political processions during and after

Members of the Ninety-First Regiment assemble around the statue of Queen Victoria. Many of Hamilton's early volunteers during the First World War were immigrants from the United Kingdom.

The Hamilton Recruitment League set up its booth in front of the statue of Queen Victoria — "Queen and Empress/Model Wife and Mother." One of the league's later signs asked young men, "Do you have a reason or only an excuse?"

election campaigns. Fresh air, music, fraternal effort, voluntary gusto and civic self-esteem were important parts of each pageant. Class consciousness among the workingmen, especially the craftsmen, was expressed at many of the occasions, but the purely recreational features of parades and carnivals also drew others into these social occasions. Radio and cinema would challenge the supremacy of the outdoor occasions, but the marketing of passive entertainment was not the only disruption. The automobile played a part. A further challenge came from advocates of a modern and efficient city and from a persistent middle-class reform emphasis on home life. The local branch of the Canadian Manufacturers Association at a 1912 meeting for the centennial considered processions and parades as disruptive of traffic and work routines.

> If Hamilton was going to be boomed it should be done on broader lines. The city has passed the stage where it was in keeping with its dignity to hold sangerfests, old boys' reunions and carnivals.[71]

Thus spoke the deadening spirit of modernization.

For most of the 1870-1920 era, the city had thriving outdoor leisure pursuits that collected throngs in parks and along streets. Music decorated public events and civic parks. The electric streetcar enhanced this aspect of popular culture by conveying thousands to local celebrations or amusement parks. On Victoria Day 1911, the HSR carried 47,866 people and the interurban lines another 19,555. By 1914, summer Saturdays at the beach found crowds estimated at more than ten thousand. On such days the radial cars were packed.

On special occasions the musical outpouring was stunning. At a two-day festival to celebrate Queen Victoria's Golden Jubilee, the Hamilton Philharmonic Society assembled a sixty-piece orchestra and a massive choir — 425 adults and 1,000 children. The program included Haydn's *Creation* and Handel's *Sampson*. The Germania Singing Society, originating in the wake of the stream of German immigrants that passed through in the 1850s, sponsored an international *sangerfest* in 1891. The militia or other volunteer bands, resplendent in uniform, played at every conceivable function from steamboat excursions to auction sales.[72]

Zestful participation also marked the city's expanding forms of amateur sport. Baseball, which had become popular in the 1860s,

evolved as a working-class recreation that blended into craft-union picnics. Rugby football, coming to prominence in the 1870s with the Tigers, originated among gentlemen. However, the sport of grunt and shove had gone plebeian by the early 1890s when the Tigers recruited beefy north-enders. The Tigers lost their first Grey Cup appearance against the University of Toronto in 1910. Another Hamilton team, the Alerts, brought the city its first Grey Cup in 1912; the Tigers won it the next year and in 1915. Soccer thrived in the early 1900s, invigorated during the industrial boom by symbolic duels between Westinghouse and "the infallible runners' up" from the ILP team.

Bicycling, an elite sport, flourished for decades. The "Wheelmen," members of a club founded in 1881 and alleged to be the most prominent club of its kind in the Dominion, included the future industrialist John Moodie and financier Aemilius Jarvis. The club raced during the 1880s and 1890s on several tracks where members pumped through sand circuits against athletes from the Ramblers and Crescents. Rowing clubs felt the impact of the bicycle craze and lost popularity between the turn of the century and the 1920s. Both the Leander Rowing Club, founded in 1877, and the Nautilus Club, established the next year, had collapsed in 1895. The latter club had drawn heavily from among the ranks of employees of a glass factory on the bay. When the company failed, so did the Nautilus Club. At about the same time, track and field became an important sport when the workingman's newspaper, the *Hamilton Herald*, sponsored the annual around-the-bay race. The first was held in 1894. Billy Sherring's victory in the marathon at the Olympic games held in Athens in 1906 and Bobby Kerr's triumph in the 220 metres in the 1908 games made Hamilton a self-conscious track centre.[73]

The industrial-city stage in Hamilton's evolution was significant in terms of achievements in institutionalized or refined cultural activity. The Mechanics Institute Hall and Crystal Palace served theatrical groups, including the Garrick Club (1875-1910). The Grand Opera House opened in 1880 and permitted the staging of elaborate productions. Other theatres, ranging from large operations booking legitimate theatrical productions — the Savoy and Bennett's Theatre — to small vaudeville theatres such as the Star, were constructed at the end of the century. On Thanksgiving Day 1908, a city record was set when all three major theatres posted standing room only during matinee and

On 14 August 1913, during Hamilton's premature centennial celebration, contractor James Bryers arranged to build a house in a day. The stunt upset the building trades because they feared speed-up methods and careless construction practices.

evening performances. Given that the Grand had a capacity of 1,800, Bennett's 1,685 and the Savoy 1,500, it was likely that 10,000 people attended theatrical performances. In prewar Hamilton, the live theatre was a thriving institution.[74]

A revitalized Philharmonic Society (1885) and the Orchestral Club (1889), aided by moderately priced instruments and sheet music, were able to create the necessary interest to support the Hamilton Conservatory of Music, chartered in 1896. The popular and enduring Elgar Choir was founded in 1906. The establishment of the Hamilton Art School (1886) did not result from the credo of art for art's sake, but from the belief that an industrial city would require draftsmen. Still, it promoted artistic development. A breakaway group formed the Hamilton Art League in 1898; this association eventually revitalized the art school. The school trained a number of prominent painters, including J.E.H. MacDonald, an original member of the Group of Seven. The Hamilton Art Gallery was founded in 1914 with thirty-two paintings donated by the family of William Blair Bruce, a son of Hamilton who had studied painting in Paris and had settled in Sweden. The small gallery was housed in the public library. The original library had opened in 1890 and moved to a new building in 1914; the older building then housed the gallery and the city health department.

In addition to the various arts-and-letters groups, there were clubs espousing ideals of public service, self-improvement or fostering a set of patriotic sentiments. The Canadian Club of Hamilton, organized in 1892, became the nucleus of a national association after 1909. Four philanthropic associations federated in 1893 to form the Hamilton and District Council of Women. The Women's Institute movement began at Stoney Creek in 1897. Hamilton's Clementina Fessenden successfully campaigned for a formal observance of Empire Day in schools (1897), and other patriotic ladies formed the first Ontario branch of the Imperial Order, Daughters of the Empire in 1900.[75]

Music, parade, sport and patriotic associations also had a sombre use — to aid in the recruitment of soldiers during the war. Until the summer of 1915, recruitment had been fairly easy, an indication not only of patriotism but of the hard times and under-employment. When "the flow of recruits began to show signs of sluggishness," concerned patriots formed the Recruiting League of Hamilton, the first association of its kind in Canada. Working with the city assessment officials, they compiled a list of eligible men to whom they would appeal (or shame). During good weather they organized rallies in the parks. Other times they met in theatres. Numerous clergymen allied themselves with the association and "used their eloquence, their influence and their example with great effect."[76] The league skilfully tapped mainstreams of popular culture, as did the authorities who devised the concept of "sportsmen's regiments." In Hamilton, the 205th, the Tigers Battalion, was born amidst a publicity campaign. Athletes were transferred from other units to give the 205th an appropriate cast of attractive local competitors. Bobby Kerr became the adjutant. Scarcely a day passed in April, 1916, without a new star being signed to convey "clean amateurism" onto the fields of Flanders. Retail shops displayed team colours and pennants; sporting contests were held against other units. When sent overseas, the Tigers were broken up to reinforce other battalions.[77]

Manipulation of popular culture, news censorship and organized ostracism supported recruitment drives. There was also a strain of British patriotism, its strength difficult to assess. It certainly appeared among qualified Hamilton voters, for in the 1917 federal election Hamilton East and Hamilton West sent Union Government candidates to Ottawa. In the working-class east, Alan Studholme's stronghold at provincial elections, the 1917 federal victor was General Sydney Chilton Mewburn, the minister of militia. Mewburn had been a Liberal. Whatever Mewburn's defection proved about weak political opposition to the conduct of the war and more narrowly to the conscription act, there are problems with any attempt to see the 1917 election as a resounding statement of popular support for the conduct of the war. The Wartime Election Act enfranchised mothers, wives, sisters and daughters of soldiers and took away the vote from naturalized immigrants from enemy countries who had arrived in Canada after 1902. Moreover, Mewburn as a Unionist had a strong Conservative organization behind him. Out of twelve federal representatives selected in Hamilton from 1878 to 1917, nine had been Conservatives. The party machine with city-hall connections and the popularity of protection in an industrial city help to account for a Conservative grip on federal constituencies.

In sum, there is no clear-cut way to summarize the domestic shock of war; there was not true confirmation from all the resi-

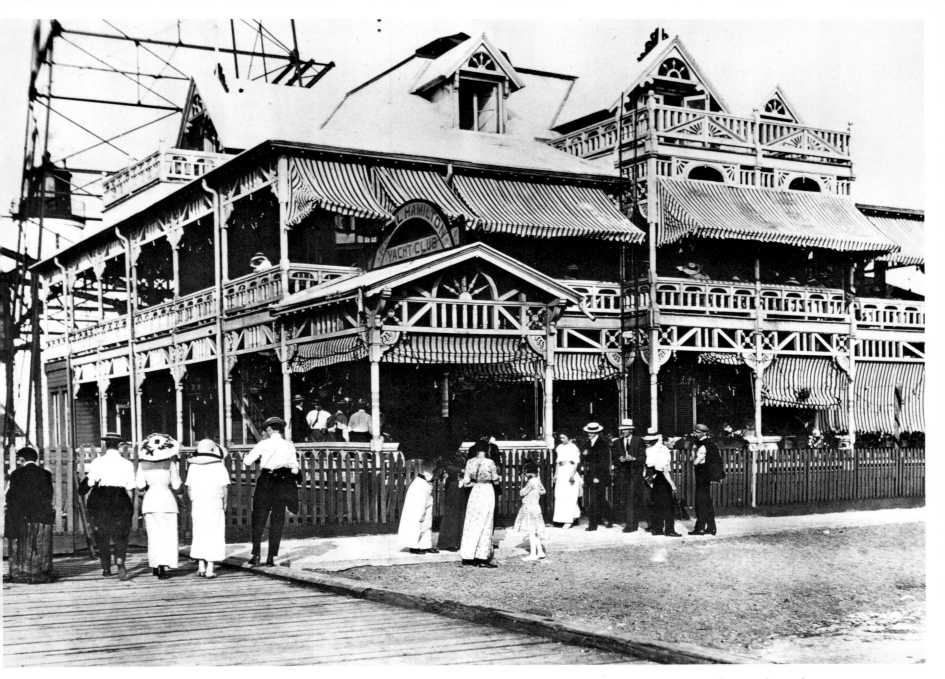

Burlington Beach remained fashionable for the elite in the early 1900s, but railway traffic, power transmission lines and crowds resulted in an exodus of the affluent. The Royal Hamilton Yacht Club near the Burlington Canal is seen on an idyllic day in 1908. It burned to the ground in 1915.

The Hamilton Herald sponsored the annual around-the-bay race. The starting line in 1908 was on King Street.

Seen here on a field trip in 1887, the Hamilton Association organized into sections to study minerals, flora and birds. Their activities combined a social-club atmosphere with the Victorian passion for natural science.

Even in the winter, celebrations such as this one around 1890 inspired floats and banners.

An urban vignette from 1919. These children were headed for the last Sunday-school picnic before having to return to school; the truck has replaced the streetcar and the carriage.

A windy day at the beach around 1912. The radial streetcar provided a special service with stops designated at mile posts. For mothers and children, the excursion permitted an escape from the summer heat of Hamilton streets.

The slope at the bottom of the escarpment near the Chedoke Ravine was and remains a locale for winter recreation.

For many years the Hamilton Tigers battled for honours on the Cricket Grounds in the west end. Septimus Du Moulin — oarsman and leading football player — is second from the right in the back row.

Uniforms, a group outing and a symetrically posed photograph like this 1890s one set on the courthouse steps were characteristics of the bicycle craze. The craze was swept away years later by automobile touring.

dents of Hamilton that the city should make continued sacrifices. On the one hand, industrialists, British patriots, the Conservative party apparatus and a poorly informed press saw little to criticize. The political arena was managed to prevent a frank discussion of much that deserved forthright condemnation. On the other hand, as the machinists' strike illustrated, there was discontent. Hamilton gained a few heroes in the war, experienced the unpleasant frenzy of patriotism and lost an estimated 1,800 men. Perhaps as many as 7,000 men serving in Hamilton units were wounded. Direct losses and incalculable emotional damage dampened the prewar gaiety of popular culture, joining other forces that seemed to erode traditional leisure forms.[78]

Sights, sounds and odours in and around 1920 Hamilton pointed to an important transition in transportation. The internal-combustion engine was becoming established as one of three means of motive power. It would become dominant during the next decade. In 1920 horses and wagons remained important in drayage and delivery. The air near the city market was still redolent with horse manure, while only a few yards away streetcars growled and sparked as they picked up speed from the passenger stops. The founders of the Cataract Power Company operated an extensive local and interurban streetcar system that converged at the Terminal Building (1908) on King Street near the Royal Connaught Hotel. The Hamilton Street Railway operated as far east as Kenilworth Avenue (1916) and soon would run a line into Westdale (1923). The Hamilton and Dundas Street Railway provided a service for the industrial labourers who resided just beyond the city limits in what was known as West Hamilton. The Hamilton Radial Electric Railway (1896) eventually swung through the industrial belt and extended into Burlington; at the peak of radial-line expansion it reached Oakville (1906). The Hamilton, Grimsby and Beamsville Electric Railway (1908) completed the system. Both horses and streetcars shared the street with dull black automobiles. Ungainly chain-driven trucks, a few now produced at International Harvester, were replacing the drays; by 1920 trucking companies had lobbied for improved roads.[79]

At the end of the war, more and more individuals placed the automobile at the centre of their leisure time. For owners the immediate advantages far outweighed disadvantages. No longer were they confined to the interurban schedule and rails for a ride in the country. Never again would they have to squeeze onto the rattling, swaying, crammed streetcar to attend picnics, band concerts or amusement concessions at the beach. Before the war, the liberation to be effected by the automobile was presaged when the Ontario Motor League went through the Hamilton region painting white bands around trees to identify major routes. Rail lines directed movement, but the automobile introduced random possibilities and required aids to prevent drivers from becoming lost.

At first the vehicle was for the affluent, and they retained the practices of bicycle clubs and group outings. The eighty-five Ford owners in the Hamilton vicinity met on 4 August 1911 for a planned journey to a banquet at Brant House. Blending traditional pageantry with the instrument which would help to challenge the very fabric of such occasions, Sir John Gibson and the Ninety-first Regiment Band opened the first Hamilton auto show at the Armouries in March, 1914. A two-edged sword, the automobile liberated individuals and even sanitized streets, but it likewise helped to jeopardize those many collective events at which the people of the city had drawn together. Eventually the automobile did more than that, because it forced physical reorganizations and burdened municipal government with hidden expenses.[80]

CONCLUSION

The Hamilton of 1920 can be viewed in retrospect as a result of highly productive economic booms like that of the late 1880s, the years of "Laurier prosperity" from 1900 to 1913 and the wartime economy of 1915 to 1918. Despite social inequalities and an often harsh set of working conditions, the city of 1920 emanated great strength. In concrete, brick, paving materials, and consumption of the new power source — hydro-electricity — the sinews of a robust city can be measured. Many structures stand today as an inheritance of these remarkable years of urban growth. The large scale of factories, apartment dwellings and office blocks represented a break from the two earlier and quite different Hamiltons that had developed on Burlington Bay. Moreover, many of the institutions of the industrial city endured; Hamiltonians have sometimes taken them for granted. Stelco, International Harvester, Westinghouse and the TH and B are prominent examples.

Much of the industrial city still functions in the midst of the contemporary city. Nonetheless, the industrial-city epoch was

"Tank Day" at Gore Park in November 1918 was an occasion for the sale of war bonds. The tank demonstration included feats such as crushing a boxcar. Gore Park was the focal point of patriotic gatherings in most of the city's eras.

only a moment in history. Some of its cultural enthusiasms and relationships with the surrounding landscape of the Niagara peninsula can stimulate nostalgia for a bygone era. The profound interest in public pageant is one such feature. Another is the way in which Hamilton once blended into rich farmland. Only a few miles east of the factories, fruit orchards and dairies occupied a green and uncluttered periphery. The extensive urban concentration reaching from Niagara Falls to Oshawa was decades away; expressways were not even remotely prefigured in the modest Hamilton-Toronto highway opened in November, 1917. The compact and vital city would experience cultural change; economic and demographic cycles would make it a different community; it would overwhelm the countryside. Despite these alterations, the kernel of industrial activity that existed by 1920 had defined the essential Hamilton for subsequent periods.

The Hamilton and Barton Incline Railway at James Street is pictured here in 1930 toward the end of its more than thirty years of service. The apartment building on the right was designed for upper-middle-class tenants and was part of the apartment construction boom of the 1920s.

Chapter Four
Hamilton, Canada: International Forces in a Local Setting, 1920-1946

The years from the end of one war to the end of the next compose an untidy interlude consisting of three distinct phases: the comparatively vigorous 1920s, the great Depression and the Second World War. Contained within the Twenties — appropriately and frequently qualified as "the roaring Twenties" — were several significant beginnings. The automobile was established as a fixture. The average of 30 fatalities and 500 accidents a year on Hamilton streets (1926-30) defined traffic as a shocking urban hazard. The city government clearly had to take the automobile into account when planning its budget for streets and policing. Radio was becoming a familiar consumer item and apartment buildings appeared in clusters along major traffic arteries. In terms of continuity, the 1920s contained some industrial growth, considerable residential construction and renewed immigration.

What distinguishes the Depression of the 1930s from earlier cyclical reversals was its duration, although that claim is slightly misleading. Excepting the noteworthy case of the construction industry, the great Depression saw some recoveries; certain categories of manufactured goods were far more vulnerable than others. Not every plant was crippled for an entire decade; some companies stayed close to full production. Nonetheless, the basic and tangible measures of urban expansion — population growth and residential construction — were a clear indication that Hamilton had stopped growing. The demographic impact would register years later, after the war, when the city's industries were held back by a dearth of skilled labour and immigration became an instrument of industrial policy. The many consequences of residential construction's being frozen for nearly two decades included short-term impacts, for it increased unemployment and soon meant a decline in housing standards. It also had long-term consequences. The inability of the existing free-enterprise arrangements to meet the housing problems, as well as the weak fiscal base of city government, brought the federal and provincial governments into urban affairs. Depression and war also brought on circumstances that revolutionized the relationships between employers and industrial labour. As was the case with prior cycles and shocks, Hamilton's history cannot be understood without persistent reference to wider economic and political systems of which it was a part.

CRISIS AND OPPORTUNITY IN THE INDUSTRIAL ECONOMY

In surface appearance, the economy ran a broken course of fluctuations great and small across the Twenties and Thirties. No single year presented an employment history comparable to another. A familiar contrast, that of prosperous Twenties and depressed Thirties, stands unchallenged as a fundamental truth. However, it presents a generalization peppered with noteworthy exceptions, since economic uncertainty affected Hamilton during the 1920s and traces of recovery came in the great Depression. Unemployment in the city reached 15 per cent of the labour force during the worst months of a recession in 1921 and 1922. Although residential construction pushed the later years of the Twenties into a boom, employment routinely dipped from October to March. The winter cut into the building trades, canning factories, nearby farm-labour opportunities and civic-works projects.[1] For workingmen and their families the checkered state of economic life in either the Twenties or Thirties translated into a need to retain the occupational and geographic flexibility of their counterparts in earlier stages of Hamilton history. They had to confront opportunities and debacles with family strategies. Therefore there were domestic dramas tied to the seasons, to

James Street, west side, looking north, 1925. A row of landmarks, from left to right: Robinson's Department Store, the Bank of Hamilton, city hall. On the right, a portion of the Canada Life Assurance Company Building and its clock tower. The impact of the automobile is now apparent.

minor business cycles and to short-term cutbacks in specific sectors.

Beyond the economic surface appearances and nearly hidden exceptions, there was another important economic feature to the interwar years. A structural transformation unfolded. The federal government increasingly intervened in the city's economic and social life through taxation of income (begun during the First World War), social and housing programs, imposition of wage and price controls and immigration policy.

We can see how events occasionally ran counter to a conventional picture of two contrasting economic epochs by tracing the corporate experiences of Dofasco and Procter and Gamble. Dofasco was established in 1912 by Clifton Sherman, an American with a background in the iron and steel industry. Once more, the entrepreneurial connection with the American iron trades was confirmed. The company flourished during the First World War and greatly increased its open-hearth facilities. Business in the 1920s proved disappointing. A plate mill constructed after the war sat idle until 1920; an expected corporate payroll of 1,000 declined to 400 in 1927 and bounced up to 1,000 in early 1930. During the Depression, the company embarked on innovative and aggressive diversification. Among several new mills, it added one for production of hot-rolled steel coils to supply automotive manufacturers. That was in 1935. Diversification and a flair for technological boldness enabled the company to employ as many or more men as it had during the 1920s, and coincidently poised it for wartime production. At Procter and Gamble, demand for a simple household item — soap — kept full employment in effect during the Depression.[2]

Still, such an unconventional view of the economy is really only a corrective to generalizations. In fact, the back-to-back alignment of potent economic disruptions — depression and war — had profound effects. These major events — especially the war — drew a reluctant federal government into involvement with the city's economy and labour force. The economic sequences also marked the composition of the city's population — size, age and origins. The disruptions from 1930 to 1945 imposed a moratorium on major housing construction and urban planning. Because of these several considerations, an examination of the economy is central to understanding Hamilton's history during this period.

The relative health of Hamilton manufacturing in the late 1920s derived from Canada's consumption of heavy capital goods. The construction of hydro-electric plants and equipment for pulp and paper mills and mining operations brought a steady flow of large orders to Westinghouse and Otis-Fenson Elevator. Construction of office towers in Montreal, Toronto and Vancouver benefited these same firms as well as the Steel Company of Canada and Hamilton Bridge. International Harvester prospered in step with prairie grain production and National Steel Car received contracts for increased rolling stock on Canadian railways. The city's industries came to rely upon two precarious conditions: sustained investment in capital goods used in the nation's resource or transportation development, and the position of Canadian wheat in the world grain market. Both broke down during the 1930s. International contraction of credit dried up demand for heavy equipment and structural steel. Poor grain harvests undercut the agricultural-implements industry. After the first year of the Depression, these collapses had forced closings at Otis-Fenson Elevator and National Steel Car; Harvester retained a skeleton crew, operating at about 20 per cent of capacity. Steel and machinery firms functioned at 40 to 50 per cent, with Dofasco faring somewhat better. Adult males in Hamilton had averaged over forty-five weeks of employment in 1921, but only thirty-eight weeks of employment from June, 1930, to June, 1931. The layoffs and reduced hours produced fewer weeks of gainful employment for a number of trades which were at the heart of the city's economic make-up: machinists averaged thirty-seven weeks, millwrights thirty-seven, sheetmetal workers thirty-six, forgemen thirty-five, carpenters thirty-two, unskilled labourers twenty-nine, masons and bricklayers twenty-eight, moulders and coremakers thirty-seven, longshoremen twenty-two. In subsequent recoveries, a few trades improved their position, but construction stayed generally depressed despite school-building efforts undertaken as a civic relief measure and erection of a new CNR station (1931) and TH and B terminal (1933). According to the 1935 Hamilton relief rolls, 60 per cent of the recipients were connected with the building trades. The transportation and commercial sectors retained a far better employment record than did manufacturing.[3]

Interestingly, women in the workforce in the period from June, 1930, to June, 1931, had an average of forty-five weeks' employment. The fact that they received about half the hourly wage rate paid to men might explain their retention, as might their concentration in textiles, which operated at fairly high levels of

The Remington Rand typewriter plant was relatively well-ventilated and well-lit for factories of the day (1947). A sign on the left declares "Silence to prevail in this department."

Foundry floors looked much the same in the 1930s as in the 1880s except for the moulding machines like the one in the centre of this 1935 picture. Such mechanization challenged skilled labour because craftsmen represented a production bottleneck and the possibility of worker control. Manual labour remained intact, as the wheelbarrow suggests.

The Second World War revived Hamilton's heavy industries. Slack employment gave way to strenuous ten- and eleven-hour days.

capacity until 1935. In December, 1930, the Hamilton textile mills operated at 60 per cent capacity, and three years later were functioning at an estimated 90 per cent. Depending on the year — 1931 was the peak — knitting and weaving mills employed from 2,500 to 5,000 women. Therefore, along with a modest income derived from approximately 10,000 lodgers, the pay envelopes from Canadian Cottons, Hamilton Cotton, Eaton Knitting, Mercury Mills, J.R. Moodie and Zimmer Knit helped support many thousands of families whose main provider sat idle for a third of the year in the worst period of the Depression. Whether labouring away from the home or tending to boarding-house chores, a good many women worked when husbands, sons and brothers could not.[4]

The Hamilton situation resembled that in other industrial and shipping centres across Canada. At full employment in 1929, an estimated 36,000 wage earners found employment in Hamilton. By contrast, the spring of 1933, the worst period of the Depression, found only 22,000 employed. The relative misery in relation to several other centres and the real drop in employment opportunities pointed up the city's vulnerability. From the employment low in early 1933, a gradual recovery built to a climax in the summer of 1937. Employment inched up to 29,000 in the spring of 1935 and reestablished the 1929 level in the summer of 1937. Another poor western harvest deflated recovery; textile production already had dropped following an onslaught of American competition and dumping. It took war to eliminate unemployment swiftly just as it had done in 1915. Textile mills undertook some of the city's first war orders in January, 1940, when they started to turn out tents and uniforms. Steel-service companies had anticipated impending shortages and launched into an abnormal forward buying of steel. Their speculation primed steel manufacture well before actual war orders.[5]

Stark peaks and troughs seen in employment statistics and figures on plant capacity in use had their counterpart in the city's relief reports. By the end of 1931, some 2,500 to 3,000 families received relief. A year later, the number had doubled and continued to rise until the spring of 1933, when it reached 8,500. During the first two years of the Depression, no more than 10 per cent of families were on relief at any one time; the worst months of 1933 raised it to 25 per cent, a figure comparable to estimates for the winter of 1914-15. That earlier depression had struck hard and fast; the great Depression ground on steadily until it arrived at a comparably demoralizing state. Fluctuations following 1933 also can be traced in the relief estimates: 4,000 families in December, 1936; 2,500 in December, 1937; 4,000 in December, 1938; 2,300 in December, 1939; 600 in December, 1940.[6]

From 1930 until the war, city hall struggled with social and fiscal emergencies arising from the unprecedented unemployment. Constitutionally, the fiscal responsibility for unemployment resided with the province, but historically the municipalities had dealt with administration of relief for the poor for as long as Upper Canada had been settled. As early as 1930, it was evident that current conditions could not be handled by local action. Civic resources were simply too limited. Therefore the federal government, in its Unemployment Relief Act (1930), indicated that unemployment, which had been a provincial and local responsibility, was to become a federal concern also. By this act and many subsequent agreements, cost-sharing programs were initiated. These usually left the city managing the administration of relief and carrying one-third of the direct costs.

The administrative burden of arranging for the distribution of groceries, clothing, rent money and fuel forced Hamilton to create a Public Welfare Department in 1933. During 1935, the department employed thirty-one investigators; each applicant for welfare was investigated at the central office, but the neighbourhood investigators delivered the first vouchers and returned at least every two weeks to check the needs of the client family. In cases where tenants were faced with evictions, a rent branch of the department determined the taxes and the water rates, added 50 per cent to the sum of these billings and divided by twelve. This amount was offered to the landlord as a month's rent. The offers were usually accepted. The Public Welfare Department's efforts represented the city's major response to the Depression. However, Hamilton also managed a rural resettlement scheme and a slum-clearance project. Both were quite limited experiments. Meanwhile, voluntary agencies increased their services. The Lions Club, for example, ran a hostel for transients at the corner of Catherine and Cannon streets. A private group attempted to generate employment for a few family men through a "Man-A-Block" scheme. Householders and businesses subscribed to a fund and in return men were assigned small maintenance chores.

Throughout the crisis, the city scraped to finance its portion of

Old men, the unemployed and benches in Gore Park — a familiar scene from 1928.

A bright and airy room typical of the new industrial architecture. Under the scrutiny of the foreman who checked on their output, cutters at Mercury Mills in 1928 shaped knitted fabric for garments. Standing all day was one of the physical penalties of this job.

the welfare department's expenditures. However, it also had to pay interest on civic bonds and meet current routine expenditures. At the same time, its tax base shrank because there was an unwillingness or inability among holders of unimproved property to launch new construction. As well, many owners defaulted on their tax payments. Between April, 1929, and April, 1938, the city sold eighty-seven built-upon properties and 3,358 vacant properties; these sales were forced by tax arrears. When the federal government established a Royal Commission on Dominion-Provincial Relations in Canada (1937), Hamilton appraised municipal responsibilities and sources of revenue and submitted a pointed brief. Arguing that senior governments had saddled the city with social-service tasks like education, policing, public health and relief administration, Hamilton appealed for additional tax powers.

There was some rationale for having property taxes carry the expenses for hard services like water and sewer, but the accumulated social functions called for a new system of taxation. In the United States, a few cities levied a local sales tax. Hamilton's requests were more modest. Specifically, the city asked for the power to tax the owners of automobiles and the properties owned by the tax-exempt Hamilton Hydro-Electric Commission. Rather than granting a greater taxing authority to cities, the federal and provincial governments eventually increased their own social-service activities or granted funds to the local relief agencies, providing these bodies accepted senior-government guidelines. Therefore, in the constitutional skirmishes ignited by the Depression, the city council of Hamilton and of other Canadian cities failed in their attempts to maintain a real measure of autonomy.[7]

The payroll reports of the city's eight leading industries collected by the Wartime Prices and Trade Board — one of Ottawa's new incursions into the local economy — chart the eventual turnaround in heavy manufacturing. In September, 1939, 35,000 worked in the eight industries. The next year brought an increase of 5,000, followed by jumps of 10,000 employees in each of 1941 and 1942. In September, 1942, the count peaked at 60,000. About 20,000 were thought to have been working directly in the production of munitions. The payroll increases in several corporations drastically affected by the Depression were remarkable. Otis-Fenson Elevator had 250 employees in September, 1939, and 4,300 in September, 1942. At National Steel Car, the increase over the same period was from 920 to 4,000. Westinghouse went from 380 to 6,750; Dofasco from 1,620 to 3,000 and Stelco from 6,500 to 9,900. The swelling ranks of labour and the longer work hours also can be seen in the increase of industrial accidents — from under 3,000 in 1939 to over 16,000 in 1945.

To thwart the inflationary pressures of a sudden influx of people and government expenditures in a community with a contracted supply of housing and with many other goods in sudden demand, the federal government turned to economic planning. An Order in Council of 3 September 1939 had established the economic regulations which were supposed to counter excessive profits and inflation. Light controls were kept until the slack in the country's labour pool and productive capacity had been taken up. At that point early in 1941, the price index moved up sharply, and in October, 1941, the government announced price ceilings. The base period of prices was decreed as September and October, 1941. Retail prices had become considerably inflated at that point and comparable wage settlements had not been achieved. Actually, wage controls had been declared in December, 1940, with 1926-1929 as the base years. Where wages in that period could be shown to be inadequate, higher increases could be granted. In addition, rises in the cost of living were to be met by cost-of-living bonuses. Hamilton labour disputed the application of these terms, alleging poor enforcement and especially protesting removal of wages from the collective-bargaining process. What had been undertaken as measures to avert the inflation and labour protest of the First World War would contribute to a climate of grievance in a 1946 summer of strikes. The federal presence stood as an important factor in civic affairs, but not even it could do much more than delay the fundamental conflict between industrial labour and management that had been brewing for decades.[8]

THE UNEVEN COURSE OF POPULATION INCREASE

A fairly high birthrate, declining mortality and immigration jointly account for an increase of city population from 114,000 in 1921 to 155,000 in 1931. A falling birth rate and relatively few immigrants during the Depression froze the city's population at roughly 155,000 until 1940. Immigration during the war was negligible, but internal migration became important and so did

In the city's primarily Anglo-Saxon north end, the rigours of outdoor work on the lakeshore (at left) contrasted with the frivolity of the 1903 St. Andrew's Society Masquerade Ball (above). Although southern and eastern European immigrants had begun to arrive before the First World War, United Kingdom newcomers dominated until after the Second World War.

a rising birthrate. These two elements carried the population to 174,000 in 1945.

Comparison of 1921 and 1931 census data show that the number of continental Europeans increased from 6,500 to 30,000. This bare fact masks an extraordinary situation when population movement in a troubled postwar world affected Hamilton. Behind the numbers were incidents of personal sacrifice and flight from European political turmoil and economic dislocation. In Hamilton's case, the arrivals from Poland and Hungary were most prominent in the 1920s, a sign of the problems of central Europe. American quotas for visas imposed in 1921 held back thousands of would-be émigrés. Throughout 1921 and 1922, quotas had been exhausted at Riga, Rotterdam, Vienna and Warsaw. Philip Onizezuk, informed by a Warsaw steamship agent that an "American visa to be obtained at Warsaw was about the hardest thing in the world," went to Canada. He set down in Hamilton because it was close to the United States. In 1924, the quotas remained fully taken at Berlin, Bucharest, Genoa, Helsinkii and Prague. As the difficulties of securing entry to the United States and the ease of access to Canada became well known, the numbers of central and eastern Europeans coming to Hamilton increased. Thus the years from 1926 to 1930 were especially active.[9]

One illicit means of gaining entry to the United States was to secure a visitor's visa. Immigrant smuggling rings operated out of Hamilton during the 1920s and 1930s. A 1923 investigation exposed a ring which forged visas, provided dress clothes and arranged transportation for a fee of $125 to $130. Several rings operated out of boarding houses in the Sherman Avenue North area, while another was found at the Mutual Steamship Agency. Railway brakemen, an investigator reported, smuggled "southern Europeans" in boxcars for $50 to $100 each. These practices declined when local economic recovery began and American officials increased border surveillance, but smuggling did not vanish, nor did the legal exodus to the United States. Perhaps several thousand individuals of foreign origin left the Hamilton region for the United States in each year of the 1920s. In 1926 alone, there were 3,000 British-born and 1,000 southern and eastern European residents of Hamilton on a waiting list for American visas.[10]

As it had in the 1850s, Hamilton again was functioning as an expedient station on the immigration trail that led to America.

While the city made a substantial gain of continental-European immigrants — about 23,000 — the actual number which set down in Hamilton could have been twice that. It is probable that many who settled in Hamilton, or merely used it as a base for preparing the final leg of their journey, had access to kinship networks or other old-country relationships that gave them assistance with job hunting or shelter while in Hamilton. The variations on such relationships are extensive: family obligation, friendship, generosity, sheer exploitation of the newcomer by steamship agents and boarding-house keepers, and political or regional connections. The sojourning male — very much an Italian phenomenon prior to 1914 — was much more a trait of Polish and Hungarian movement during the Twenties, when Italian immigration achieved a near balance of males and females.

Natural increase became an important component of population growth during the 1920s, perhaps for the first time in the history of the city. The birth rate increased slightly at the end of the war, a result of the return of husbands and fiancés. In addition, the infant mortality rate fell and stayed constant at a reduced rate. In 1905 and 1908, approximately 150 out of every 1,000 infants born alive had died during their first year of life. The sanitary reforms and the volunteer work of the Babies' Dispensary Guild (incorporated in 1911) were credited with reducing the rate to 54 deaths per 1,000 births by 1931. Improved nutrition and better housing conditions may have assisted the direct efforts of the health department and the guild. Whatever the cause, the city's overall mortality rate was brought down from 15 per 1,000 before the war to 10 per 1,000 during the Twenties.[11]

Economic decline and demographic contraction tend to occur together. That fact certainly applied to Hamilton during the Depression as natural increase faltered. The birth rate had been close to 30 births per 1,000 residents in 1920, dropping to 18 by 1936. Ironically, during the period of a naturally declining birth rate, a handful of affluent women formed the Birth Control Society of Hamilton. Founded in 1931, the society owed its guiding spirit to pseudoracial theories and eugenics based on a hereditarian rather than an environmental social philosophy. A stated purpose was to awaken the people of Hamilton to birth control's "beneficial effects upon the race." The society's references to the cases of large families on welfare and statements about the cost of maintaining asylums for the mentally deficient further defined the bent of the group. The society's opposition to abortion as a birth-control measure (as its members saw it) and concern about venereal disease stood as laudable causes, but the belief in birth control as a remedy for social distress was simply naïve and tainted with condescension.

In terms of the city's demographic profile, it is unlikely that birth-control publicity and a clinic for married women altered the birth rate as much as did the hardship and pessimism, circumstances leading to postponement of marriages, to desertion of spouses and to more rigorous birth-control regimes among some couples. The 15,000 excess of births over deaths in the ten years of depression could not keep pace with migration out of the city. The city actually was losing population, possibly to the United States or to the hometowns and farms from which some migrants had come during the Twenties. Indeed, some United Kingdom immigrants returned to the British Isles. Furthermore, immigration restrictions were introduced in 1931. They were tightened during the Second World War with regard to immigrants from any country that threatened national security.[12]

ARRESTED DEVELOPMENT AND A HOUSING CRISIS

As in prior eras, the mountain affords the best place to embark on the exploration of physical attributes. Seen from lookouts at different times, the city's land-use characteristics and architectural forms can be detected through the foliage; they make statements about Hamilton's economy and even its culture. Thus to have scanned the urban landscape in 1930 and to have repeated the exercise in 1946 would have indicated a city frozen by the collapse of the construction industry and the shortages of wartime.

The mid- and late 1920s had promised a different story. Housing went up at an impressive rate. The decade had not begun that well. In fact, to assist a flagging construction industry, the federal government had made its first contribution to the city building process in Hamilton via a 1919 housing act. Through the provincial government, Hamilton was to receive a quarter of a million dollars to be lent at low interest to building contractors and potential home-owners by a civic housing commission. Additional funds sponsored an Ontario housing office that drafted plans for economical houses. It designed the "A1" Hamilton bungalow. Slightly over 100 dwellings were constructed under the auspices of the federal-provincial arrangement, and fifteen years would

elapse before the federal government would again act to stimulate home construction. Yet a hesitant step had been taken toward a federal presence in local housing concerns. Also, the conditional grant used here became the essential device of senior-government influence in provincial-municipal and federal-municipal relations.

The massive land-assembly project begun in the west end just before the First World War, on what became the model suburban community of Westdale, illustrates the construction situation of the 1920s. At first a few of the "A1" bungalows were constructed on the less attractive land of the tract. By the mid-1920s, whole blocks of more expensive dwellings were being erected by a score of building contractors. The suburb was taking on its character as an enclave of middle-class Protestant Hamilton, adding to the segregated land use of the modern city. The securing of parkland along Coote's Paradise and the 1930 opening of McMaster University enhanced the west end and strengthened the appeal of Westdale for more affluent home-owners. A related development, insofar as west-end beautification was concerned, was the 1930 establishment of the Royal Botanical Gardens' rock garden in what had been a quarry.

The quarry redeveloped as a rock garden had been used during the construction of the Hamilton-Toronto highway, built to accommodate the proliferation of automobiles. Automobile registration in the city tripled from 1920 to 1930. In 1925, Hamilton purchased its first automatic traffic signals and the city was compelled to invest in continuous street improvements. Appropriately, the residents of South Wentworth were represented at Toronto from 1923 to 1934 by Thomas J. Mahony, active in the Hamilton Automobile Club and known as "Mr. Good Roads." The automobile insinuated its way into being more than a concern of government and a factor in the physical reorganization of urban space; it became entrenched in the structure of the urban economy in the form of garages, salesrooms, parts manufacture, parking lots and gas stations.

Along with the suburban trends represented by Westdale and the city's growing traffic concerns, the 1920s were significant for one further dimension of modernization in the urban form. Sudden bursts of construction along several main arteries heralded the advent of the apartment building. By contrast, office-building construction was minimal. In 1928, the gothic-styled Pigott Building became a modest contribution to the modern skyline. After the Pigott Building opened, construction collapsed. For fifteen years the essential story of Hamilton's physical qualities was one of arrested development. Eventually an area of disrepair, blight and overcrowding formed around the northern edges of the central core. By 1946, the visual impression — seen from street level — demonstrated the cyclical economic disaster and the world-wide crisis that had continually afflicted the city. The urban economy was not ill-served by war, but the physical quality of the city was far less fortunate. Except where war industries were concerned, construction was frozen.

The subject of apartment living affords an introduction to the physical condition of the city on the eve of collapse. Apartment living in 1900 was rare, though not unknown. A few living quarters had been included in commercial structures such as the Lister Block; the pre-1914 expansion of the city had included the construction of scattered tenements. Gradually, prestigious structures for middle-class occupants joined the housing stock. Opened in 1914, the elegant Herkimer was one of the first. Located in a pleasant district, it boasted assorted conveniences: offices for doctors and dentists, a service elevator, refrigerated food lockers and a basement laundry area. At completion, it was the best of about thirty structures of uneven quality. War and recession forced cutbacks until 1923, when work began on an extraordinary forty-eight structures.

There is no single explanation for this phenomenon. No doubt the 1923 peak expressed the number of projects that had been planned several years prior but held back by tight credit. The still-born Board of Trade housing scheme of 1912 had made moderate-cost housing a topical issue among realtors, contractors and investors. The scarcity of land along major arteries focussed additional interest on high-density dwellings. What is more, investors in rental accommodation found apartments to be a better class of investment than individual houses. To have an apartment building partly empty and cared for by a resident janitor proved more economical than maintaining separate houses with a comparable tenancy rate.

City residents generally accepted apartment living. This developed along with and due to the independence of young couples, the provision of newly marketed domestic conveniences, and apartments' reputation for respectable living. Names imparted sophistication: the Alexandra, Asquith, Carlton, Elodian, Forest, Noble, St. Deny's, Victoria, Windsor. The names and sound build-

ing construction projected the solidity of gentlemen's clubs, ladies' hostels or respectable hotels. In 1921, as many as seven out of ten household heads living in apartments were between the ages of twenty-nine and thirty-nine; among household heads at large the proportion was probably about four out of ten. The disproportionately youthful tenants were joined by a second and quite different group — two households in ten were headed by widows, surely including a portion of war widows. Clerical workers and skilled labourers were more evident than in the general population. Concentrated along Main Street East, apartments had handy access to public transit that could move occupants to commercial and industrial nodes. The turnover rate of occupants was high. In a sample of ten buildings from 1917 to 1937, 95 per cent of the tenants moved within a two-year period. Apartment dwellers sought shelter in accord with a particular stage in their life cycle.[13]

The increment in apartment dwellers during the 1920s was significant. In 1921 only 4 per cent of Hamilton households resided in apartments, but in 1931 the apartment portion had increased to 15 per cent. Given the collapse in construction after 1929 and wartime shortages in building materials after 1940, the apartment buildings raised in the 1920s dominated the architectural form of this type of dwelling for a quarter-century. Apartment dwellers would increase between 1929 and 1945, but additional accommodation often came about by the conversion of existing structures — homes and commercial properties. The three-storey brick apartment buildings with such occasional flourishes as truncated balconies, stained glass, gumwood interior trim and gas or electric fireplaces were hallmarks of the Twenties. Wartime conversions and a postwar flurry of construction doubled the number of apartment units between 1941 and 1951, but the scale of apartment structures remained relatively small.

The composition of apartment residents was tied to the health or distress of Hamilton's economy. The Depression impeded many tenant families from attempting home ownership. Having set up apartment households as young couples, the typical tenants of the 1920s were locked into renting a flat. In the 1941 census, exactly half of all heads of apartment households were forty-five years of age or more, marking a considerable aging of the apartment population. Ten years later, after prosperous times, the proportion of older households in apartments had declined. Nonetheless, the prolonged housing problem of 1930 to 1945 had warped

The Pasadena Apartments on Bold Street, photographed around 1940, were somewhat more ornate than others built between the wars.

Flanked by the Sun Life Building and Robinson's Department Store, the Pigott Building was Hamilton's sole example of the soaring office-tower architecture of the 1920s and 1930s. Its Art Deco decorative features incorporated medieval motifs. Stained-glass panels inside the entrance depicted the construction professions. Strong vertical lines, an elongated middle and stacked segments draw viewers' eyes upward.

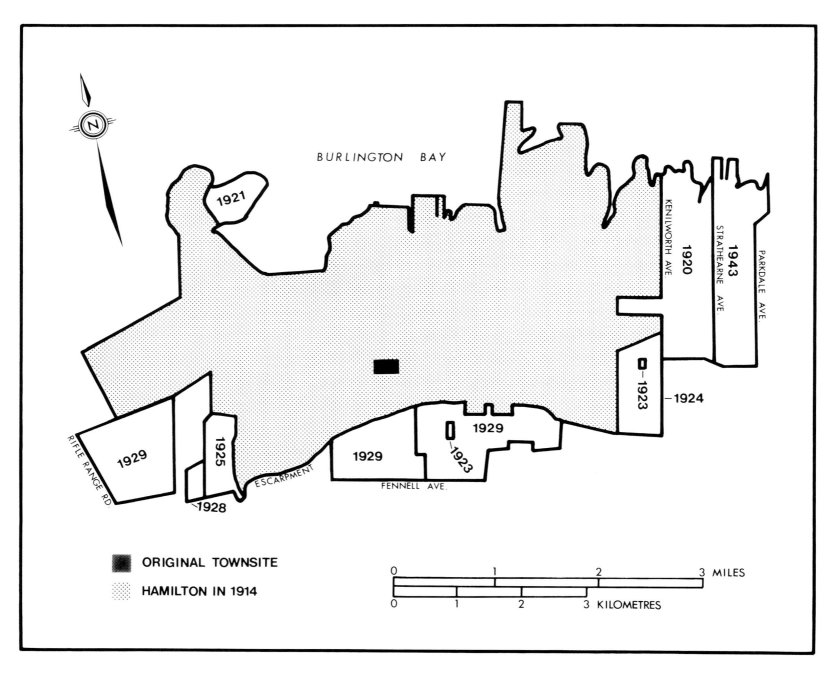

7 Hamilton's Boundary Extensions, 1915-1943.

the housing experiences of thousands of families; the situation made the Twenties shine in retrospect. Even the 1935 Dominion Housing Act and the 1938 National Housing Act failed to stimulate the critically depressed building trades because they required that prospective home-buyers possess considerable cash and a steady income. Until the 1950s, low-cost housing received limited federal attention. A series of Hamilton housing studies conducted under assorted auspices from the mid-1930s to the mid-1950s chronicled the problem.[14]

An impressionistic description of working-class housing appeared in the 1933 Hamilton novel *Forgotten Men*:

> Shabby houses jostled one another on either side of narrow streets. Occasionally one found an attempt to beautify the front garden, by coaxing a sparse lawn to grow upon ground which was a mixture of sand, and slag from nearby furnaces, and pitiful beds of geraniums and begonias grew straggly and soon became blackened by soot from neighbouring smoke-stacks.[15]

A 1941 special housing-atlas study prepared by the Dominion Bureau of Statistics reinforced contentions of depression shabbiness. About 18 per cent of the city's dwellings needed external repair. Of course, this assessment failed to include interior conditions or sanitary facilities; it also failed to state whether poor housing was concentrated in a slum or scattered throughout the city. A 1937 survey which had covered these issues concluded that Hamilton did not have an obvious housing problem. There were no extensive slums. The poor housing tended to be scattered in depressed pockets. In the spring of 1936, a team of investigators had combed a twenty-block neighbourhood of older dwellings and low-cost apartments, an area of households burdened with poverty. Located north and east of the central business district, it was a region where nearly two-thirds of the families were on part or full relief. Only one in ten of the houses was occupied by an owner. Apartment dwellings here were carved out of converted houses, rooms above stores or situated in tenements. Eighty per cent of toilet facilities were defined as unsatisfactory; 78 per cent of apartments lacked central heating. Vermin infested over a third of the flats. Houses tended to be in better condition, but lumping together both forms of dwelling, a quarter of the households were lodged in unsatisfactory accommodations.[16]

The war effort packed more individuals into a welter of rental facilities. Federal reviews of conditions in June, 1940, and January, 1941, reported no Hamilton vacancies. Stretched to capacity, an aging house stock was officially deemed inadequate to absorb an estimated 5,000 men who were due to arrive during 1941 and 1942. Not only did the situation threaten to form a minor bottleneck in the war effort, but a 1942 survey by the Hamilton Council of Social Agencies alleged overcrowding in the central city to have "endangered the welfare of a known 1,500 of the population and from 20-30 per cent of the homes in that area."[17] Determined to avoid the sorts of housing problems that had occurred during and immediately after the First World War, the federal government sought to handle an influx of munitions workers by creating a Crown corporation in 1941. The government charged the Wartime Housing Limited and its president, Hamilton contractor Joseph Pigott, with meeting shelter needs across the country. Hamilton's concentration of heavy industry made it an exceptional recipient of WHL housing (1,700 units). Even so, as late as January, 1945, official appeals were being made to home-owners to take in boarders.[18]

The WHL accommodations demonstrated government fretting about labour disturbances during the war and about a peacetime recession. Wartime housing policy was framed to avert these problems while meeting the current crisis; the government took little heed of advice to introduce a comprehensive housing program that would recover the lost decade of the Depression and anticipate future demands from veterans. As a result, all WHL units were to be temporary. Pigott and Hamilton authorities forced exceptions but could not reverse the thrust of this deliberate policy, in spite of the fact that permanent housing was only slightly more expensive and would endure as an asset. The Department of Finance wanted to force an eventual housing construction boom to alleviate a postwar recession and it opposed meddling likely to antagonize the private sector. The temporary-housing solution was shown to be unfeasible at war's end, when Hamilton had desperate need of permanent rental accommodations. Another attribute of WHL housing was the attempt at social control. Dormitory halls for single men were outfitted with recreational facilities. For its temporary housing developments, WHL formed a tenants' relations department with social workers. Since most munitions workers requiring WHL shelter were uprooted,

In 1943, Wartime Housing Limited operated these barracks on Kenilworth Avenue to house a few of the thousands of out-of-city labourers.

A typical Hamilton house on Balsam Avenue South around 1920-1930. Most working-class neighbourhoods in the east had been surveyed during the real-estate boom before 1914. Lots were narrow — no more than fifty feet — and the two-and-a-half-storey plan was commonplace. In 1930, about one in five households had a boarder. The attic was a source of income.

"they provided a fertile breeding ground for discontent" — which the WHL claimed was kept in hand by the special department.[19]

TOWARD A NEW CIVIC CULTURE

The quarter-century of international crisis was also a period of crisis for the old civic culture of amateurism and outdoor gatherings. These did not vanish, but their status as integral parts of city life ran into stiff competition. Some activities, especially sports, rebounded vigorously after the war. In the sporting events that had evolved during the industrial-city era from gentlemen's recreations to more democratic contests, the move toward spectator events with professional athletes was now clear. The Tigers football club attracted its first American recruit during the 1930s; the city had a professional NHL franchise which it lost in 1925 when the league-leading hockey Tigers went on strike for higher wages. The franchise moved to New York. Parades, bands, excursions and picnics endured, but cinema, radio and the automobile challenged these traditional activities. As well, it was through amateurism in sports in the late 1920s and early 1930s that Hamilton truly made its mark as a city known for athletic achievements.

War casualties blunted amateurism in many areas of recreation, but by the mid-1920s the activity in athletics had surpassed that of the prewar years. A sportswriter recalled that 1925 "was one of the busiest years in sports the city has seen, before or since, with every vacant lot, rink or indoor court humming with activity in all divisions of all sports." The Leander rowing club, which faded in the 1890s due to the bicycle rage, was revived in 1927. The playground program and the track-and-field club added appreciably to the city's reputation, so that in 1929 the United States Recreational Association reported that for its size Hamilton had the best arrangements for sports in North America.[20]

In two sports, football and track, the city's accomplishments in the late 1920s and early 1930s were exceptional. The Tigers football club had lost twenty-five players and former players in the war; however, a revived club won the Grey Cup in 1928, 1929 and 1932. Unfortunately for the club, the West won its first Grey Cup in 1935, when Winnipeg defeated Hamilton. The popularity and recognition accorded track also led to significant achievements. In the years following the First World War, the Ninety-First

Highlanders' athletic club organized its famous annual track meets; the Finnish star Paavo Nurmi was the main attraction in 1925. One of the dedicated promoters of track was Captain John Cornelius, who coached local track teams after the war, participated in the formation of the Hamilton Olympic Club and coached the track team that represented Canada at the 1928 Olympic Games. The Hamilton Olympic Club (HOC) revived the around-the-bay race in 1926; the 1927 run was recognized as Canada's marathon trial for the Olympics. The HOC conducted all of the Canadian track-team trials for the 1928 and 1932 Olympic Games. To keep its Olympic-calibre athletes in international competition, the club sponsored a dual track-and-field meet against the Oxford-Cambridge team in 1929. In 1930 Hamilton hosted the first British Empire Games. From August 16 to August 23, Hamilton attracted Empire athletes, dignitaries and international press attention. Captain Cornelius and M.M. "Bobby" Robinson, who had managed Canada's track team at Amsterdam in 1928, had promoted the notion. Hamilton council helped to finance the games. The city had just completed a new indoor swimming pool; it increased the seating capacity of the stadium. The athletes were placed with city families or lodged in city schools. Thus, for a very small expenditure, Hamilton sponsored Canada's first major international athletic event. Significantly, the entire endeavour had arisen because of the city's well-known commitment to track.[21]

The amateur performances of the Garrick Club had stopped during and immediately after the war. Reorganized in 1926, the club took the name Hamilton Players' Guild. However, its days in the mainstream of civic culture had passed, and the 1920–1945 era belonged to the motion picture and radio. The Grand Opera House continued to stage live performances, but the cinema theatres were more popular houses. Moreover, the structure of the motion-picture and theatre industry, like so many other concerns, shifted from independence to consolidation around the time of the First World War. Locally the process crested when the city's four major theatres — the Palace (seating 2,300), the Capitol (2,300), the Tivoli (1,300) and the Savoy (1,300) — were taken into a pooling arrangement by Famous Players. Only a few suburban independents, including the Empire, Delta and Queen's, escaped direct control. Even so, the independents had to agree to accept a set of films selected by distributors. In effect, what the

Hamilton social life during the 1940s included evenings at the Brant Inn on Burlington Beach, a fashionable club that sponsored facsimiles of the big band sound.

Hamilton public could see was controlled commercially by American consortiums. That may well have loosened the cultural ties with the British Empire; it certainly integrated North American culture as well as exposed audiences to middle-class conveniences, language and lifestyle. The cinema introduced and disseminated new concepts of the good life.[22]

As for radio, it had an early beginning when CKOC received its licence in 1922. At five watts, it broadcast baseball scores and music for the owners of crystal sets. Raising its power to fifty watts in 1925, it moved toward commercialism by inserting limited advertising. The 1940 studio housed a 250-seat auditorium, recording facilities, production staff and sales representatives. CHML had gone on the air in 1927, the year when radio truly became a fixture of popular culture. Less than a decade after the licensing of the first local station, about 40 per cent of the city's households had receivers.[23]

The demise of a competitive daily press was another way in which the cultural texture of earlier eras was squeezed out of the city. The *Times* failed in 1920. More importantly the *Herald* ceased publication in 1936. Founded in 1889 as the city's first penny daily, the *Herald* had an illustrious history of covering local and labour news and supporting urban reform in the industrial-city period. Only a few years after the competition had collapsed, an American report concluded that the *Spectator*, which had survived, was "weak editorially for the reason that it is operated as a business enterprise hence its general policy is to offend no one."[24] That could never have been said about the partisan press of the mid-nineteenth century nor the sensational journalism of the late nineteenth and early twentieth centuries. Hamilton thus became the first medium-sized Canadian city to have had daily press coverage by a single newspaper. The overlap with the Toronto metropolitan region was a possible factor.

Industrial society and immigration fostered clashes with traditional Ontario Protestant culture. One of these clashes assisted the rise of organized crime and also magnified its significance through racial slurs. Traditional acceptance of alcohol by European immigrants, the constraints imposed on social activity by shift work and a rigorous enforcement of liquor laws in the 1920s led to crime. After-hours drinking was a natural but legally proscribed conclusion to a late shift. Bootlegging and gambling flourished, with three gangs emerging to control the lucrative

business. Two were Italian and one was Ukrainian. A savage contest waged among them claimed the life of several people, including Bessie Perri who was murdered in 1930. Her husband Rocco, the king of bootlegging, was apparently murdered in 1944. Violence remained a part of Hamilton's organized-crime scene when gangs expanded into narcotics and extortion. As a medium-sized city with few countervailing claims to fame in the news, Hamilton became identified as crime-riddled. Both the influence of mob elements and erroneous racial slurs would assume a greater share of public attention than in other Canadian cities.[25]

The shock of war intervened and distorted the course of urban history. War's impact on the economy, immigration and housing has been mentioned. Sports were interrupted too. There would be no HOC trials for the Tokyo Olympics in 1940. The new forms of media became agents of information and propaganda. Nonetheless, the civic regime was less strident and the attrition of local men less catastrophic than during the 1914–1918 conflict. Recruitment by the city's two regiments went extremely well in the early months of war. In the summer of 1940, with the German army occupying most of western Europe, the Argyll and Sutherland Highlanders' recruiting tent in Gore Park — the scene of similar drives during the previous war — drew as many as ninety recruits a day. Ranks were filled in sixteen days. Until 1943, the Argylls had an extended repose from combat when they attended to garrison duty in Jamaica. They went ashore in Normandy on 21 July 1944 and fought at Falaise and Caen; they were in the Netherlands campaign and, after the German surrender, they were selected for police duty in Berlin. The Royal Hamilton Light Infantry (the Thirteenth) had been bloodied in earlier combat. The RHLI sustained 480 casualties during the disastrous Dieppe raid of 19 August 1942. After rebuilding and training, the regiment would distinguish itself in the liberation of the Netherlands. But the Dieppe raid stood as the war's most devastating jolt to the city. Except for this action, most of the grief that affected Hamilton families came in the ten months of combat on the western front. The swiftness of sustained combat contrasted with the prolonged attrition of the previous war. Conceivably, this condition accounted for the fact that the ugly side of patriotic zeal was less apparent. Many foreign-born residents had been disenfranchised for the 1917 federal election; when a candidate for the 1941 Board of Control ran on a platform of disenfranchising the city's Italian-

The renowned Captain John Cornelius is seen here with his Hamilton Collegiate Institute relay team in 1922. Hamilton's amateur athletic groups have long encouraged international competition.

The YMCA gym in 1935. With the decline of child labour and the rise of a belief in social improvement through education, a variety of agencies took an interest in organizing the summer recess. The YMCA and Hamilton Playground Association attracted and guided children from a variety of backgrounds.

For over a century, the elegance of thoroughbreds, the gambling impulse, the thrill of a close finish, and the banter of the crowd made horse racing a popular entertainment. The sale of the Hamilton Jockey Club track for a shopping centre with ample parking symbolized the cultural impact of the automobile.

The Homeside neighbourhood that sponsored this women's team was well known for its British working-class character.

born population, he ran last. An all-stops-pulled approach to local recruitment, a frantic endeavour that included the search for "cowards," was not the widely condoned practice that it had been in the First World War.[26]

LOCAL POLITICS, INDUSTRIAL UNIONISM AND A SWING TO THE LEFT

The Depression upset industrial employment and construction; it also broke a Conservative hold on public life that had come in the wake of the ILP collapse in the early 1920s. The gregarious Thomas Jutten provides the clues for the staying power of the Conservative Party until the early 1930s. A former machinist and boat builder who had retained union membership and had supported public ownership of utilities, Jutten functioned like many "workingmen's friends" in other cities. He resided in the working-class north end and was a leader in the North End Improvement Society. He remained in the neighbourhood even when nearby landfill operations placed him next to what was a refuse dump complete with stench, rats and fires. He was remembered for having endured the situation with the other north-enders. In the 1920s, he claimed membership in at least ten clubs or lodges; he had joined the Orange Lodge at age sixteen. As an alderman (1906-1913), controller (1914-1921), mayor (1923-25) and MPP (1926-1934), Jutten repeatedly demonstrated the staying power of his organization and the role of the fraternal attitude.

But after years of success, the Tories were shut out of the three provincial ridings in 1934. Labour candidate Sam Lawrence carried Hamilton East, a Liberal defeated Jutten in Hamilton Centre, and Liberal T.B. McQuesten carried Hamilton West. Lawrence lost to a Liberal in 1937. Meanwhile, a 1931 by-election in Hamilton East returned labour candidate Humphrey Mitchell to Ottawa. Mitchell sat as an independent labour representative, refusing to join the CCF. This union official from Hamilton was defeated in 1935 and became a civil servant until a by-election win at Welland in 1942. He would stay in Parliament and become Minister of Labour. Depression challenged the political *status quo*. A growth in labour-organization activity in the late 1930s and during the war did more than that, since it radicalized significant numbers of industrial workers.[27]

Hamilton experienced fundamental changes in labour relations between 1940 and 1946. Labour historian David Millar has summarized that "until 1939 most union organizers were fired, most forms of picketing were illegal, and union security was a pious hope. Only the railwaymen and AFL (American Federation of Labor) crafts had unions, but their wages, dues and membership fell sharply in the depression."[28] A chain of forces reversed the demoralized state of labour. The more important ones were attempts at industrial union organization in the late 1930s, the leverage offered labour by wartime production and the threat of left-wing votes in the mid-1940s. In many industries, unions succeeded in establishing their security only after tough conflicts with antiunion employers. Bitter strikes divided the city, particularly in the summer of 1946. A few large and many small firms escaped union organization altogether. Within the union movement itself, all was not harmonious. The rivalry of the American Federation of Labor and the Congress of Industrial Organizations divided the local labour movement until the two groups merged in 1956. On the whole, organized labour gained enormously — even if it frequently had to grapple with industry resistance. At the level of the wage earner, unions had won pay increases and fringe benefits. The improvements extended to the major unorganized industry, Dofasco, which followed negotiations between Stelco and the United Steel Workers with its own benefits to retain worker loyalty.[29]

Preparations that resulted in union advances in the 1940s had commenced in 1935-1937. A brief economic recovery and industrial-labour organization activity in the United States by the newly formed CIO emboldened Hamilton labour activists to press for the recognition of unions as bargaining agents. A 1935 strike of Stelco Sheet Mill workers ended in a union defeat and the recognition among the strike leaders that to be effective they had to organize skilled and unskilled men into one union. Union recognition and higher wages precipitated a complete walkout of all 450 employees at Dominion Glass in August, 1936. The unsuccessful strike was not a craft action alone; it involved the entire plant. Management brought in strikebreakers under police escort. Hamilton industries resisted so successfully that in 1939 the American CIO leadership considered a retreat for want of results.

As well as management resistance, the CIO had to weather hostility from the leadership of the international unions of the AF of L. In May, 1937, an international organizer from the AF of L attended a regular meeting of the Hamilton Trades and Labour Council and demanded that representatives "affirm their unswerving loyalty to the American Federation of Labor."[30] When the CIO delegates and AF of L delegates who were sympathetic to the CIO refused, the organizer split the meeting and walked out with half the union representatives. Political differences accentuated the conflict. The AF of L wanted no part of the socialist or communist politics of the CIO. The new council, with Sam Lawrence as president, rejected the old craft-union policy of political neutrality, which usually meant support for Conservative candidates. In 1941, the CIO movement in Hamilton consisted of unions whose titles described their objective — to organize entire industries rather than separate trades within a plant: the Amalgamated Clothing Workers of America, the United Steelworkers of America and the United Electrical, Radio and Machine Workers of America.[31]

The early CIO attempts to organize workers at Stelco, National Steel Car, Hamilton Bridge and other plants were not protected in Canada by the type of legislation that had sheltered American counterparts since 1935. No law provided Canadian workers with the right to join unions; no law obliged companies to recognize a duly certified union as the employees' bargaining agent. When federal authorities acted on labour relations during the early war years, it was not with the aim of introducing these conditions but to maintain steady industrial output and regulate prices and wages. In January, 1943, the federal government altered this policy by making mandatory a set of guidelines, including the right of workers to form their own unions.[32]

The first major definition of labour's rights and management's responsibilities that applied in Hamilton were spelled out in the Ontario Collective Bargaining Act (OCBA) of April, 1943. A labour court was established to hear the arguments of companies and unions through legal counsel and determine who would represent employees in negotiations with employers. One hotly contested case which eventually tested the constitutional basis of the OCBA originated with Stelco. For several years the company had tried to avert CIO organizing efforts by an employees' council consisting of eleven men elected by the employees and eleven from management. In the event of a tie vote, the council turned the matter at hand to the president of the corporation for a decision. A November, 1942, election for council returned eight members of the United Steelworkers. All eleven employee members of the council subsequently recommended to management that the USW be recognized as the collective-bargaining agent. The inevitable tie vote put the matter before the president, who rejected the workers' proposal.

Next the Steel Company of Canada reorganized the system of employee representation and permitted the formation of "a company union" — the Independent Steelworkers Association. It was formed just in time for a hearing at the Ontario Labour Court; the court had to decide who should represent the workers — the USW or the ISWA. The court ordered a secret ballot to select the bargaining agency. In the February, 1944, vote, 3,781 ballots were cast. The USW received 2,461 and the ISWA got 889. This did not clear the air. Stelco management thought the union could be broken. Major questions remained awaiting collective bargaining. Neither USW Local No. 1005 nor any other recently certified local had the authority to negotiate wage settlements because of the controls on war industries. However, locals could work on behalf of members to secure legal bonuses and fringe benefits through the War Labour Board.[33]

War had created special ground rules. Labour and management wondered about peacetime revisions. The CIO pressed ahead with the organization of more plants — Westinghouse, Frost Wire and smaller industries like Hoover Vacuum and Hamilton Cottons. Urgency in organizing and collecting dues was dictated by the realization that wage controls would end soon and wrangling over new contracts containing wage components would begin. Certified locals braced for the tough negotiations that would set precedents by yielding the first peacetime contracts between major Hamilton manufacturers and industrial unions. During the winter of 1945-1946, both sides moved toward confrontation. One labour expert was "puzzled as to why, with all the strikes going on in the States, there is little trouble going on the labour front. Some of the people here are afraid there is going to be a sudden blow up one of these days."[34]

Showdowns testing labour's wartime gains and fixing much of its long-term status were numerous in the spring and summer of 1946. In May, the membership of USW Local No. 1005 voted 3,114 to 80 to enable their executive to call a strike against Stelco if necessary to enforce demands. In June, Westinghouse workers voted 2,811 to 630 to use the strike if required. Firestone negotia-

The Stelco picket line in the summer of 1946 severed friendships and families. Workers who stayed inside the plant were not quickly forgiven after the strike.

Liberal party publicity or public information? With displays such as this one at the Hamilton Public Library, the federal government advertised its price controls during the Second World War and reminded the public about inflation during the First World War and the crisis of the Great Depression. Although women had replaced men in many industrial positions, the information program still dealt in stereotypes of women as frivolous consumers.

The summer decorum of labour's Mayor Sam Lawrence (right) provided a hierarchical contrast both with the vice-regal formality of Alexander of Tunis and the khaki-clad troops, at Hamilton's centennial celebration of 1946.

tions also were underway. By mid-July, 5,000 had struck at Stelco, 4,000 were out at Westinghouse and another 1,500 at Firestone. Before the headline-grabbing strike had broken out at Stelco on July 14, there had been signs of a hard contest ahead. Stelco had laid in supplies of food and bedding for workers — perhaps a third of the labour force — who stayed on the job. On October 20, after eighty-one days of friction and stalemate, a contract was agreed upon. Over the next six months, the example of the Stelco-USW contract had its influence on agreements signed between CIO affiliates and a number of Hamilton factories. In the mass-production industries, the CIO had won recognition and secured an "American" standard of living which included vacation with pay. The triumph, however, was not universal. The female workforce, white-collar, service and retail employees were unorganized.[35] In addition, cold-war tensions, the purge of Communists, the decline of CCF votes, the continued rivalry of the AF of L and CIO and the sheer size of big unions brought new problems in the late 1940s and early 1950s.

The recurrent ambition of organized labour to gain direct political influence yielded disappointing results. The majority of unionists and their families had not necessarily voted for the union-supported CCF-NDP. This fact contrasts with the expectations of activists in the mid-1940s when left-wing politics spread enthusiastically over the local arena. The brief ascendancy of the CCF constituted the major political expression of a leftward movement in public opinion — a movement which encouraged the CCF to present a slate of twelve aldermanic candidates at the December, 1943, civic election and to have Sam Lawrence stand as CCF candidate for mayor. As the ideological heir of the ILP, the local CCF aspired to the political successes of 1919–1923. The party had just swept Hamilton in the August, 1943, provincial election, which had brought the CCF within four seats of forming a provincial government. Further, the CCF had improved its share of the municipal vote from 20 per cent in 1939 to 39 per cent in 1942; it had returned at least three aldermen in each of the intervening years.

During the intense 1943 campaign, the party ran into rigorous resistance from business interests, which financed advertisements alleging that socialism was akin to Hitlerism. A number of municipal candidates campaigned against the idea of a disciplined party's entering civic affairs and claimed that nonpartisanship would ensure neighbourhood service, rather than simple loyalty to a party. This was a specious attack because civic politics always had been meshed with provincial or federal partisan groups. The upshot of the 1943 showdown was a failure of the CCF to break beyond a socialist base in east-end wards. Sam Lawrence was elected mayor and three CCF aldermen were returned; party finances had been drained. Labour would continue to endorse aldermanic candidates, but the effort to present a full slate of party candidates did not bring the anticipated success. Gradually, in elections during the late 1940s, civic candidates from the left dropped the party tag.[36]

A secondary but important current in the left-wing strivings of the 1940s came from the Communists. Legitimized by the status of the Soviet Union as an ally, Communists also had been energetic organizers of CIO locals, especially Local No. 504 of the United Electrical Workers. They had built a base of municipal electoral support in Ward Seven. Their cells at the height of party influence in 1946 included several clubs. The Electric Club was a cell in Local No. 504 and led by that local's organizer, William Walsh, who had been interned until the Soviet Union became an enemy of Germany. There was the Stelco Club, a cell within Local No. 1005, USW. The Matthew Popovich Club catered to the Ukrainian population; the Croation Club and Hungarian Club likewise had ethnic membership. The Sam Scarlett Club was largely Anglo-Saxon. It was claimed that Communists had infiltrated the Dale Community Centre; except for Ukrainians and Yugoslavs, the eastern Europeans of Hamilton were generally considered anti-Communist. The East Hamilton and Wentworth Club was the association for staunch party members, including the several candidates at municipal elections.

Among these candidates, Helen Anderson exemplified the swift rise and decline of civic Communists. Sent by the party to Hamilton from Prince Rupert, she was an attractive and intelligent advocate of popular measures like an improved labour code, a higher minimum wage, the forty-hour work week, two weeks' vacation with pay and free milk for schoolchildren. From the 1946 civic contest which brought out a record 65 per cent of the voters, she emerged with a seat on the Board on Control. For a year, the Communists had Anderson and a representative from Ward Seven on council, a number of cells and capable organizers in union locals. Within a year their position had con-

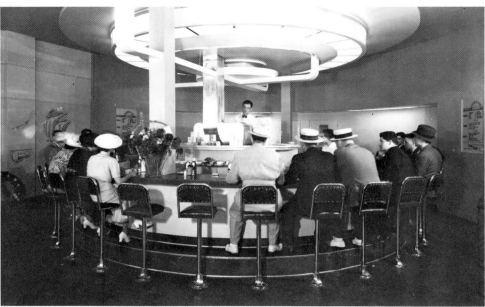

The automobile and modernism in decor inspired the Motor Bar, photographed in 1937.

The automobile had numerous influences on urban form. In the planned suburb of Westdale, seen here in 1937, the central shopping area provided parking space.

tracted. Anti-Communist sentiment increased in part because of international affairs; anticommunism found expression in newspaper articles, city council debates and the Hamilton District Labour Council's move to "box in" members of party cells. Helen Anderson was defeated in the 1947 election, described as "an abrupt swing to the right." From that year forward, Communists who undeniably contributed to industrial unionism were removed from the prominence they had briefly enjoyed.[37]

A clear cultural shift was related to the labour and political scene we have discussed. Certainly one part of the new cultural pattern was the vacation with pay, viewed as a real measure of social progress. War production plants in Hamilton gave their first vacations with pay in 1943. The exodus to the Muskoka and Parry Sound districts strained accommodations at hotels whose clientele had been exclusive. Hamilton's elite had established summer homes in Muskoka since the turn of the century; now the area was opening to other city dwellers. The postwar combination of contracts that surrendered two weeks' vacation with pay and the revived state of automobile sales effected a social change involving recreational space and thereby the character of Hamilton. Labourers and their families could escape from the industrial environment. In terms of time and distance, their recreational excursions began to rival those of the elite and an affluent middle class. The drain of leisure activity away from the city was compounded by its stark industrial image and lack of amenities.[38]

The union and socialist activism that climaxed in the 1940s stands unchallenged as a paramount social event in civic affairs. However, less dramatic sociopolitical alterations began during the period. From the annual local elections of the 1930s and 1940s, two accomplished public figures emerged to dominate civic news and prefigure important aspects of local government in the postwar decades. Nora Frances Henderson broke the male monopoly to become the first woman on council. William Morrison became the first mayor to hold office for a relatively long period (1936–1943) and to implement a program — austerity and the securing of a quality credit rating for Hamilton.

Henderson's career epitomized a social transition. Whatever her own contribution to her achievements — she was a very feisty woman — she succeeded because of an overdue improvement in the status of some women that allowed them to assume circumscribed roles in community leadership. The many women's groups founded locally in the 1890s formed a wedge for leadership in patriotic and social-service functions. The social crises of the industrial city, including health concerns, education, assimilation of immigrants and child welfare, assisted the legitimacy of allowing women to hold a narrow field of leadership in civic life. The First World War intensified this process. Henderson was in the right place at the right time. Like her friends Agnes MacPhail and Charlotte Whitton, she made use of journalistic talents. Her position as woman's-page editor for the *Herald* brought her public notice in the late 1920s. On its pages, she advocated that more women should hold responsible offices in the city.

In 1930, she helped found the Women's Civic Club to further the cause and urged the Council of Women to nominate a member as a candidate for city council. They asked her. Thus in the municipal campaign of late 1931, a women's political machine, the Civic Club's "Bell Ringers," went after female voters. Successful in 1931, she was elected to the Board of Control in 1934. This made her chairman of the city relief committee. She became the first woman to preside over a meeting of council in June, 1946, when she was acting mayor. Her defiant stroll through the picket lines at Stelco later that summer, to demonstrate what she believed was the right of city residents to move as they pleased within the law, gained friends and enemies. For a while, union men sang "We'll hang Nora Frances from a sour apple tree." Shortly after leaving civic politics in 1947 to become secretary of the Children's Aid Societies of Ontario, Henderson died. For her personal achievement and her efforts on behalf of public health, the city honoured her memory by naming a new hospital Henderson General.[39]

CONCLUSION

By the end of 1946, Hamilton wore a down-at-the-heels demeanour. The labour disputes of the summer had polarized residents and disrupted retail commerce. The worn-down physical qualities that contributed to a loss of civic esteem were the consequence of long-term tendencies that had accented wartime industrial additions without corresponding residential or commercial building. Hamilton had no extensive slum area, but scattered

V-E Day on King Street at Gore Park. The war for democracy was over. Soon many women would hand their work back to men and the city would have its baby boom and suburban expansion. Nonetheless, the industrial work experience stood as a precedent for women to use in seeking non-traditional employment.

throughout the north and east were pockets of urban blight. About a quarter of the city's residential blocks were considered to be in a state of deterioration. Heavy traffic — 1,100 vehicles per hour passed through the Cannon Street and Victoria Avenue intersection — contributed to the already considerable noise and hazard of living near the industries and the transportation arteries of the east end.

With the more desirable regions between the mountain and Duke Street (the Durand district) and Westdale occupied by low-density housing, the city below the mountain had reached its limits. Future housing would have to be placed on the mountain. The crisis in residential facilities fostered a nagging concern among many labourers. Worried about the continued deterioration of old housing, desiring something better than homes near coke ovens and traffic and concerned about the high land costs if speculators developed the mountain, organized labour recommended in 1944 that the mountain be planned along the lines of garden-city communities in the United Kingdom. This was one recommendation for regenerating Hamilton that was not pursued. The fact that the left could claim a mayor and several aldermen meant little beyond their symbolic support for the unions during the 1946 strikes. Sam Lawrence was a cautious mayor and not given to initiating capital expenditures or experiments in planning. Lawrence was long past his fighting prime, and his council was an odd mixture of conservatives and radicals. City government marked time.

Other circumstances troubled Hamilton residents. The city's sports program had fallen on hard times; supervisors had been drawn into service or war industries and the recreational grant had become a victim of austerity. The beach facilities, cut up by road and rail or given over to industry, were a reproach to a lake city. For the culturally minded, the cramped library, antiquated art gallery and lack of proper symphony hall defined Hamilton as a city without refinement. A 1945 planning report on existing conditions singled out these and many other complaints. The report implied a real crisis in civic morale. It certainly expressed an inferiority felt by the civic elite. The booster elements unhappily acknowledged that the fourteen-storey Pigott Building was the city's sole skyscraper. Except for the Tuberculosis Sanatorium and McMaster University (1930), "the ambitious city" exerted no social service or cultural impact on the province.

Fortunately for the comfort and pride of all, the industrial and construction sectors were preparing to move again in powerful ways toward increased industrial capacity and housing. The fifteen-year lull in major growth was about to end. Hamilton began to move as it always had after setbacks. Still, the distribution of power among Canadian cities was continually evolving to Hamilton's disadvantage. The apprehension and gloom apparent at the end of the war yielded immediately to the construction booms and the immigration waves of the contemporary city (1946-1980), but the deep-seated structural problems inherent in Hamilton's geographic location and its middle-size status in the Canadian urban system were never overcome. The city had begun to shed its arrested development in the early 1950s, but then it also began to evolve new and sometimes perplexing economic, physical and cultural attributes.

Gore Park and King Street looking east, 1948. The enlarged Connaught Hotel is the largest structure on the right; immediately west of it is the block-long Canada Public Building. The construction of the Woolworth's store at the lower left was one example of the renewal of building projects after years of arrested development.

Chapter Five
Hamilton-Wentworth: The Contemporary City, 1946-1980

Depression, war and a traumatic labour dispute have placed the years from 1929 to 1946 in the mainstream of city lore. Hard times and struggles are remembered. In terms of systematic urban history, however, these years presented many static conditions. The structure of the economy, the composition of the population, and residential construction held fast for about two decades. Of course to the individuals witnessing and living the events of 1929-1946, the historic weight of the era was profound and unforgettable. On the other hand, the seemingly tranquil and relatively prosperous circumstances of 1946 to 1980 actually furthered structural changes so that the postwar years assume greater urban significance. Not since the industrial city's shifting from small artisan shops and foundries to large industrial enterprises had a truly major economic reorganization taken place. But after the war, the steel companies did more than expand; they exploded into new product lines and searched for additional land to place mills and furnaces employing state-of-the-art technology. The unprecedented expansion of one industrial sector and the comparative or absolute decline of others allows a new description of Hamilton: a company town. The description is not wholly flattering and it is not without important exceptions. No single company dominates. There has never been the extension of corporate control over the home life of workers. Company housing has been a rare phenomenon in Hamilton's development.

All the same, the notion of Hamilton as a company town akin to Sudbury, Ontario, or the steel town of Gary, Indiana, is a plausible one. Among Canada's ten largest cities, Hamilton had the largest percentage distribution of its labour force in manufacturing, according to the 1971 census. The fact that steel, of all manufacturing sectors in Canada, is the most concentrated in terms of corporate control of production and that two of the big three

companies are centred in Hamilton confirms the company-town image. The probable status of Hamilton has had a glittering backdrop for comparison — Toronto. Always the superior rival in the past, Toronto's metropolitan power in economic matters and culture was accented in the postwar decades by the concentration of corporate headquarters and the reach of the electronic media.

Increasingly the steel town, Hamilton became more aware of environmental hazards so that the city's most obvious detraction began to be discussed openly; public pressure forced reluctant companies to abide by environmental standards. Nonetheless, a company-town attitude has complicated pollution and occupational-health controversies. Jobs in the steel mills have appeared as immediate benefits whereas health hazards have seemed remote. Costly pollution-control devices have been introduced gradually. These actions, coupled with a long string of corporate denials of wrongdoing, a local sensitivity about criticism from outside observers, and a capacity for self-deception among residents, have generated a peculiar mentality about one of the contemporary city's more readily discernible traits — its polluted air. This mentality of suppressed complaint, as much as the contribution of steel to the Hamilton economy, defines Hamilton as a company town.

Of course, there have been other formative events; the company-town trait is not the sole ingredient of the civic image. Hamilton has become a multicultural community in the sense that its immigrant groups have been drawn into the mainstream of political life and aspects of their culture have been accepted as part of the city's valued character. The relaxation of rigid immigration guidelines after the war permitted a resumption of the cultural and religious diversification which had begun before the First World War. Stelco could boast in 1954 that over half of the nations of the world were represented among its 15,000 employees. Fraternal clubs, frequently focussing as much on regional identity as national patriotism, became legion across the east end.

In comparison to the previous four chapters of this book, this final chapter has a somewhat different focus. Accounts of the earliest decades bristled with characters whose actions defined a townsite and its ambitions. Their political commitments, modes of business and even recreation loomed over the confines of a courthouse town or frontier community. The prominence of personages in the early years was not just a matter of scale; the fact that the aggregated experience of thousands has replaced vignettes is more than a condition of growth. The contemporary city is described by reference to collective terms: the corporation, union local, mass media, the suburb. These phenomena can be explained if we see the city as the place where evolutionary advances in capitalism are concentrated. Contemporary cities, whether prospering or faltering, are creations of corporations — banks, industries, communications firms and land developers. The introduction of urban planning and regional government to the contemporary city have been less significant in terms of shaping the city than the elements of modern capitalism. Yet together they point to a distinctive period in Hamilton's history.

THE ECONOMY OF A STEEL TOWN

Unlike the economy of the 1920-to-1945 period, that of the postwar decades experienced only mild fluctuations, but the local economy underwent a structural reorientation. The fundamental changes to Hamilton's economic base occurred between 1945 and 1965. The process was twofold. The steel companies expanded enormously; other industrial sectors remained static, collapsed or grew only marginally. The progress of the steel industry in the postwar years constituted more than a simple multiplication of existing processes and products, for technology and the product lines altered. Basic shapes like rods, bars, hot-rolled plate and wire products had been the significant items manufactured by Canadian firms. After the war, tin plate and annealed steel grew in conjunction with the appliance and automotive industries. Research and development were acknowledged as vital to production efficiency and to the anticipation or creation of new markets. To these ends, the steel companies expanded their engineering and scientific staff and strengthened associations with McMaster University.[1]

The close identification of Hamilton with steel has centred on two companies, but it is important to distinguish between the east-end siblings in terms of technology, product lines, labour relations and public image. As in the 1920s and 1930s, Dofasco remained the smaller and more daring corporation. Unlike Stelco, which had originated as an amalgamation including a local rolling mill, a blast furnace and mills in other centres, Dofasco began as a local foundry that used pig iron and scrap steel. The former was an integrated corporation and included an iron-making facility; the latter was a specialized manufacturer that purchased iron and scrap. At the end of the war, Dofasco planned a sequence of expansions that carried its operations backward into iron production even as it carried forward improvements in the processes that made it a major manufacturer of tin plate. Due to the additions at Dofasco, its production of steel increased 400 per cent from 1945 to 1960. The growth also meant qualitative changes in the company's operations. Dofasco began to use water transport and to invest in mines. In terms of local employment — and this was true of Stelco too — the jobs created tended to be less subject to the seasonal or even the cyclical events which precipitated layoffs in the farm-machinery or textile industries. More and better jobs — at least in terms of security — had been gained, although a handful of fatal accidents and the environmental issues raised questions about the social costs of progress.[2]

The decision to expand into iron production with a blast-furnace operation came as a consequence of the war. Homemakers had been denied appliances and automotive production had been stopped. These conditions fostered pent-up demand for steel products. Industries eager for new equipment to develop peacetime markets added to the call for steel.[3] Dofasco responded and strengthened its position as a tin-plate producer with the 1949 completion of a new plant that replaced the hot-dip process with electrolytic tin-plating. The postwar shortage of scrap steel created a bottleneck in the company's operations. The obvious remedy was to manufacture new steel from iron, but the implications were far-reaching. To receive the necessary coal and iron ore, the company had to shift from rail to water transportation. This required the construction of a large facility on the waterfront; that could be achieved only by landfill and alterations to

The industrial concentration on the harbour looking east toward the Burlington Skyway Bridge in 1970. International Harvester is in the centre and directly behind it and also around it to the right is Stelco. The narrow landfill strip east of Stelco was constructed for Dofasco's dock and blast furnaces.

Hamilton's harbour. Moreover, to guarantee supplies Dofasco would have to acquire new expertise and properties. In connection with these new supply requirements, Dofasco received the first shipment of Labrador iron ore to be made within Canada (1954). Iron making also demanded experience with the production of coke and the operation of a blast furnace. In late 1949 Dofasco announced plans to construct coke ovens and a blast furnace; the furnace began production in August, 1951. Another was fired in 1956 and a third in 1960. A fourth was added a decade later. Dofasco's commitment to expansion led to its becoming the first on the continent with an oxygen furnace in 1954. Dofasco entered the 1960s with purchases to diversify its operations. In 1961, the company bought into the Wabush Iron Company of Labrador. The next year it purchased control of neighbouring National Steel Car.[4]

The recasting of Dofasco was a bold venture into new undertakings. It was this novelty of the postwar plans, not just the scale of physical expansion, that accounts for reviewing Dofasco's growth before that of Stelco. In terms of scale, Stelco's additions were larger. In the late 1940s, the city's senior iron and steel manufacturer prepared plans for massive construction. Throughout the late 1940s, the most serious obstacles to industrial expansion in Ontario were the shortage of skilled labour and the inability of steel producers to meet orders without delay. With the exception of the 1946 strike at Stelco, the steel producers worked at near capacity; by 1948 both Hamilton steel companies had reached the emergency levels of output attained in 1944 with virtually the same physical plants. At Stelco, one battery of open-hearth furnaces had been functioning since 1900. They were the oldest functioning open hearths on the continent. Even the 1895 blast furnace was called upon to fill orders for foundry iron. After planning and preliminary engineering studies, the company announced in 1951 its program for a 1,000-foot dock, a battery of eighty-three coke ovens, a blast furnace of the maximum size and four 250-ton open-hearth furnaces. Further additions in the late 1950s resulted in Stelco's raising its steel output by 200 per cent from 1950 to 1962 and in its keeping abreast of the latest technology in finishing its product lines. Just months in advance of Dofasco in 1949, Stelco had completed an electrolytic tin-plating mill. In 1955, it opened a new wire-making plant at its Parkdale works in Hamilton. Completed in 1968, blast furnace "E" was the largest in North America. In the 1960s and 1970s, Stelco converted to oxygen injection in its furnaces, developed new instrumentation and accelerated its research endeavours. A tangible expression of the research emphasis was the research centre opened in Burlington in 1967. The point is that innovation became routine as both steel companies sought to stay ahead of foreign producers.[5]

Research and development extended to widening product lines. Both firms experimented with putting more steel into home and commercial construction. Following the course of its Hamilton ancestors, Stelco remained a major supplier of nails. There had been no redesign of these humble fasteners since the late-nineteenth-century shift from cut nails to wire nails. Stelco's spiral nail, introduced in 1953, changed that condition. The company also began to market a self-colouring steel for building exteriors in the mid-1960s and used it on the Stelco Tower in downtown Hamilton. Coloured siding was introduced to compete with aluminum siding. Dofasco demonstrated the versatility of steel by constructing an all-steel head office. With a federal housing loan granted in 1972, Dofasco built sixty-six homes in Bellewood Heights; all had steel floors and walls.

Along with the growth and diversification, the steel companies increasingly encountered environmental criticism.[6] Stelco's operations, perhaps more than those of Dofasco, had provoked a questioning of the city's cooperation with the steel makers. Air pollution and the dumping of acid into the harbour came under the critical scrutiny of the press and interest groups. Stelco had been meeting some complaints about air pollution since 1953 when it reduced dust in blast-furnace operations. Efforts to reduce emissions were costly and often a step behind the rising standards. The situation appeared more acute at Stelco; in 1973, that company produced twice as much steel as Dofasco and, according to one study, five times as much sulphur dioxide daily. Accident rates at both companies were low, but the handful of dreadful fatalities and occupational-health concerns added to a general awareness of hazards.

Controversy about Stelco peaked in 1968. The announcement of a decision to construct a new facility on Lake Erie and of another to transfer the corporate headquarters to Toronto outraged Hamiltonians. John Munro, who represented Hamilton East in Ottawa, was "damn mad." The *Spectator* published a stinging

Work at United Smelting in 1946 demonstrated a basic foundry practice. Molten metal was directed into ingot moulds. Cooled ingots were removed and rolled or forged into desired thicknesses.

Dofasco's first blast furnace under construction, June, 1951.

editorial — "Hamilton's harbour is murky and its air is foul because this is a steel town. Stelco plans its next plant in Nanticoke and soon will send its managerial brains to Toronto." The headquarters transfer was an indication of Hamilton's weakness in contrast to the metropolitan giant, but the Nanticoke plant was a blow to the economic confidence built on steel since the end of the war. The *Spectator* admitted to the company-town status conferred upon Hamilton by the situation. "We are just one of the many places where Stelco does business and that is that." Of course, another side of the company-town relationship was quickly stated: corporate patronage of arts, education and urban renewal. Mayor Vic Copps — frequently the spokesman for Stelco's contributions — reminded the city that Stelco had made large philanthropic gestures and that the move to Toronto was to be balanced by the presence of Stelco as a major tenant in a new office tower in Hamilton's urban renewal scheme. A slowdown in the construction of the Nanticoke plant and expenditures on pollution abatement moderated criticism. Nonetheless, the shocks of 1968 had demonstrated that Hamilton had grown only to slip into the position of Canada's largest company town — though admittedly a company town that had received high-paying jobs and gifts from admirably efficient and technologically alert steel producers.[7]

Labour relations and paternalism have considerable visibility in a company town. Judged by that, Hamilton again has qualified as a special city within the Canadian urban system. Even though Stelco and Dofasco had different approaches to labour and community relations, their every move in these matters has transcended the attention accorded to labour issues in more diversified urban economies. The fact that Stelco workers have been represented by a union and those at Dofasco have not been so represented accounts for a unique labour and image situation. From the first Stelco-United Steel Workers contract in 1946, Dofasco chose to match pay terms. Even before that policy of meeting the wage settlement of the union factory, Dofasco had initiated a profit-sharing program. The company's annual Christmas party, claimed to be the world's largest, and the Dofasco Choir have played up the image of a pleasant family operation. The fact that members of the founding Sherman family retained a management interest and resided in Hamilton added credibility to the Dofasco family image. As the product of an externally financed consolidation and as the firm that carried the brunt of labour negotiations for the entire industry, Stelco has had a more controversial position. The contractual relations at Stelco and the paternalism at Dofasco have provided ample basis for a running debate among city residents as to the better system for employees. The four-month strike at Stelco by Local 1005 of the United Steel Workers in the fall of 1981 stoked up the controversy. Striking workers sacrificed savings and several thousands faced layoffs after the settlement. Dofasco employees were thousands of dollars ahead; they undoubtedly gained from the presence of a steelworkers' union in the city, but they assumed none of the risks of the struggle.[8]

With sales that rank it just behind the top twenty Canadian corporations, Stelco has been a visible giant with all of the organizational traits of a modern corporation. It has engaged in takeovers and expansions; its stock has been accumulated by trust and insurance companies; it maintains interlocking directorships with financial corporations. At times, Stelco's scale and relationships with other companies has caused concern about excessive influence. In fact, neither Stelco nor Dofasco (ranked in the top forty) have such close relations with financial institutions that they would have improper access to sources of capital. They have strong credit worthiness because of good returns on investment in the 1960s and, to a lesser extent, the 1970s. Moreover, both firms have remained apart from the trend of corporate consolidation represented by major holding companies like Canadian Pacific Investments (which controls Algoma Steel) or by the Argus or Power corporations. As of 1982, Stelco and Dofasco were run by management personnel familiar with the industry and were not cogs in financial empires.[9]

The notion of Hamilton as a company town stems from the postwar expansion and the overwhelming press coverage granted to the two giants. Meanwhile, the other industries have declined relative to growth in steel, although postwar beginnings at many factories were auspicious. Postwar consumer spending raised the hopes of Hamilton manufacturers. In a publicity gesture reminiscent of the 1911 tour of the industrial east end, Stelco held an open house in 1948. Under tents on Wilcox Street, manufacturers displayed electric stoves, refrigerators and machinery. Over 25,000 visited the displays and five CNR coaches were reserved for an excursion from Toronto.

The optimistic secondary manufacturers whose peacetime wares were on view undertook plant expansions in the next few years. Hoover, the vacuum-cleaner manufacturer, doubled its Hamilton plant size between 1945 and 1960. The example of Westinghouse more completely described the maturation of a consumer-durables producer in ways that did not always benefit Hamilton. At first Hamilton remained favoured. Westinghouse acquired a wartime plant on Longwood Road and converted it into an electric-stove department. A four-storey addition followed in 1951, but in 1953 Westinghouse opened branches at Brantford and Trois-Rivières. By the late 1950s and early 1960s, the company's radio division began to feel the competition from Japan; by the late 1970s a decision made by the American parent corporation resulted in the withdrawal of the firm from appliance manufacture and led to a struggle to keep the Longwood plant open under new ownership and the Hotpoint brand name.[10]

Corporate events at Firestone formed a sequence comparable to those at Westinghouse. The immediate postwar years brought plant additions to Hamilton, but being free from a need to locate either near resources or a terminal capable of handling bulky resources, Firestone could establish branches near markets. Therefore, from 1954 to 1964, it increased its employees in Canada from 2,400 to 3,150, but in Hamilton the gain was only from 1,625 to 1,800 because of the 1959 opening of a Calgary branch plant. The Calgary plant was expanded in 1969 and 1972; another plant opened in Joliette in 1967. An eight-month labour dispute in 1975 and the recall of a line of radial tires in 1977 were reversals that left the company with a rebuilding chore for the 1980s.

The experiences of Westinghouse and Firestone with respect to their establishing branches outside Hamilton contrasts with the experience in steel. Important technical reasons have made it advantageous for steel producers to expand at one site rather than decentralize. The production of iron and steel necessitates such large expenditures on land and dock facilities that duplication is rarely contemplated. The production of steel shapes benefits from concentration at a single location where gases from furnaces can be used to heat ingots in soaking pits before rolling; continuous casting from new furnaces also offers production efficiencies. In sum, there have been benefits from concentration at one site in the steel industry. This has not been the case with consumer durables.[11]

At International Harvester, there has been a parallel history of initial growth within the city followed by decentralization, for

the company built a Chatham assembly line and a major-parts depot in Burlington. From the standpoint of the Hamilton economy, the fact that Harvester's Hamilton labour force never grew beyond its wartime high of over 3,000 between 1945 and 1970 was only part of the picture. The farm-implements industry traditionally operated with a work rhythm of full production and overtime followed by layoffs; that unsatisfactory labour condition remained in the postwar years. Droughts and changing agricultural practices caught Harvester with a surplus inventory in the early 1950s; there were layoffs in 1953, followed by hirings a year later. A new round of layoffs in 1955 dropped employment to a third of what it had been just after the war. Like the neighbouring steel mills, Harvester began in the early 1950s to invest in research and development as well as product diversification. In conjunction with Rolls-Royce, Harvester moved into the development of heavy-duty trucks; the first of these was delivered to Dofasco in 1959. During the mid-1960s, the firm began to market its recreational vehicles. The diversification helped to bring stability to an industry long plagued with seasonal layoffs, but the economic problems of the 1970s — the recessions and energy costs — reintroduced major layoffs.[12]

To be able to discuss so much of Hamilton's economy through the corporate histories of the steel companies, Westinghouse, Firestone and International Harvester confirms the importance of the industrial boom of the early twentieth century. Only one new group of large-scale manufacturers seemed ready to consider Hamilton as a base in the postwar period of industrial planning. Two automobile manufacturers purchased wartime facilities. Studebaker took over an antiaircraft-gun plant and began to manufacture passenger vehicles in 1948. For several years, it appeared likely that the Austin Motor Company of the United Kingdom would open a branch factory, for it had acquired the Canadian Army Trades School and began to refit it for automobile assembly. After investing several million dollars, the financially troubled Austin Company had to withdraw. Indicative of the failure of the automotive sector and the complete success of steel, Dofasco purchased the Austin property in 1967 for its own expansion. Studebaker, by contrast, began on a solid footing. The Champion, an inexpensive model with advanced styling and engineering, was a company mainstay. About 8,000 passenger cars were produced annually until 1957. Along with trucks, total Hamilton production reached approximately 15,000 units an-

Some industrial jobs were retained by women in the postwar years. These women wound transformer coils at Westinghouse.

nually during the early 1950s. The company purchased land in Nelson Township in 1952; had it not failed, Studebaker would have contributed to the phenomenon of industrial decentralization. Despite the fairly successful introduction of the compact Lark in 1958, the company derived less and less profit from its automotive division. The American plant closed in 1963. The Hamilton branch factory stayed open until 1966. Providing work for between 600 and 800, Studebaker had been the city's tenth-largest employer.[13]

Nothing in the Hamilton economy contrasted so completely with the success of steel as the failure of textiles. In 1941, 15 per cent of all manufacturing jobs were in the city's spinning and knitting mills. Half of all women employed in manufacturing worked in textiles. At the end of the war, there were eleven mills; textiles ranked third among all industrial groups in terms of payroll. By the mid-1950s, most mills struggled to stay open as competition from countries with low labour costs took half of the Canadian market. Chipman-Holton and Mercury Mills merged and battled foreign competition with new equipment. The effort failed. Eagle Knit, still managed by the Moodie family, ceased its spinning operations in 1956 and shut down entirely in 1958. Cosmos-Imperial closed out its Hamilton operation in the same year. By the early 1960s, the Young family cut back on textile manufacture at their Hamilton Cotton Company mills and successfully reorganized the firm as an equipment-leasing enterprise. Thus in 1961, textiles provided work for less than 3 per cent of the city's manufacturing labourers; only about 10 per cent of all women in manufacturing worked for textile firms.[14]

Steel's triumph and the declines in other sectors can be observed in the status of Hamilton as a port. In terms of tonnage, it now figures as one of Canada's most active. Only Vancouver, Montreal and Thunder Bay rank ahead of Hamilton. The Atlantic-region ports and Toronto have fallen behind Hamilton. Of course, the explanation for this surprising showing by the steel city becomes apparent when the overall statistics are broken into components. Roughly 50 per cent of the tonnage entering Hamilton's harbour consists of iron ore or iron concentrates.[15]

Finally, what of long-term changes in the relations between employer and employees? Amidst the growth and consolidation of industry that has characterized Hamilton since 1900, the workplaces have become vastly different from the small foundries and modest offices of the turn of the century and earlier. Today large numbers of employees work for huge corporations with numerous subsidiaries or branches in other centres. Whereas foremen once flaunted dictatorial authority over work practices on small shop floors, there now exist elaborate chains of command within the industrial organization. On the one hand, the relations between foremen and workers have been the achievements of organized labour. On the other, corporations have become more skilled in handling authority and fragmenting the foreman-versus-workingmen confrontation by instituting a less polarized system of job classifications. Additionally, the clerical and bureaucratic elements in industrial concerns have swollen considerably to the extent that they now present liabilities to corporations during downswings in the business cycle. For example, management had to terminate the jobs of managers at Westinghouse in the late 1970s; the social disruptions of economic crises now disturb the lives of more than the city's blue-collar workers. The scale and complexity of personnel matters have grown in all major industries in the period since 1945.

THE MULTICULTURAL CITY

Given the barrier to European immigration imposed by conflict, Canadian-born migrants added to Hamilton population during the early and mid-1940s. War production as well as the solid position of steel and urban construction in the postwar economy drew considerable numbers from the more depressed regions of the country. Between 1941 and 1951, the relatively small population pool of the Maritimes region provided the city with nearly 5,000 newcomers; roughly 1,000 came from Alberta and British Columbia. Depressed conditions in Manitoba and in Saskatchewan were evident in the fact that 3,000 emigrated from these provinces. Over 2,000 arrived from Quebec. This increase was sufficient to place French as the third most-cited mother tongue in the 1951 census — behind English and Italian. Quite likely French had been second to English during the war years, but much of the migration came in the form of temporary allocations of manpower to war industries. Veterans were slated to replace the stand-in labourers from Quebec.[16]

From 1946 until 1957, the restrictive immigration policy was replaced with an expansionist approach which, according to the

1961 census, already had brought in such a volume of continental European immigrants that for the first time they outnumbered residents born in the United Kingdom. Rapid economic progress and low unemployment had followed the war. A tight labour market prevailed because of rapidly expanding development in construction and consumer durables as well as the slow-growing domestic labour force. The latter was a demographic consequence of the low rate of natural increase during the 1930s. To expand the labour force, the federal government adopted a set of regulations relaxing admission requirements. The changing immigration policies can be seen in terms of when the non-native-born Canadians who resided in Hamilton in 1961 had first come to Canada. The estimates include both United Kingdom and European immigrants. Those who had arrived before 1921 accounted for nearly 22 per cent of a total immigrant population of close to 86,000. Arrivals from 1921 to 1930 made up 16 per cent; from 1931 to 1940, under 3 per cent; from 1941 to 1945, negligible; from 1946 to 1950, 13 per cent; from 1951 to 1957, over 35 per cent; from 1958 to 1961, 11 per cent.[17]

The federal policies influenced ethnic composition as well as the volume of immigrants who established themselves in Hamilton. There was a sequence to the arrivals. Among the first were the refugees from countries occupied by the Soviet Union or from countries where the political climate was hostile. The former included Lithuanians, Latvians and Estonians; most came between 1948 and 1952. The political émigrés embraced Poles, Serbs and Croatians. All groups maintained cultural establishments: churches, recreation halls, newspapers and pressure groups. In the mid-1950s, there were nineteen Polish organizations claiming a total membership of 3,000. The Serbian League of Canada had its headquarters in Hamilton. The political impact was as marked as the cultural since the anticommunist proclivities of the arrivals were uncompromising. Beyond the celebration of national independence days, the flying of national flags and demonstrations against Soviet imperialism, newcomers helped to tip the political scales in a conservative direction. The example of the Hungarian community is illustrative. In the mid-1940s, Communists had become entrenched in the Hungarian clubs. They had gained control of the Hungarian Mutual Benefit Society and the Hungarian-language press. A campaign led by the Protestant and Catholic Hungarian churches accompanied by the ideological persuasion of newcomers eliminated the Communist influence even before the 1956 Budapest uprising solidified anticommunist nationalism.[18]

In early 1947, the federal government loosened a prohibition against the entry of unskilled or general labour. Then in 1950, it revoked the order blocking immigration from former Axis countries. This act introduced a sudden increase in immigration to Hamilton from Italy in 1950-51. A backlog demand for visas had been building for several years. In 1951, the Italian-immigrant population was close to 6,000. It had surpassed 17,500 by 1961 and comprised 6 per cent of the city's population. The first Germans had arrived in April, 1951. By 1954, the Lutheran Church had opened an immigration service centre; in three years it handled 15,000 people, not all of whom were necessarily German or Lutheran.

During the 1960s, the scale and composition of immigrants changed once more. Fewer arrived and, except for citizens of the United Kingdom who always led in numbers of immigrants, the mix of nationalities was different from the 1950s. Yugoslavs, Greeks and Portuguese became more prominent; Italian and German numbers fell. One measure of the contrast between the initial volume and diversity and the later moderate gains was the demand for special citizenship and English classes. In early 1952, new Canadians from thirty-two countries attended language courses in the evening at Central Secondary School. Enrolment reached 3,000. By the mid-1960s, only a few comparable courses were being presented; there was a feeling among school officials that Toronto had become the haven for immigrants. The educational pressures of the 1950s seemed remote.[19]

Postwar European immigration rearranged the denominational composition of the city. Roman Catholics surpassed Anglicans to become the largest religious denomination. The patterns of immigration formulated in Ottawa also had an influence on Hamilton's cultural make-up, as can be seen in the experience of one neighbourhood comprising approximately 100 households. Somerset Park, in the heart of the Gibson district (bounded by Main, Sanford, Barton and Gage), was, in 1961, a typical subdivision in an area with a high concentration of Italians and Poles. Surveyed in 1909, Somerset Park emerged as one of those housing districts characterized by parallel streets and rows of modest brick houses that attracted predominantly semiskilled occupants.

A Dutch war bride and her baby in January, 1947.
The Red Cross helped to relocate many European newcomers in Hamilton.

Ethnic diversity and a spirit of national strength were celebrated
on this float prepared for Hamilton's centennial in 1946.

Anglo-Celtic surnames dominated from the period of construction until the 1940s, when the largely Protestant body of English-speaking residents slipped from comprising 80 per cent of the neighbourhood households in 1940 to 45 per cent in 1960. The Polish and Ukrainian components had a strong minority representation in 1950, because they accounted for 17 per cent of households, but that increased to 24 per cent over the subsequent ten years. Italian households only appeared during the post-1950 surge of Italian immigration; by 1960 they constituted 21 per cent of the households.

Catholicism in the Sixties cut deeply into the once-Protestant neighbourhood and the city more generally. Whereas only 15 Somerset Park households claimed Roman Catholic affiliation in 1930, the number stood at 77 in 1960. A five-minute stroll down to Barton Street brought residents into contact with a progression of national churches: St. Ann's had been the original Italian church; St. Stanislaus had been the first Polish church; Holy Spirit Ukrainian Church was constructed in the mid-1960s; St. Anthony's, another Italian church, was erected in the mid-1950s. Here within a few blocks, churches mirrored the history of the city's two great eras of immigration — the pre-1914 and the post-1945 movements. The institutional bases of immigrant communities remained along these blocks, set in the rows of brick commercial structures which held ethnic grocery stores, apparel shops, travel agencies and fraternal clubs. By the Seventies, immigrants and their children had begun the move to suburban subdivisions in Stoney Creek and the mountain, leaving the Barton Street commercial and religious strip as a distant and shrinking anchor.[20]

HOUSING AND PLANNING IN THE POSTWAR CITY

At all earlier stages in urban expansion, the entire scope of Hamilton's residential and commercial or industrial landscape could be recorded by water colours, oils or photographs from overlooks on the mountain. With the urbanization of land on the mountain itself, the all-encompassing view was lost; only an aerial survey could capture the city's forms. The landfill operations of the steelmakers jutted into the harbour; the Longwood Road division of Westinghouse as well as extensions to Slater Steel added a minor industrial belt in the west. More impressive, however, were the suburban additions — some arranged on a grid plan and others employing curved streets and dead-end courts. The explosion of new housing began almost immediately after the Second World War. Between 1947 and 1957, Hamilton had nearly doubled its acreage through annexations of parts of Barton and Ancaster townships.

The suburban trend was forecast at the end of the war by the federal authorities responsible for reconstruction of the economy. In fact, they dearly hoped for a housing boom to soak up any excess labour created by peacetime. When the armed forces demobilized, an estimated 12,000 servicemen were due for discharge in Hamilton; roughly 30 per cent were believed to require local accommodations. The estimate on the number staying in Hamilton was low, for in 1951 there were 12,400 veterans who headed households in the city. In addition, industrial workers had done well and Ottawa officials calculated that 15 per cent of Victory Bond holders would convert these assets into housing. True to the implications of these estimates, the demand for housing created both a construction boom and a drastic shortage of decent rental accommodations.

In a whirlwind of activity, an estimated 4,500 detached dwellings were erected between 1946 and 1951. Many were placed on old subdivisions where for fifteen years or more the vacant lots functioned as informal playgrounds. As construction exhausted the surplus lots on older surveys, new land developments radiated into the countryside. In 1951, the Hamilton Home Builders Association claimed that the city had a shortage of serviced lots. Hence there was a spread into Stoney Creek and Ancaster as well as along the mountain in between. Generally in the postwar years, land developers were local men with a related occupation; attorneys, realtors, building-supply dealers and building contractors were drawn to the opportunities of urban expansion. Significantly, in view of the theme of senior government involvement in local concerns, federal housing authorities assembled such large surveys as Murray Park, Mahony Park and Corman Park. Many new surveys such as the 600-lot Mount Royal Court (1953) and the 540-lot Huntington Park (1954), both on the mountain, departed from grid street plans. In tandem with the apartment tower, the gently curving street contributed to a physical definition of the contemporary city.[21]

To a degree the federal government spurred housing construction through its Central Mortgage and Housing Corporation, which took over WHL assets. Yet the CMHC role was not a powerful one because, as one alderman complained, CMHC plans "were out of sight as far as the veterans are concerned."[22] The value of houses that it would help to finance was relatively steep and so were down payments. The more dynamic ingredient of the building boom derived from enforced savings. The impossibility of purchasing a new automobile or new home during the war permitted enormous savings. An indication of pent-up demand and capital accumulation can be traced in a few statistics. In Hamilton, home ownership increased from 49 per cent of the city's households in 1941 to 64 per cent in 1951. Among the 1951 home-owners, only half had a mortgage. The war had converted Hamilton into a city of proprietors, a residence phenomenon without parallel in any of the city's previous eras. By 1961, approximately 70 per cent of household heads owned their dwellings. That would be the highest level of home ownership in the city's history; the advent of numerous highrises in the 1960s would depress home ownership to 60 percent in 1971.[23]

New home construction was accompanied by innovations in building materials, heating and domestic conveniences. The fact that nearly half of the city's housing in 1961 had been constructed since 1945 affected the urban energy metabolism. Fewer instances of doubling up of families, the decline of boarding, the formation of separate households by young men and women as well as senior citizens, and consumer marketing escalated the installation of appliances. More important for energy consumption was the geographic transformation of the city; the suburban form with curving streets, larger lots and distance from place of employment increased automobile population. Furthermore, new homes introduced a shift in the type of energy consumed. Coal and even coke had heated most Hamilton homes during the Depression. Oil heated less than 2 per cent of the city's dwellings in 1941, but accounted for 25 per cent in 1951 and 75 per cent in 1961. Welcomed as an environmental boon, oil reduced winter soot, but twenty years after its general adoption, concern about long-term supply and price forced conversions to natural gas.[24]

Suburban tracts stimulated retail decentralization. Hamilton's first large venture, the Greater Hamilton Shopping Centre, opened in the east end in 1955 with parking facilities for 25,000 automobiles daily by 1960. The spread of retail activity reflected mass consumption of assorted conveniences and luxuries that now were within reach of most consumers. Depression barred the application of convenience devices to a majority of households. Ice-boxes had dripped relentlessly in most kitchens until well after the Second World War, when sheet-metal production could be reintroduced to appliance manufacture. By 1951, three-quarters of the city's households had dispensed with the iceman.

The appliances and retail facilities changed women's functions but not their status. Wives and mothers ceased being domestic producers — sewing and canning — and became domestic consumers. Women certainly had supplemented family income, as confirmed by their work in textile mills during the Depression and their munitions labour in the war years. In the postwar years, they increasingly found themselves as clerical workers and typists. During all periods they were the backbone of teaching and nursing. Adding to family income at low wages and often by work in unglamorous situations, women were defined as dependent upon a male household head.[25]

In some ways suburban expansion improved the housing situation at the end of the war, but there was also a negative aspect to housing in the 1950s. A postwar housing shortage created both home-construction opportunities and a scarcity of low-rental accommodation. So acute and lingering had the situation seemed in 1951 that the city organized a fact-finding survey. Reports of evictions and inadequate shelter already had moved Mayor Lloyd D. Jackson to tears and anger. "Damnable greed has created the horrible conditions under which some people in this city have to live." Frame barracks that formerly had served the wartime Canadian Army Trade School provided emergency housing as late as 1952. Hamilton Council appointed a housing authority and made use of a provision in the National Housing Act to borrow funds for a low-rental housing project at Roxborough Park. Completed in 1952, it contained 496 single-family dwellings. Within five years, the city was managing five housing projects largely financed with federal and provincial loans and had started to plan a project in the north end. In 1964, in what stands as one of several losses of civic autonomy to the senior governments, the administration of the public housing was transferred to a provincial agency.[26]

The 1950 construction of an east-end low-rent project repre-

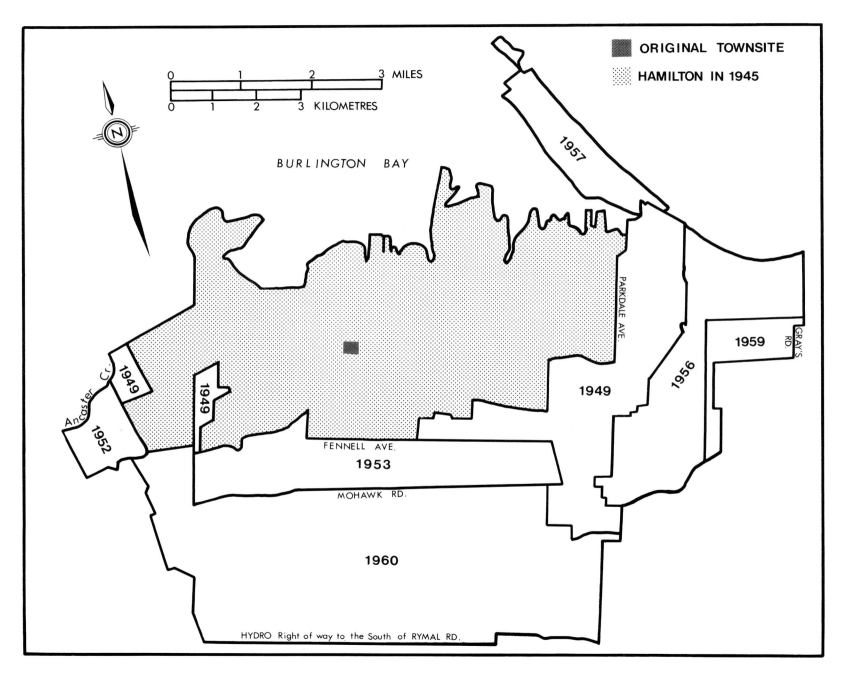

ORIGINAL TOWNSITE

HAMILTON IN 1945

BURLINGTON BAY

1957

PARKDALE AVE.

GRAY'S RD.

1959

1956

1949

Ancaster Cr.

1949

1949

1952

FENNELL AVE.

1953

MOHAWK RD.

1960

HYDRO Right of way to the South of RYMAL RD.

0   1   2   3 MILES
0   1   2   3 KILOMETRES

8 Hamilton's Boundary Extensions, 1946-1960.

sented a new trend in architecture because this city-managed complex included two seven-storey structures. The highrise had arrived. When a 1961 alteration to the zoning bylaw allowed these buildings in the central city, many older semidetached dwellings were demolished so that a spurt of construction from 1962 to 1968 generated 12,000 units of apartment dwellings — 70 per cent of all city dwellings created during those years. Residential towers encroached upon streets in an old elite area south of Main Street near Central School; they replaced the southern half of Corktown; they advanced along arterial streets on the mountain and were constructed on Main Street West. The visual result was stunning from a distance, but uninspiring at street level. By 1980, the view from mountain overlooks presented a scene of apartment buildings towering over the nineteenth-century church spires and outnumbering the few new office buildings: Alexandra Square (1967), the IBM Building (1970), the Stelco Tower (1972) and other commercial or government structures.

The highrise had gained status as an architectural symbol for a distinct decade of growth, the Sixties. Additionally, its dominant position on the Hamilton skyline demonstrated the singular condition of Hamilton. The minor contribution of commercial and hotel space to the skyline emphasized the city's proximity to Toronto. In 1970, Hamilton had less than half the average number of hotel rooms available in the five cities of comparable size: Quebec, Ottawa, Winnipeg, Calgary and Edmonton. Hamilton's hotel-occupancy rate was the lowest of all Canadian medium-sized cities, reflecting the absence of tourism and the concentration of corporate headquarters in Toronto.[27]

In terms of spatial configuration, the postwar period was notable because, for the first time, a housing-construction surge had rolled back the city's urban fringe beyond the face of the mountain. The east and west ends added new suburban tracts, but the most dramatic additions extended southward. The mountain became Hamilton's "upper bunk." From the peak of speculative real-estate action in 1912 until 1945, only modest interest and development had focussed on the mountain. At war's end, some 10,000 to 12,000 resided above the city. In 1952, the estimated population stood at 25,000; at the end of the decade it had doubled to at least 50,000. By 1970 it was close to 100,000. The five schools open in 1946 had grown to fifteen in 1960. The

process of residential expansion was typical of North American suburban sprawl. Streets were constantly in a state of disrepair; trunk-line sewers and sidewalks pushed up local improvement taxes. Industry was excluded and commercially zoned land was snapped up by shopping plazas. Most large new suburban tracts on the mountain had no neighbourhood stores. The main artery, James Street, became a commercial strip. These suburban forms shared attributes with the fringes of other Canadian cities, although a unique circumstance intervened. The mountain presented an obstacle to the flow of commuters.[28]

The closing of the incline railways during the Depression cost Hamilton a local novelty, but they never could have assisted with the movement of tens of thousands of cars in the 1950s. The burden fell on a handful of two-lane roads. As early as 1945 an engineering study had recommended a tunnel leading from James Street to the mountain; the idea was based on a Pittsburgh plan since that city had a similar topographical problem. Instead the city chose to improve the existing roads. In 1950, one road, the Jolley Cut, was widened to four lanes. A four-lane approach in the east end, the Kenilworth-Flock Road access, was constructed in 1958, but the central and western access roads — Claremont Hill, James Street and Beckett Drive — remained unimproved and inadequate. Furthermore, the crumbling of the escarpment face forced annual repairs to the Jolley Cut and endangered other routes. Altogether, the mountain roads carried an estimated 75,000 automobiles daily in 1960; this burden choked the access points during the rush hours. The impatience of mountain residents renewed interest in the tunnel concept. But again the remedy chosen called for massive expressway construction that changed both the mountain face and several city blocks at the foot of a crisscross of concrete-supported roadways. By 1972, when four years of construction on the new Claremont Access ended, all mountain routes carried a total of 130,000 automobiles per day.

Meanwhile, a provincial highway in the far west had been carrying traffic through the Chedoke Ravine and up the mountain to the expanding suburbs of the west mountain and Ancaster since 1963. Pressure for a further expressway in the extreme east, through the Red Hill Creek Valley, provoked conservation groups to protest the sacrifice of further recreational land to traffic. As with industrial growth, the pressures of suburban traffic began to run into environmental protest during the 1970s. The

A west Hamilton subdivision. The curving streets and scale of housing construction were characteristic of the postwar suburban housing boom.

The Hamilton Trades School, operated by the Ontario Department of Labour, prepared veterans and war-industry labourers for the planned boom in construction after the Second World War.

Innovations in construction methods and a minimal scale contributed to the expansion of home ownership in the late 1940s.

Home ownership and appliance purchases were vigorously promoted. The end of wartime controls and the existence of considerable personal savings produced the desired economic effect, pushing Hamilton industries into boom growth.

Apartment-tower construction during the 1960s and early 1970s overwhelmed the city between James and Queen streets.

scrambling to improve roads and the political wrangling over the pressures imposed by mountain housing came during decades when urban planning made its first inroads into Hamilton civic affairs.[29]

Unlike the unplanned expansion of the industrial city, a hallmark of the contemporary city has been the participation of all levels of government and a host of consultants in urban design. An advisory planning board with no powers had been the city's only flirtation with planning throughout the 1920s. Finally, council officially recognized planning as a civic responsibility and organized a Town Planning Committee in January, 1930. Economic problems precluded planning action until the 1940s, when two studies helped to cast the physical future of Hamilton for thirty years. The planning committee hired a consultant who compiled a 1945 *Report on Existing Conditions*. The report's compendium listed city problems: east-west traffic congestion, numerous level closings, inadequate mountain-access roads, lack of an auditorium for symphonic or dramatic performances, a cramped library, an obsolete art gallery and an abused beach. It had faithfully described the drab industrial centre.

In response, the city hired another consultant — one of many during the next three decades. The resulting 1947 plan guided successive councils into major alterations to the city. The plan proposed a new city hall and courthouse; both were constructed. A recommended cultural centre with library, art gallery, auditorium and adult-education facilities was realized piecemeal. The city pursued suggestions for housing redevelopment, better mountain access, the widening of several east-west arteries and replacement of streetcars by buses. For recreation it singled out the potential of the Red Hill Creek and Van Wagner's Beach. Finally, the report proposed regional planning and suggested boundaries almost identical to those proposed in 1969 for the new regional municipality of Hamilton-Wentworth.[30]

In 1951, the city adopted zoning — the intricate designation of land use to protect residential areas against undesirable development. The zoning arrangements were made highly mutable by appeal procedures and amendments. The volume of spot changes drastically altered original zoning maps. Another specialized consideration entered the repertoire of planning during the 1950s, namely calculating facilities needed for automobiles. Automobile registration held steady during most of the Depres-

sion, rising marginally in the 1935-1937 recovery. The number stayed constant until the end of the war, when conversion of several wartime assembly lines to passenger-car manufacture increased registration during the 1950s. Traffic and parking problems forced the city to commission studies beginning with a 1937 study on mountain transportation. Another in 1957 led to the institution of a one-way street plan.[31]

Zoning and urban renewal schemes aroused intense spates of civic controversy from the early 1950s into the 1970s. Tussles on zoning related to revisions permitting the creation of a downtown highrise district. Private developers and concerned neighbourhood groups clashed. Urban renewal was a different matter. It involved the additional factor of federal intervention. Federal funds set against a backdrop of depression and wartime privation made monumental action feasible. In 1957, the National Housing Act was amended to permit use of federal funds in renewal projects. North American planners, who thought that poor environmental conditions bred social problems, had influenced Canadian urban policy. Hamilton civic leaders and planning consultants bought the argument — and maintained naïvely that pulling down old shops and dwellings would trim social-work cases. Other benefits were alleged to flow from renewal, including a central-city challenge to the commercial pull of the shopping centres, higher tax assessments, beautification and cultural facilities. In the case of Hamilton's civic-square redevelopment, an overly optimistic sketch of a future core was something which sparked imagination in 1965. The realization of the plan included a disillusioning series of revisions that did not measure up to promised benefits, although the completion of a cultural heart for the city answered the 1945 report's notice of poor facilities.[32]

Except in haste to obliterate structures erected before 1900, the city's major planning endeavours failed to come to terms with the past. Hamilton was singled out in a Canadian handbook for architectural preservation as a disaster area. "In Hamilton, Ontario, it was estimated in early 1973 that, at the current rate of demolition, every designated heritage building would be gone in fifteen years."[33] The prediction proved premature. After bulldozers had cleared space for the civic square and had flattened properties assembled for highrises, a few Hamiltonians strove for the revitalization of the built environment through restora-

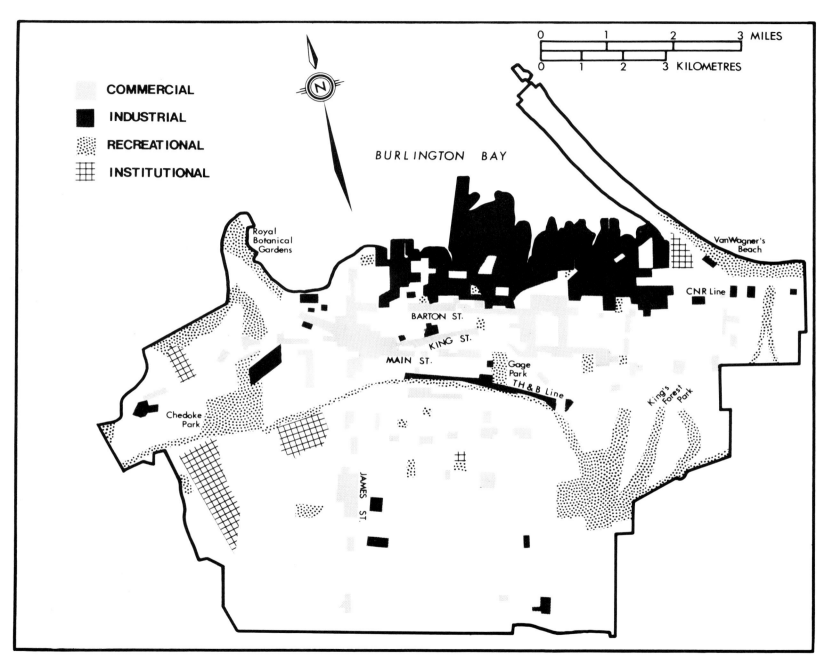

COMMERCIAL

INDUSTRIAL

RECREATIONAL

INSTITUTIONAL

BURLINGTON BAY

Royal Botanical Gardens

VanWagner's Beach

CNR Line

BARTON ST.

KING ST.

MAIN ST.

Gage Park

TH & B Line

King's Forest Park

JAMES ST.

Chedoke Park

0   1   2   3 MILES

0   1   2   3 KILOMETRES

9 Land Use in Hamilton, c. 1968.

To accommodate the traffic between work and the increasing number of homes on the mountain, the access roads had to be improved both in 1955 and 1975.

tion. Work on Dundurn Castle in the mid-1960s already had stimulated interest in older buildings. In a backlash against renewal by demolition, heritage struggled forth as a civic force. Heritage Hamilton was formed to save older buildings; private development restored a section of Hess Street for fashionable shops; the 1974 Ontario Heritage Act prompted formation of a Local Architectural Conservation Advisory Committee in 1976.

In the half-century since the appointment of a city-planning committee, Hamilton had digested an assortment of planning fads. Planning revealed itself to be less a science and more a guise for the age-old study of immediate problems in terms of current wisdom and politics. Allegedly the contemporary city had secured through planning an objective means of collecting and evaluating superior information upon which to base rational decisions of long-term importance. There have been several problems with this conception of planning. First, the projections upon which future growth has been predicted have been in error. Second, at the level of policy implementation, political wrangling and special-interest lobbying have come into play.

However, in one very innovative episode, Hamilton broke away from the usual planning pattern and experimented with neighbourhood initiatives. It must be conceded that this provincially inspired notion was, like prior planning enthusiasms, a fad. It grew out of 1960s American critiques of centralized urban planning. For some neighbourhoods, the scheme worked well because of dedicated local leaders. The elite Durand district, for example, was well served. In the working-class Gibson district, residents secured a park and a recreation centre because a few forceful individuals set these as goals for their neighbourhoods.[34] The experiment alters premature judgment of Hamilton civic affairs as being manipulated by the influence of the mob, the media and the political machines. Hamilton civic affairs have had their dynamic and radical side; the city has not been without citizen influence on neighbourhood facilities.

RECREATION, ENTERTAINMENT AND CULTURE

The post-1945 era brought considerable changes in recreation, entertainment and culture. Widespread purchases of automobiles, the introduction of television and professionalism in sport charted the direction of popular culture. The ability to purchase the hardware for the new leisure pursuits was related to credit and an extended period of time when real wages were rising. The layoffs and recessions between 1946 and 1970, not to mention the inflationary problems of the 1970s, make typical family budgets and wage-and-price indices crude measures of the standard of living. The fact remains that most Hamilton residents enjoyed nearly three prosperous decades in which they shared the wealth to an unprecedented extent. From the mid-1940s to the mid-1970s, the cost-of-living index increased at a slower rate than the wage index. By the mid-1970s, the index numbers had drawn closer together.

Leisure activity was influenced by technology, a new affluence and capitalism. Paradoxically, as these forces and the emergence of Hamilton as a company town developed, formal culture — the arts — gained proper facilities. Thus it is risky to conclude that the automobile and electronic media absolutely dominated culture or that the cultural shadow of Toronto had completely overwhelmed Hamilton's formal culture. In general, both propositions held true except for the set of new cultural facilities: Hamilton Place theatre (1972), the Art Gallery of Hamilton (1977) and the new public library (1980).

By the same token, it is too sweeping to claim that amateurism in sports was struck down by television and professionalism. Amateur track and field remained important in Hamilton, more so than in most cities. The Hamilton Olympic Club supervised the 1952 Olympic team trials — as it had on several previous occasions. The annual indoor track meet at the Armories and the annual CANUSA games held in competition against Flint, Michigan, maintained civic interest in amateur sports. On the other hand, it is true that the postwar years brought reorganization in the one other sport that had a strong local following when senior football became openly professional. In 1943, a combined-services football team, the Hamilton Flying Wild Cats, defeated the Winnipeg RCAF Bombers and brought Hamilton its last amateur Grey Cup. The fading Tigers and the new Wild Cats merged in 1949 to form the professional Tiger-Cats, who won their first Grey Cup in 1953 and then dominated eastern football in the late 1950s and early 1960s. The purchase of the Tiger-Cats by Toronto's Harold Ballard in 1978 fits into the proposition that Hamilton has continually ceded autonomy — financial, political and cultural — to Toronto. Furthermore, the professional game struck sportswriter Ivan Miller as a quite different affair from contests during amateur days. "No longer do football teams ride from station to playing field in the horse-drawn tally-hos that made players open targets for disgruntled fans."[35]

In the 1950s and 1960s, the recreational focus of Hamilton residents no longer had to fix on the city's facilities. By 1971, 5,700 Hamilton households owned a vacation home. Admittedly, few cottages were likely to have belonged to industrial labourers. On the other hand, the figure indicates a considerable investment in escape from the city. The taste was established and the automobile represented an increasingly common expression of the possibility of leisure beyond local boundaries. Every automotive statistic emphasized the abundant access to private mobility. In 1951, automotive ownership still reflected the wartime interlude; hence there were about 27,000 passenger cars, 23 new car dealers and 146 service stations. By that time Hamilton possessed its own automobile factory, for in August, 1948, the first Studebaker came off the assembly line. In 1961, 34 new car dealers and 274 service stations operated in a city with 81,000 passenger cars. Rare in 1961, the two-car family became established in subsequent years so that about a quarter of Hamilton's 117,000 cars in 1971 were second vehicles.

The recreational potential was as obvious as the traffic congestion on Labour Day weekends. The automobile more than any other cause shattered the civic culture of parades, rallies, picnics, band concerts, excursions and amateur sports. The annual Dofasco picnic, for example, was discontinued after the war when workers had cars and statutory holidays. The car changed streets and forced conversion of some open spaces and dwellings to traffic areas. In contrast to the streetcar lines that could control movement and carry crowds to specific destinations, thereby complementing public assembly, the automobile was hostile to public space — it required parking and clashed with demonstrations and parades.[36]

Television sped the decline of traditional recreation and entertainment. Less than ten years after local station CHCH began broadcasting (1954), over 90 per cent of Hamilton households possessed television sets. Competition from television pared down motion-picture theatre attendance during the 1950s. In 1950, the city had 18,000 theatre seats; 34 per cent of this capacity was being used. Peak attendance was achieved in 1952. By 1959, the number

of seats had fallen to 15,000 and occupancy to 17 per cent. The authorization of Sunday cinemas by municipal plebiscite in 1962 could not save several of the largest theatres in Canada. The Palace and the Capitol theatres were demolished in the early 1970s. Despite initial setbacks inflicted by television, the cinema remained an attraction; new facilities were constructed in suburban shopping centres and in the Jackson Square area of the urban renewal scheme.

The electronic media revealed a further dimension of the city's cultural situation and of Toronto's metropolitan outreach. Hamilton in 1960s and 1970s came to occupy a unique position in relation to the five Canadian cities of comparable size — Quebec, Ottawa, Winnipeg, Calgary and Edmonton. All had two or more television stations in 1970. Hamilton had one. Hamiltonians have claimed that the city possessed the most varied selection of television viewing on the continent, but this has been another way of stating that Hamilton was not the dominant broadcasting force within its own immediate area. Radio broadcasting supports this contention. All medium-size Canadian cities in 1970 had one or more radio station (AM, FM and university stations included) per 100,000 residents, except Hamilton.[37]

The arts had minor successes during the postwar years. Visiting orchestras and opera companies staged productions at the Palace. The Hamilton Philharmonic Orchestra, reborn in 1949, performed in a variety of auditoriums. If the theatre situation was considered unsatisfactory, the gallery problem was far worse. Other galleries refused to lend collections to a gallery located in the decrepit and unsuitable 1890 library building. Since the 1920s, there had been discussions about the need for a proper gallery. Not until 1953 was a modern facility built near McMaster University and the Royal Botanical Gardens's sunken garden. Even with the new gallery, Hamilton had aging or uninspiring cultural facilities. Perhaps imaginative revival of older buildings would have given the city suitable theatre and appealing gallery space at the centre of the city, but renewal programs focussed exclusively upon demolition and new construction. Therefore, in relatively quick succession, the city acquired a theatre, an art gallery and a library.[38]

It is easy to tally up the city's cultural amenities acquired in the 1970s and to praise modernization; it is legitimate to accept the automobile and television as potentially instructive and liberating.

The 1946 centennial briefly recaptured some of the Victorian era's carnival spirit, love of parades and use of streets for entertainment. The Jackson Square shopping complex — to be built adjacent to this site twenty-five years later — deliberately separated pedestrians from streetscapes and, along with too many barren new structures, effaced the human scale of the city centre.

The Funland amusement strip along Burlington Beach struggled to survive against the pressure of intercity traffic and commuter trips. The city was being cut off from its greatest recreational areas — the bay and beach.

But nothing is without its price, and one price exacted for these gains has been a growing separation between the city streets and the city residents. It was a sensible decision and a comment on the times that the new Art Gallery of Hamilton and Hamilton Place theatre share a parking garage. One of the major projects of renewal involved the destruction of the old York Street commercial district. In both cases, the automobile had dictated urban form. Another price, if one yields to nostalgia, is the loss of texture in modern theatre buildings, whether they are cinemas or Hamilton Place. The Capitol and Palace, once among the largest theatres in Canada, had romantic paintings above the proscenium arch as well as orchestra pits and house organs.

A study of the city's past is not meant to be an indictment of the present. However, it can tell us what cultural forms were once valued by urban citizens for whom the possibility of a trip to Florida, a second car or a colour-television set did not exist. It can explain why former recreations and entertainments declined. It can imply that much of the culture in the urban past was quite remarkable — perhaps not in sophisticated art and invention but certainly in its capacity for pleasure and in promoting contact with the city itself. The contemporary city is unfortunate in lacking an outdoor pedestrian culture that would encourage an interest in the city's architecture and streetscapes. Architecture and civic culture, therefore, have been connected in a profound structural transition whereby the automobile and mass media have alienated the public from multiple contacts with city streets and buildings. It is worth reflecting on what remains, what was lost, what was gained. The transition is still visible, for the monumental and often impersonal scale of new construction, meant to be viewed from a distance or from a vehicle, contrasts with a precious few survivors from an earlier pedestrian culture.

CONTINUITY AND CHANGE IN URBAN POLITICS

Urban politics can be described on two levels: those of institutions and of conduct. The former often have been revised, though the latter tend to be resilient to change. The institutions have been tampered with in minor ways on innumerable occasions: the number of wards have been increased (1846, 1873, 1919); the selection of the mayor had been taken from city council and made

elective (1876); a board of control was added (1910). In the era of the contemporary city, comparable changes included the introduction of biennial civic elections (1958) and the elimination of a board of control (1980). A 1960 realignment of wards disturbed a traditional concept of representative democracy, one proposing that a constituency have some community cohesion. Instead, the new wards were simply strips running from the mountain to the bay without regard for historic or neighbourhood groupings. Aldermen who had a neighbourhood following in the north end or in the northeast working-class or ethnic areas had to fight in a new game. Ostensibly the strip wards were to guarantee that aldermen would represent a cross section of the city and not work for a particular neighbourhood or interest group. Class and ethnic segregation within the city was being artificially countered by gerrymander. As a result, half of the aldermen for the 1961 council were newcomers. The 1960 shifting of ward boundaries was a significant measure that ignited little controversy. The introduction of regional government also constituted a major innovation, yet it fanned local passions in a way that was wholly unique in the history of local government at the Head of the Lake.[39]

Annexations made from 1949 to 1957 had doubled the city's size and exhausted possibilities for large additions without confronting strong resistance. The Hamilton urban fringe had bumped into established towns. Neighbouring communities expanded as dormitories for the city; postwar Hamilton generated new jobs, but many who worked in plants serviced by the city or who travelled city streets paid taxes to other municipalities. As one of the new structural circumstances of the contemporary city, the townships, villages and towns around Hamilton gained as many residents as the city itself between 1951 and 1966. The city's population during that period increased by 35 per cent; population rose by 150 per cent in surrounding municipalities. The fact that the Head of the Lake, including Burlington, formed an economic unit seemed to demand a new initiative in the structure of local government. Efficiency and equitable sharing of costs in road maintenance, provision of water and sewer lines, public safety and social services were to be sought in some metropolitan form of government.

The problem had been faced elsewhere in urban Canada and in 1967 it was Hamilton's turn. A three-man provincial commission heard briefs and studied assorted schemes. Hamilton's presentation argued for a single urban government embracing Hamilton, Ancaster, Dundas and Burlington. Toronto's two-level structure and the chorus of protest from fiercely independent municipalities that opposed Hamilton's alleged empire building tipped the balance in favour of a two-tier system for what became the regional municipality of Hamilton-Wentworth. The city did not surrender easily; county as well as city councillors went to Winnipeg in 1973 to study that city's "unicity" government. None of the visitors budged from their prior positions. In the meantime, another controversy had erupted. About half of the jobs supporting the suburban community of Burlington were in Hamilton, but most of the residents felt that association with Hamilton would be an unworthy and costly fate for their relatively posh suburban retreat. After some prevarication at Queen's Park, Burlington got its way and was attached to the Halton region. From the perspective of Hamilton Council, the truncated region with its awkward two tiers was a flawed compromise. After the proclamation of regional government on New Year's Day 1974, the city repeatedly endeavoured to strengthen centralization.[40]

The conduct of civic politics in the contemporary city retained a few features from earlier decades and shed others. Elections to council remained potential springboards for political careers at Queen's Park and Ottawa. A handful of careerists made the progression; a few others aspired but failed. The important observation is that links between party machines at the civic level and national parties held as firm as ever, but Liberal and Conservative partisans perpetuated the fantasy that there was no real party involvement in civic elections. Civic politics was not as purely non-partisan as many politicians and newspaper editorials proposed. A final significant ingredient that carried over from earlier decades was the occasional contest between a left-wing labour faction and the other political interests. Labour endorsement continued to be a factor in the east-end wards. Therefore, in large measure, civic politics was conducted as before the war and even before the Depression, but in several regards the prewar conditions had fallen apart. The traditional conception of local politics was one that largely excluded women; another part of the tradition was that two or three one-year terms for a mayor were sufficient for such an honorary or part-time vocation. These two givens were questioned during the 1930s and 1940s by the careers of Nora Frances Henderson and Mayor William Morrison. These people were exceptions; in the postwar years what they represented became more commonplace. The notions of women in civic affairs and of the career mayor with a program grew into civic trends.

Three public figures illustrate the connections between civic politics and the other levels of government. The progress of William Warrender indicates the ideal career advances open to a Hamilton Conservative. Elected to council in 1940, Warrender served in the RCAF for three years before returning to civic politics as an alderman and controller. In 1951, he carried the provincial constituency of Hamilton Centre. Like most Hamilton politicians regardless of party, Warrender held a union card (in the Brotherhood of Railway Signalmen) and broadcast the fact. In contrast to such token union memberships, CCF or NDP candidates often held union executive positions. Warrender had held four cabinet portfolios before his 1962 appointment to the bench.

John Munro has demonstrated the ascent from a well-organized local base to the Liberal cabinet in Ottawa. A perennial candidate in high school and university and elected as an alderman in 1954, young Munro took up progressive causes, proposing a women's centre in 1954 and pressing for the development of a working-man's recreational area at Van Wagner's Beach. After building a rapport with ethnic clubs in the east end, he succeeded in winning the Hamilton East constituency from the Conservatives. In Ottawa, he associated with the radical wing of the Liberal party. He received his first appointment to the cabinet in 1968, as minister without portfolio. As Minister of Health and then of Labour, he retained the populist image cultivated when he was an alderman. Of course, he also played the major role in distributing federal patronage in the city.

The routes to the bench and to cabinet were closed to the third individual, Reg Gisborn. Praised even by opponents as a voice of reason at Queen's Park, Gisborn ran unsuccessfully as a candidate for alderman on four occasions. Each time, he had the backing of organized labour. His interest in civic affairs was further expressed in 1954 when he served on a citizens' committee to examine the city-manager form of government for possible application in Hamilton. In 1955, he was elected as one of just three CCF members in the provincial legislature. He held his riding until cancer forced his retirement in 1975. Warrender,

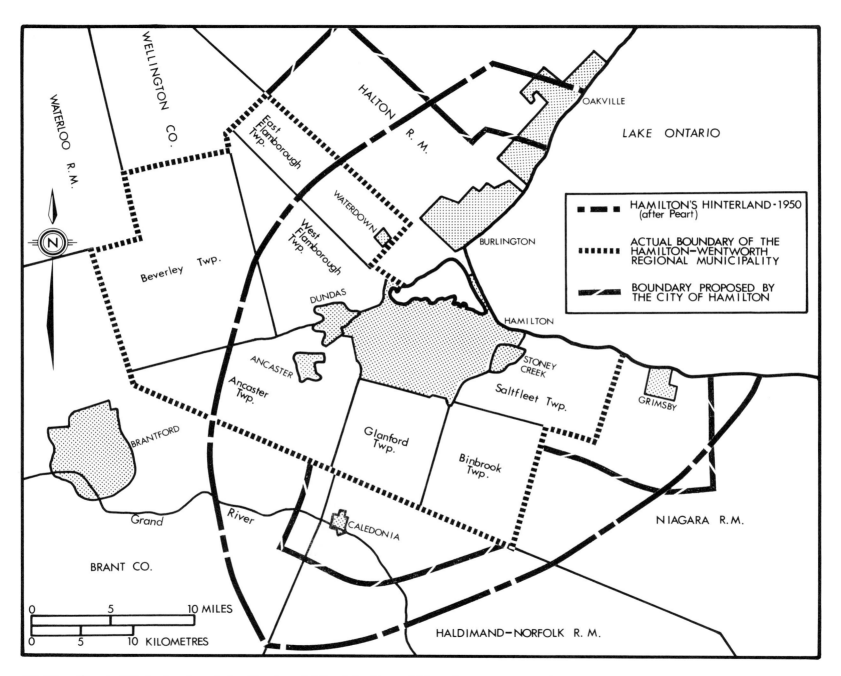

WELLINGTON CO.

WATERLOO R.M.

HALTON R.M.

OAKVILLE

LAKE ONTARIO

East Flamborough Twp.

WATERDOWN

West Flamborough Twp.

Beverley Twp.

BURLINGTON

DUNDAS

HAMILTON

ANCASTER

STONEY CREEK

Ancaster Twp.

Saltfleet Twp.

GRIMSBY

BRANTFORD

Glanford Twp.

Binbrook Twp.

NIAGARA R.M.

Grand River

CALEDONIA

BRANT CO.

HALDIMAND-NORFOLK R.M.

N

	HAMILTON'S HINTERLAND-1950 (after Peart)
	ACTUAL BOUNDARY OF THE HAMILTON-WENTWORTH REGIONAL MUNICIPALITY
	BOUNDARY PROPOSED BY THE CITY OF HAMILTON

0   5   10 MILES

0   5   10 KILOMETRES

10 Hamilton's Hinterland and the Regional Municipality of Hamilton-Wentworth.

Munro and Gisborn had progressed as far as any member of their respective parties from Hamilton and all had begun with a hand in civic affairs.[41]

Despite the overt links between parties and contests in the civic arena, city politicians have been leery of accepting a party label. The press, business leaders and many members of council have kept alive the notion that city government must be maintained as a uniquely nonpartisan affair more akin to a large corporation than to the government in Toronto or Ottawa. Since several extremely successful public figures — Nora Frances Henderson and Lloyd D. Jackson — campaigned as independents, running under the nonpartisan label has remained an attractive way to seek city office. The fact that the CCF had run candidates in the 1940s and that the NDP organized a full slate in 1970 helps explain the vigour with which many civic leaders vociferously embraced the concept of nonpartisanship while often retaining ties with the Liberal or Conservative party and harbouring aspirations for higher political office. Being accused of "partyism" in city elections was one of the sins ascribed to the left in Hamilton. Indeed, experienced civic politicians on the left — men like William Powell, who was active in the 1960s and elected mayor in 1980 — tried to avoid the party label while welcoming labour's endorsement. Essentially, the political culture of Hamilton resembled that in other Canadian cities where a person's activities in the wards launched lifetime careers and where the deceit about nonpartisanship made for shapeless statements by candidates. The lack of profound policy discussions in a one-newspaper city (with the exception of 1947 to 1955, when the *News* was published) with a nonpartisan tradition may help to explain Hamiltonians' apathy during municipal elections. In the midst of a commonplace political arena, there were two types of civic figures who added novelty to an otherwise familiar tale: women and mayors with programs and long periods in office.

The late 1940s and the 1950s were a heyday for women in local politics. A special situation developed in 1946 when three women sat on council: "do-gooder" and feminist Nora Frances Henderson, dedicated Communist Helen Anderson and deep-blue Tory Ellen Fairclough. Fairclough was appointed to council to fill the seat vacated by the resignation of the man who narrowly defeated her in the 1945 civic election. She won her subsequent civic elections and carried a 1950 by-election to become the first woman to represent a Hamilton constituency. During the years of the Diefenbaker government she attained two national firsts: she was the first woman cabinet minister and the first woman to be acting Prime Minister. When she lost her seat in the Diefenbaker debacle of 1963, her successful opponent was Joseph Macaluso, the first Liberal MP of Italian descent.[42]

The number of women who ran for council varied from four to seven at each election until the early 1960s, when their participation declined. There are several explanations for the early enthusiasm. Henderson's example certainly helped. The wartime service groups like the Red Cross and the postwar creation of new neighbourhoods with a need for schools and community services provided situations that brought women into quasi-political activities which then blended easily into civic campaigns. In the case of several women like Ellen Fairclough, the dedication to a party was very much a contributing element. Typically, the female candidates belonged to several community or women's groups. For example, Ada Pritchard, one of the most astute civic politicians during the 1950s, developed an interest in local issues through her position as president of the Hamilton branch of the Canadian Association of Consumers. During the 1960s, the most consistently successful woman at city hall — the successor to Nora Frances Henderson and Ada Pritchard — was Anne Jones. After more than a decade in council, she accepted appointment as the first chairman of the Regional Council of Hamilton–Wentworth in 1974. Generally, women became active once again in the civic elections of the 1970s. The three elected in 1978 matched the 1946 number, but there were none surviving the 1980 civic contest.

From 1949 to 1977, Hamilton had two mayors. With their long tenures in office and their identification with specific programs, both Lloyd D. Jackson and Victor K. Copps represented a different breed of chief magistrate. The legacies of most Hamilton mayors had been trivial; the position had been largely honorific and the opportunities for placing a personal stamp on the city were minimal. Sewage plants, schools and new railway stations were worthy achievements, but scarcely monuments for civic immortality. Old-time mayors, admitted former mayor Thomas Jutten, loved to lead parades and preside over public gatherings. By contrast, postwar mayors had a penchant for action. Jackson, an owner of a city bakery with roughly 500 employees and no prior experience on council, won a four-way contest in 1949. He had

York Street looking west, 1953. The chaotic collection of shops was not a stunning entrance to the city centre. Shopping-plaza competition helped to undermine small business areas in the older urban areas.

York Street looking west, 1975. The sterile concession to the efficient movements of cars and trucks carved up inner-city neighbourhoods.

promised a new administration without ideological or political bias, but rather one dedicated to running the city like a business. In contrast to the overly cautious and frugal administration of CCF mayor Sam Lawrence, Jackson proposed large expenditures on streets, sewers, recreational facilities and city beautification. His call for an end to austerity coincided with industrial and suburban growth.

Additionally, Jackson made contact with the city's ethnic communities, a sound practice adopted by many postwar politicians. For the 1950 inaugural meeting of Hamilton Council, Jackson invited eight representatives from the city's ethnic groups. Jackson's successor, Vic Copps, continued the process of symbolic bridging and in 1966 paid a visit to Gagliano Aterno, Italy. The town with 900 citizens had been a major source of immigrants before and after the war. About 5,000 former citizens and their descendants were alleged to reside in Hamilton.[43]

Victor Kennedy Copps came to prominence as a skilled campaigner with a definite platform. His position as a salesman for radio advertising furnished him with abundant business contacts, a knowledge of economic problems in the city core and an appreciation for campaign advertising gimmicks. These attributes, along with a personal enthusiasm for campaigning and 800 poll workers, secured him a seat on the Board of Control in 1960. His first election had a startlingly professional quality. When Copps toppled Jackson in 1962 and became the first Roman Catholic mayor, he had campaigned as someone who recognized that the economic boom of the immediate postwar years had run into difficulties. The loss of industries and stores was undeniable, but Copps's answer of massive urban renewal never addressed the primary malaise — the drawing power of Toronto.[44] Copps accurately observed that "while other cities have skyscrapers going up in the downtown area, Hamilton has 147 parking lots."[45] However, as an eager civic politician of the 1960s, he could not see the virtual inevitability of Hamilton's predicament, for he was infatuated by the idea of downtown urban renewal as a cure-all. He welcomed an end to federal renewal aid's being tied to housing. From the viewpoint of the new mayor and supportive downtown businessmen, the housing crisis of the postwar years had ended and the core of the city now required assistance. Securing a new central city with cultural amenities dominated the nearly fifteen years of Victor Copps's public life, though as an ambitious

Liberal he became a candidate for the provincial leadership in 1964. The hypocrisy of the nonpartisan cry in civic elections had no better example than the city's Liberal machine's dropping its Liberal banner when working to elect the mayor. Undoubtedly, there was more behind the success of Copps than the call for urban renewal, a smooth campaigning style and a Liberal machine. Since the war, the Roman Catholic proportion of the populace had increased and Copps derived some benefit from the shift.

As for the economic benefits of overhauling Hamilton by urban renewal, they may prove ephemeral; the architectural losses caused by renewal will be lamented by many residents for generations. Nevertheless, the Copps years provided the city with splendid facilities for its cultural institutions. The political problem, as successor Jack MacDonald discovered, was what to do after the Jackson administration had overseen the remaking of the urban fringe and the Copps administration had redone the core. In politics as in the economy, population and construction, profound growth had slowed; the 1980 civic election produced an upset victory for a mayoralty candidate devoid of bombast and pledged to conservation and to a reassessment of costly schemes. Whether the slower pace on all fronts indicates a passing fad, a cyclical movement or the beginning of a structural change for Hamilton is an essential question for the future.

CONCLUSION

After we have considered five stages in Hamilton's development from village to contemporary city, there are some summary questions. Is Hamilton to be seen as a unique place or in terms of urban themes familiar to other centres across the country and throughout North America? Can the historical record assist with a forecast of the next era? The questions are related.

The city must be understood as both unique and typical. The important point is to understand how and where the singular and commonplace are expressed in the city's make-up. To a considerable degree, local economic events, housing attributes, cultural features, themes in labour organization and political practices have had and will continue to have counterparts throughout the North American urban system. As a middle-size Canadian city in the central region and as a smaller North American urban

To the east of the Hamilton Public Library and below Central School, there was an old, established neighbourhood, seen here in 1957. This was the site for a new city hall.

The new city hall built in 1959 offered comfort and space. Architecturally it had no connection with the historic stone and brick of Hamilton's built environment. Its cool white appearance and use of glass prefigured the spread of less accomplished modernism — the new apartment towers.

centre in the Great Lakes area, Hamilton will evolve much like its counterparts in these associated groups of cities. The historic losses of fiscal decision making through the intervention of senior levels of government and the erosion of industrial decision making through consolidations have combined with recent increases in energy costs to leave the smaller central Canadian and Great Lakes cities vulnerable to unfavourable economic decisions. By contrast, Toronto and Chicago are sure to persist as metropolitan titans of the region. Political frailty is a further measure of Hamilton's current status, for the provincial government determined the shape of the Hamilton-Wentworth regional municipality and nearly succeeded in foisting its elevated transit system on the city. The experience of Hamilton with senior governments is broadly typical of the struggle between cities and states or provinces across North America. The specific issues vary, but city governments frequently have found themselves in a conflict for home rule against a distant bureaucracy.

There is a spatial counterpart to the loss of economic and political power to greater metropolitan centres. As small cities in densely occupied regions lose their identity as financial or wholesaling centres, so too are they failing to retain a clear physical shape. Not only has Hamilton become a part of the Hamilton-Wentworth region, but its situation in the central Canadian urban corridor has meant a blending into an extended urban cluster. More than most Canadian cities, Hamilton is a participant in urbanization without clearly separated cities. The entire golden horseshoe of southern Ontario, from Niagara Falls to Oshawa, comprises an urban expanse fragmented by jurisdictional boundaries and by lingering expressions of local boosterism. The new urban form and old boundaries coexist in a complicated way. The city as place and concept remains, especially to the core of long-term residents and established institutions. As a smaller city, Hamilton retains an intimacy at many levels. However, the reality of region and urban corridor present competing urban forms.

In what ways has Hamilton been distinctive? The city's singular features have included its proximity to Toronto. No Canadian city has had to endure comparable rivalry from a nearby metropolis. As well, Hamilton's unique economy developed from a long association with foundries and then steelworks. The topography has also been a special challenge and asset. All of these local features have been both cursed and praised. What cannot be in dispute is the fact that these conditions impose strictures on local initiatives to shape the city. The weight and direction of the historical record draw attention to the metropolitan shadow cast by Toronto and to the significance of corporate decisions often made outside the city. As for the mountain, it obstructs; it also erodes enough annually to cause hazards. In sum, nothing about Hamilton's shared or unique qualities recommends civic complacency. Indeed, the analysis of five eras often has had to centre on vulnerability. There is no other prediction for the future.

The city centre has remained about where it was over a century and a quarter earlier. Gore Park is still surrounded by retail shops, banks and office space. The Stelco Tower (beneath it is Jackson Square) overwhelms the old Bank of Hamilton (Bank of Commerce) Building and the Pigott Building to the left in this 1977 photograph.

Appendix
Statistical Tables

TABLE I
Population Change and the Rank of Hamilton[1]
in the Canadian Urban System, 1834-1981

Year	Population	Per Cent Change	Rank
1834	1,367	—	—
1837	3,188	133.0	—
1839	2,895	-9.2	—
1841	3,414	17.9	—
1848	9,889	190.0	—
1852	14,112	42.7	—
1857	25,000	77.2	—
1861	19,096	-23.6	5
1871	26,880	40.8	6
1876	32,641	24.4	—
1881	36,661	12.3	5
1886	41,712	13.8	—
1891	48,959	17.4	4
1896	51,527	5.2	—
1901	52,634	2.1	5
1906	54,956	4.4	—
1911	81,969	53.4	6
1916	104,330	27.3	—
1921	114,151	9.4	5
1926	128,875	12.9	—
1931	155,547	20.7	5
1936	153,358	-1.4	—
1941	166,337	8.5	5
1946	175,000	5.2	—
1951	208,321	19.0	5
1956	239,625	15.0	—
1961	273,991	14.3	6
1966	298,121	8.8	—
1971	309,173	3.7	6
1976	312,003	0.9	7
1981	306,434	-1.8	—

[1]The city and not the Greater Hamilton area is covered in this table.

Sources: PAC, RG5, B26, Upper Canadian Population Returns; *Census of Canada, 1842-1971; Annual Report of the Registrar General of Ontario, 1876-1946.*

TABLE II
Life Cycle Index for the Incorporated City of Hamilton, 1851-1971[1]

Year	Index Number	Remarks
1851	.21[2]	Youthful population of immigrant centre and boom town
1861	.24	
1871	.31[3]	
1881	.33	
1891	.38	
1901	.70	Impact of declining birth rate of depression of 1890s
1911	n.a.	
1921	.73	
1931	.89	
1941	1.67	Impact of declining birth rate of Depression of 1930s
1951	1.23	
1961	.94	Impact of postwar "baby boom"
1971	1.14	

[1]Life cycle index = % of population over 45 / % of population under 15

[2]The index responds well to changes in birth rate and declines in death rate. For the early census years it indicates Hamilton's status as an immigrant centre receiving youthful arrivals.

[3]The 45-to-50 age cohort had to be estimated by arbitrarily dividing into two the 40-to-50 cohort cited in the census. The under-15 population had to be estimated from a 0-to-16 cohort.

TABLE III
Number of Adult Males
per 1,000 Adult Females, 1834-1901[1]

Year	Number of Males
1834	1,500
1837	1,600
1840	1,010
1852	870
1861	1,088
1871	926
1881	870
1891	1,040
1901	1,030

[1]Adult is defined 16 and over except for 1891 and 1901, when it is taken as 15 and over.

Sources: PAC, RG5, B26, Upper Canada Population Returns; *Census of Canada, 1852-1901.*

TABLE IV
Increases in Hamilton Dwellings and the Changes in the Number of Occupants and Level of Home Ownership, 1834–1971

Year	Number of Inhabited Dwellings	Average Number of Occupants per Dwelling Unit	Percentage of Dwellings that were Owner-occupied
1834	180	8.0	—
1836	290	11.0	—
1839	460	6.0	—
1841	545	6.3	—
1844	760	—	—
1848	1,637	6.0	—
1852	1,950	7.2	26.5
1861	3,271	5.8	25.6
1871	4,830	5.6	23.7
1881	6,800	5.4	30.5
1891	9,222	5.3	34.5
1901	10,802	4.9	33.3
1911	15,157	5.4	51.4
1921	28,984	3.9	50.4
1931	35,117	4.4	50.9
1941	39,889	4.2	48.7
1951	55,340	3.8	65.0
1961	73,829	3.7	69.3
1971	94,590	3.3	57.9
1981	113,926	2.7	—

Sources: PAC, RG5, B26, Upper Canadian Assessment Returns; *Census of Canada, 1842–1981;* Michael Doucet, "Working Class Housing in a Small Nineteenth Century Canadian City: Hamilton, Ontario, 1852–1881," *Essays in Canadian Working Class History*, ed. Gregory S. Kealey and Peter Warrian (Toronto: McClelland and Stewart, 1976), pp.83-105.

TABLE VI
Land Speculation and Development in the Greater Hamilton Region[1] Measured by Registered Surveys, 1851–1980

Years	Number of Surveys Registered[2]	Remarks
1851–55	34	Railway boom
1856–60	33	
1861–65	6	Collapse
1866–70	24	Industrial recovery
1871–75	35	
1876–80	27	
1881–85	45	Industrial growth during 1880s
1886–90	38	
1891–95	39	
1896–1900	9	Reaction to depression of early 1890s
1901–05	21	
1906–10	63	Speculative expansion of second industrial boom
1911–15	129	
1916–20	11	
1921–25	10	Overspeculation of 1911–13 created a surplus of lots
1926–30	3	
1931–35	4	
1936–40	6	Stagnation in Depression
1941–45	42	
1946–50	78	Postwar housing boom begins
1951–55	121	
1956–60	114	Recession of 1958–61
1961–65	134	
1966–70	103	Adverse industrial announcements
1971–75	132	
1976–80	132	Despite or perhaps because of inflation, suburban growth has continued

[1]All plans of surveys bordering on Hamilton were included. With a few exceptions, the Wentworth County registered plans were in or contiguous to Hamilton. Stoney Creek, Dundas and Ancaster were excluded from the tally until 1946, by which time they were being drawn into the fabric of Hamilton as suburban communities.
[2]In some cases surveys were reregistered with new plans. Since this represented a speculative or development action, these surveys were included to reflect the volume of activity or anticipated expansion.

Sources: From 1851 to 1940, there were duplicates of Wentworth County surveys in the McMaster University Map Library. The *Plan Index* at the Wentworth Courthouse was used for 1941 to 1967. In 1967 a new registration system was adopted and all of the 300 plans (1967 to 1980) were examined in the Land Records Division, Wentworth Courthouse.

TABLE V
The Labour Force of Hamilton by Occupational Category, 1851–1941[1]

	1851		1861		1871		1881		1911		1921		1931		1941	
	n	%	n	%	n	%	n	%	n	%	n	%	n	%	n	%
Agriculture	22	1.3	38	1.3	136	1.6	91	0.7	393	1.0	218	0.5	562	0.9	529	0.8
Building Trades	277	15.1	406	13.9	886	10.2	1,200	9.6	4,059	10.6	2,744	6.8	4,711	7.6	3,880	5.6
Manufacturing	477	26.0	760	25.9	2,769	31.9	4,417	35.6	18,978	49.6	19,229	47.7	18,094	29.3	26,560	38.1
Transportation	10	1.0	91	3.1	434	5.0	692	5.6	2,431	6.3	3,078	7.6	4,646	7.5	3,926	5.6
Trade and Commerce	494	26.8	718	24.5	1,496	17.3	2,334	18.8	5,494	14.3	7,637	19.0	7,784	12.6	8,045	11.5
Professional Services	80	4.3	127	4.3	397	4.6	593	4.8	1,640	4.3	1,746	4.3	4,147	6.7	4,229	6.1
Domestic and Personal Service	6	0.3	24	0.8	1,259	14.5	1,574	12.7	4,057	10.6	3,026	7.5	5,577	9.0	6,681	9.6
Government	32	1.7	89	3.0	89	1.0	184	1.5	1,252	3.3	2,605	6.6	586	1.0	789	1.1
Labour (Unspecified)	432	23.5	676	23.2	1,204	13.9	1,332	10.7	—	—	—	—	10,219	16.6	6,616	9.5
Clerical	—	—	—	—	—	—	—	—	—	—	—	—	5,462	8.8	8,448	12.1
Total	1,830	100.0	2,929	100.0	8,670	100.0	12,417	100.0	38,304	100.0	40,283	100.0	61,788	100.0	69,712	100.0

[1]Due to changing classifications of occupational groups, comparison across time periods will be imperfect.

Sources: Michael Katz, *The People of Hamilton, Canada West: Family and Class in a Mid-Nineteenth Century City* (Cambridge, Massachusetts: Harvard, 1975), p.52; *Census of Canada, 1871–1941.*

TABLE VII
Birthplace of Hamilton's Population, 1871–1911

	1871		1881		1891		1901		1911	
	n	%	n	%	n	%	n	%	n	%
CANADA:	(13,969)	(52.8)	(22,082)	(61.4)	(31,649)	(67.1)	(39,070)	(71.7)	(49,545)	(64.3)
Ontario	13,569	51.2	21,402	59.5	30,732	65.1	38,200	70.1	48,497	62.9
Other	400	1.6	680	1.9	917	2.0	870	1.6	1,048	1.4
UNITED KINGDOM:	(10,639)	(40.2)	(11,242)	(31.3)	(12,506)	(26.5)	(10,335)	(19.0)	(19,852)	(25.8)
England	4,781	18.0	5,502	15.3	6,536	13.9	5,626	10.3	13,146	17.0
Scotland	2,315	8.7	2,397	6.7	2,571	5.4	2,120	3.9	442	5.8
Ireland	3,543	13.5	3,343	9.3	3,389	7.2	3,524	4.7	2,023	2.6
Other	—	—	—	—	10	0.0	65	0.1	211	0.3
EUROPE:	(586)	(2.2)	(642)	(1.8)	(939)	(2.0)	(2,054)	(3.8)	(4,206)	(5.4)
Austria	17	0.0	—	—	—	—	—	—	253	0.3
Germany	518	2.0	557	1.5	758	1.6	—	—	629	0.8
Hungary	—	—	—	—	—	—	—	—	435	0.6
Italy	—	—	5	0.0	17	0.0	—	—	1,191	1.6
Poland and Russia	14	0.0	16	0.0	113	0.3	—	—	1,227	1.6
Rumania	—	—	—	—	—	—	—	—	—	—
Yugoslavia	—	—	—	—	—	—	—	—	—	—
Other	37	0.2	64	0.3	51	0.1	—	—	471	0.6
UNITED STATES	1,227	4.6	1,755	4.9	1,140	3.9	1,933	3.5	2,880	3.7
ASIA	—	—	—	—	7	0.0	32	0.0	362	0.5
OTHER	72	0.2	220	0.6	246	0.5	1,049	2.0	225	0.3
TOTAL	26,493	100.0	35,941	100.0	47,187	100.0	54,473	100.0	77,070	100.0

1921–1971

	1921[1]		1931		1951[2]		1961		1971	
	n	%	n	%	n	%	n	%	n	%
CANADA:	(69,805)	(61.2)	(94,580)	(60.8)	(149,609)	(71.8)	(188,253)	(68.6)	(215,810)	(69.8)
Ontario	67,241	58.9	90,855	58.3	130,937	62.9	164,764	60.0	188,505	61.0
Other	2,564	2.3	3,825	2.5	18,672	8.9	23,489	8.6	27,305	8.8
UNITED KINGDOM:	(33,044)	(28.9)	(42,947)	(27.6)	(33,233)	(16.0)	(34,901)	(12.7)	(30,230)	(9.8)
England	22,638	19.8	27,947	17.9	21,819	10.5	20,857	7.6	—	—
Scotland	7,695	6.7	12,237	7.9	9,768	4.8	11,430	4.2	—	—
Ireland	2,183	1.9	2,497	1.6	1,561	0.7	1,862	0.7	—	—
Other	528	0.5	266	0.2	85	—	752	0.3	—	—
EUROPE:	(6,544)	(5.7)	(12,985)	(8.4)	(20,823)	(10.0)	(46,045)	(16.8)	(54,565)	(17.6)
Austria	539	0.5	495	0.3	—	—	—	—	—	—
Germany	380	0.3	480	0.3	711	0.3	5,288	1.9	4,305	1.4
Hungary	102	0.1	1,626	1.0	—	—	—	—	—	—
Italy	1,885	1.7	2,433	1.6	3,813	1.8	13,307	4.8	18,995	6.1
Poland and Russia	2,317	2.0	4,487	2.9	9,146	4.5	10,029	3.7	10,190	3.3
Rumania	407	0.4	866	0.6	—	—	—	—	—	—
Yugoslavia	97	0.1	803	0.5	—	—	—	—	—	—
Other	817	0.7	1,796	1.1	7,153	3.4	17,421	6.4	21,075	6.8
UNITED STATES	3,894	3.4	3,995	2.5	3,591	1.7	3,133	1.1	3,000	1.0
ASIA	450	0.4	460	0.3	593	0.3	751	0.3	2,605	0.8
OTHER	414	0.4	580	0.4	472	0.2	908	0.4	2,970	1.0
TOTAL	114,151	100.0	155,547	100.0	208,321	100.0	273,991	100.0	309,180	100.0

[1]The changes in European boundaries from 1911 to 1921 pose an obstacle to a wholly consistent series of data, but the fact that the 1911 census divided the Austro-Hungarian empire into component parts which generally corresponded to the new national categories described in the 1921 census allows a reasonable comparison.

[2]The data for 1941 was omitted because of the low number of immigrant arrivals during the 1930s. See Table XI.

Source: *Census of Canada, 1871–1971.*

TABLE VIII
Major Religious Affiliations of Hamilton's Population, 1852–1971[1]

	1852 n	1852 %	1871 n	1871 %	1891 n	1891 %	1911 n	1911 %	1931 n	1931 %	1951 n	1951 %	1971 n	1971 %
PROTESTANT:	(9,945)	(70.5)	(20,480)	(76.6)	(36,735)	(75.0)	(59,139)	(76.7)	(114,322)	(73.4)	(140,629)	(67.5)	(152,190)	(49.2)
Anglican	4,364	30.9	7,463	27.9	11,821	24.1	21,134	27.4	45,637	29.3	52,215	25.0	52,095	16.9
Baptist	535	3.8	894	3.3	1,912	3.9	4,477	5.8	8,029	5.2	10,529	5.1	12,125	3.9
Lutheran	—	—	506	1.9	776	1.6	1,212	1.6	1,931	1.2	3,755	1.8	7,860	2.5
Presbyterian	2,668	18.9	6,014	22.5	10,189	20.8	16,369	21.2	26,647	17.1	25,791	12.4	28,325	9.2
United Church[2] (Methodist)	2,378	16.9	5,603	21.0	12,037	24.6	15,947	20.7	32,078	20.6	48,339	23.2	51,785	16.7
CATHOLIC:	(3,981)	(28.2)	(5,659)	(21.2)	(8,557)	(17.5)	(12,810)	(16.6)	(28,866)	(18.6)	(51,025)	(24.5)	(120,544)	(39.0)
Roman	3,981	28.2	5,659	21.2	8,557	17.5	12,810	16.6	28,709	18.5	47,866	23.0	112,190	36.3
Greek	—	—	—	—	—	—	—	—	157	0.1	3,159	1.5	8,354	2.7
JEWISH	4	—	131	0.5	316	0.6	1,681	2.2	2,609	1.7	3,158	1.5	3,080	1.0
OTHER	182	1.3	446	1.7	3,351	6.9	3,442	4.5	9,750	6.3	13,509	6.5	33,370	10.8
TOTAL	14,112	100.0	26,716	100.0	48,959	100.0	77,072	100.0	155,547	100.0	208,321	100.0	309,184	100.0

[1]The major shifts are illustrated as clearly and as completely by using twenty-year cross sections as by ten-year ones.
[2]This figure includes Methodists and Congregationalists from 1931 onward.

Source: *Census of Canada, 1852–1971.*

TABLE IX
Alterations in the Size of Hamilton Accomplished through Annexations, 1846–1966

Year	Acres Added	Total Acreage	Remarks
1846		3,050.0	City incorporation
1891	924.0	3,974.0	
1902	17.3	3,991.3	International Harvester
1903	694.7	4,686.0	
1908	30.0	4,716.0	
1909	1,272.0	4,988.0	East end roughly from Sherman to Ottawa
1910	89.0	6,077.0	
1912	170.0	6,247.0	
1913	14.5	6,261.5	
1914	869.0	7,130.5	Westdale
1920	767.9	7,898.4	
1921	99.4	7,997.8	
1922	7.6	8,005.4	
1924	253.8	8,259.2	
1925	86.2	8,345.4	
1928	470.5	8,815.9	
1929	878.5	9,694.4	The last additions for over a decade
1943	638.3	10,332.7	
1948	293.1	10,625.8	
1949	3,431.0	14,056.8	
1952	2,715.0	16,831.8	
1956	2,600.1	19,431.9	
1957	400.8	19,832.7	
1959	1,165.5	20,998.2	
1960	8,521.2	29,519.4	Barton and parts of Saltfleet and Ancaster
1961	2,047.2	31,566.6	
1962	158.1	31,724.7	
1965	-127.0	31,597.7	Annexed by Burlington
1966	3,244.9	34,842.6	Burlington Bay

Source: Hamilton, *Report of City Assessor's Department, 1968.*

TABLE X
Immigrant Population of Hamilton in 1931 by Period of Immigration

Year	Number	Per cent
Before 1901	4,210	6.9
1901–10	13,954	22.9
1911–15	14,020	23.0
1916–20	6,032	9.9
1921–25	9,295	15.3
1926–30	13,456	22.0
Total	60,967	100.0

Source: *Census of Canada, 1931.*

TABLE XI
Immigrant Population of Hamilton in 1961 by Period of Immigration

Year	Number	Per cent
Before 1921	18,538	21.6
1921–30	13,612	15.9
1931–40	2,422	2.8
1941–50	11,770	13.7
1951–61	39,396	46.0
Total	85,738	100.0

Source: *Census of Canada, 1961.*

TABLE XII
Value of Building Permits Issued in Hamilton,[1] 1897–1976
1897–1942

Year	Value of Permits ($1,000)	Value per Resident ($)	Remarks
1897	363	7	
1898	427	8	
1900	335	6	
1901	308	6	
1902	597	11	Expansion of second industrial revolution begins
1903	786	14	
1904	946	20	
1905	1,511	28	
1906	2,124	39	
1907	3,030	52	
1908	1,331	22	Brief recession
1909	1,547	26	
1910	2,546	32	
1912	4,173	50	
1913	5,110	51	
1914	3,704	37	Depression of 1913–15
1915	1,522	15	Depression of 1913–15
1916	2,410	24	
1917	2,747	26	
1918	2,472	23	
1919	5,087	47	Postwar factory expansions
1920	4,340	38	
1921	4,639	41	
1922	4,928	41	
1923	5,452	45	Peak for apartment construction
1924	3,310	27	
1925	2,676	22	
1921	3,129	24	
1927	3,837	30	
1928	6,342	50	Residential construction boom
1924	7,008	52	
1930	6,291	44	
1931	5,026	32	Construction slump begins
1932	1,424	9	
1933	510	3	
1934	772	5	
1935	1,888	12	Minor recovery begins
1936	1,467	10	
1937	1,694	11	
1938	2,326	15	
1939	2,265	15	
1940	5,562	36	
1941	4,980	30	
1942	3,304	20	Wartime controls and shortages begin

TABLE XII (continued)
1943–1976

Year	Value of Permits ($1,000)	Value per Resident ($)	Remarks
1943	2,217	13	
1944	3,289	19	
1945	5,558	32	
1946	6,468	37	
1947	7,946	44	
1948	17,696	97	
1949	18,442	96	Base year for price-and-wage index (1949=100)
1950	18,255	93	
1951	24,934	120	
1952	24,227	116	
1953	31,056	143	
1954	32,743	148	
1955	32,892	147	
1956	35,675	149	
1957	39,385	160	
1958	43,440	180	
1959	46,682	188	
1960	53,335	210	
1961	34,500	126	Recession
1962	42,781	160	Building materials index =200; building wages =130
1963	50,951	188	
1964	54,861	200	Office-tower and apartment construction
1965	61,969	221	
1966	58,271	195	
1967	56,638	183	
1968	60,462	196	
1969	76,355	246	
1970	70,379	224	
1971	69,103	224	
1972	84,453	271	Urban renewal construction begins
1973	83,306	266	
1974	123,637	398	
1975	148,186	476	
1976	104,591	336	

[1]The rises in the wage-and-price indices in the postwar years along with the impossibility of determining the relative contribution of each to construction costs prevent an accurate comparison of the value of building permits across time. Abrupt shifts are more readily interpreted.

Sources: *Reports of the Building Inspector, City Council Minutes, 1897–1913; Canada Yearbook, 1914–1978.*

TABLE XIII
Noncommercial Passenger-vehicle Registration Statistics for Hamilton, 1919–1968
1919–1941

Year	Number of Vehicles	Number of City Residents per Vehicle
1919	4,948	21.8
1920	6,662	17.2
1921	n.a.	n.a.
1922	n.a.	n.a.
1923	9,627	12.7
1924	10,790	11.5
1925	11,524	10.7
1926	13,608	9.5
1927	n.a.	n.a.
1928	17,057	7.5
1929	19,653	6.8
1930	20,562	7.0
1931	20,846	7.5
1932	20,080	7.6
1933	19,319	8.0
1934	n.a.	n.a.
1935	21,066	7.3
1936	21,208	7.2
1937	23,264	6.6
1938	24,504	6.3
1939	24,825	6.2
1940	25,902	6.0
1941	28,183	5.9

TABLE XIII (continued)
1942–1968

Year	Number of Vehicles	Number of City Residents per Vehicle
1942–1948	n.a.	n.a.
1949	32,929	5.8
1950	39,016	5.0
1951	42,528	4.8
1952	47,004	4.5
1953	51,501	4.2
1954	54,898	4.0
1955	58,473	3.9
1956	61,213	3.9
1957	n.a.	n.a.
1958	64,037	3.8
1959	67,028	3.8
1960	69,633	3.7
1961	72,037	3.7
1962	71,616	3.7
1963	73,807	3.7
1964	77,379	3.6
1965	n.a.	n.a.
1966	n.a.	n.a.
1967	88,783	3.4
1968	96,706	3.1

Sources: *Reports of the Ontario Department of Highways, 1919–1956; Reports of the Ontario Ministry of Transportation and Communications, 1958–1968.* The ministry ceased publication of local data after 1968.

TABLE XIV
Population of the Greater Hamilton Area and of its Constituent Municipalities, 1901–1966

	Municipality	1901	1911	1921	1931	1941	1951	1956	1961	1966
CITY:	Hamilton	56,254	86,479	124,316	158,842	172,898	219,630[2]	247,989[2]	273,991[2]	298,121[c]
TOWNS:	Dundas	3,173	4,299	4,978	5,026	5,276	6,846	9,507[3]	12,912[3]	15,501
	Stoney Creek	—	—	—	877	1,007	1,922	4,506[4]	6,043	7,243
	Total-Towns	3,173	4,299	4,978	5,903	6,283	8,768	14,013	18,955	22,744
VILLAGE:	Waterdown	622	756	754	921	910	1,347	1,754	1,844	1,935
TOWNSHIPS:	Ancaster	3,863	4,136	5,586	4,596	5,259	7,648[2]	11,304[2 3]	13,338[2 3]	14,960
	Beverly	3,999	3,629	3,516	3,514	3,428	4,138	4,559	5,023	5,520
	Binbrook	1,403	1,254	1,260	1,175	1,186	1,384	1,865	2,557	3,131
	E. Flam.	2,522	2,646	3,008	3,686	4,034	7,045	11,895	4,334[5]	5,089
	W. Flam.	2,822	2,736	2,840	2,809	2,869	4,229	5,753[3]	7,001[3]	7,928
	Glanford	1,585	1,413	1,409	1,356	1,641	2,444	4,039	4,714[2]	5,763
	Saltfleet	3,209	4,458	5,900	7,217	8,213	9,450[2]	13,067[2 4]	16,424[2]	17,984
	Total-Townships	19,403	20,272	23,519	24,353	26,630	36,338	52,482	53,391	60,375
TOWN:	Burlington	3,895	4,741	6,065	6,828	7,984	14,210	22,056	47,008[2 5]	65,941[c]
TOTAL: GREATER HAMILTON AREA		83,347	116,447	159,631	196,847	214,705	280,293	338,294	395,189	449,116

The geographic boundaries of the Greater Hamilton area are consistent throughout. The boundaries of most of the constituent municipalities, however, have undergone varying degrees of alteration from time to time. These changes are given in the footnotes below:

[1] Including Barton Township.

[2] Annexations to the City of Hamilton: Parts of Ancaster Township 1947; 1952; 1960. Parts of Barton Township 1947; 1949; 1952; remainder 1960. Parts of Saltfleet Township 1943; 1949; Feb. 15, 1956; 1959; 1960. Part of Glanford Township 1960. Burlington Beach Commission and parts of Nelson Township and Burlington Town (Halton County) 1957.

[3] Annexations to the Town of Dundas: Parts of Ancaster Township 1952; 1954; 1960. Parts of West Flamborough Township July 1, 1951; 1953; 1955; 1960.

[4] Annexations to the Town of Stoney Creek: Part of Saltfleet Township 1953.

[5] Including Nelson Township.

[c] Annexations to the Town of Burlington: Parts of Nelson Township 1944; 1947; 1950; Dec. 1, 1951; 1953; remainder 1958. Part of East Flamborough Township 1958. Part of the City of Hamilton 1965 (less than 500 residents involved in the reallocation).

Source: *Census of Canada, 1901–1966.*

Notes

Abbreviations

HPL   Hamilton Public Library
MLSC Mills Library, Special Collections, McMaster University
MTPL Metropolitan Toronto Public Library, Baldwin Room
NA   National Archives, Washington, D.C.
OSP   *Ontario Sessional Papers*
PAC   Public Archives of Canada
PAO   Public Archives of Ontario
SPC   *Sessional Papers of Canada*
UDC   Urban Documentation Centre, McMaster University

INTRODUCTION

[1]William Noble, "The Neutral Indians," *Essays in Northeastern Anthropology in Memory Marian E. White*, ed. William M. Engelbrecht and David K. Grayson (Rindge, New Hampshire: Occasional Papers in Northeastern Anthropology No. 5).

[2]Herbert Fairlie Wood, "The Many Battles of Stoney Creek," *The Defended Border: Upper Canada and the War of 1812*, ed. Morris Zaslow (Toronto: MacMillan, 1964), p. 58; Ernest A. Cruikshank, *The Documentary History of the Campaign upon the Niagara Frontier*, (The Lundy's Lane Historical Society, n.d.), vol. 6, pp. 7-16.

[3]Frank L. Jones, "The Burlington Races," *Wentworth Bygones*, vol. 5 (1964), pp. 18-22.

[4]Peter Baskerville, "Allan MacNab," *Dictionary of Canadian Biography*, vol. 9.

[5]For a biographical sketch of Markle see PAC, MG24, B69. References to his defection appear in RG5, A1, vol. 16, Richard Hatt to Captain Loring, 22 June 1814; RG5, A1, vol. 28, Samuel Andruss (?) and Samuel Tisdale, 2 June 1816. William Renwick Riddell, "The Ancaster 'Bloody Assize' of 1814," *The Defended Border*, pp. 241-50.

[6]John C. Weaver, "James Durand's Eventful Careers, 1802-1834: An Adventurous Englishman on the Upper Canada Frontier," *Wentworth Bygones*, vol. 13 (1981), pp. 42-9.

[7]Extract from the appeal to the electors of Wentworth published in the *Spectator*, 4 February 1817, and printed in the Journal of the House of Assembly of Upper Canada, 1 March 1817, *Ninth Report of the Bureau of Archives for the Province of Ontario, 1912* (Toronto: King's Printer, 1913), p. 340.

CHAPTER ONE

[1]Douglas McCalla, "The Wheat Staple and Upper Canadian Development," *Historical Papers, Canadian Historical Association, 1978*, p. 34.

[2]For Robert Hamilton's business see Bruce Gordon Wilson, "The Enterprises of Robert Hamilton: A Study of Wealth and Influence in Early Upper Canada: 1776-1812" (University of Toronto, Ph.D. dissertation, 1978).

[3]PAC, RG5, A1, vol. 41, George Hamilton to Civil Secretary, 11 December 1818; 14 July 1820.

[4]Some early land transactions appear among the first 250 memorials recorded in the Gore District Land Registry Records microfilmed by the Genealogical Society of the Church of Jesus Christ of the Latter Day Saints. See PAO, G.S. microfilm 1411. The initial townsite promotion by James Durand and Nathaniel Hughson is discussed in Marjorie Freeman Campbell, *A Mountain and a City: The Story of Hamilton* (Toronto: McClelland and Stewart, 1966), p. 52. For Durand's instructions see PAO, RG1, A-1-6, Nathaniel Hughson to James Durand, 14 February 1816.

[5]Unrecorded sales appear in PAO, Askin Papers, Deed for Lot 14 in Town of Hamilton; HPL, Robert Jarvis Hamilton Papers; *Hamilton Spectator*, Carnival Edition, 1903.

[6]HPL, William Hardy Papers, two letters, n.d.; Peter Baskerville, "Sir Allan Napier MacNab," *Dictionary of Canadian Biography*, vol. 9.

[7]Ernest Cruikshank, "The Government of Upper Canada and Robert

Gourlay," *Ontario Historical Society, Papers and Records*, vol. 23 (1920), pp. 75-132; Charles Durand, *Reminiscences of Charles Durand of Toronto, Barrister* (Toronto: Hunter, Rose, 1987), pp. 105-109. The demise of Beasley is evident in PAO, Abraham Nelles Papers, Militia Correspondence, James Fitzgibbon, Acting Deputy Judge Advocate, to Major Abraham Nelles, 15 January 1820. Also see PAO, William Lyon Mackenzie Papers, George Tiffany to Mackenzie, 6 January 1825.

8MTPL, W.W. Baldwin Papers, Desjardins Canal file.

9The volume of traffic on the canal is found in PAC, RG11, vol. 59, Imports and Exports by the Desjardins Canal from . . . 16 August 1837 to . . . 23 November 1844.

10Edward Talbot, *Five Years Residence in the Canadas*, (London: Longman, 1824), Vol. I, p. 120.

11Charles Durand, *Reminiscences*, p. 207.

12PAO, Gilkison Papers, William Gilkison to Jasper Gilkison, 15 December 1832.

13*Christian Guardian*, 7 November 1832.

14Concerning peddlers see PAC, RG5, B9, vols. 50-2, Bonds of Pedlars and Hawkers. Smuggling is mentioned in RG5, A1, vol. 27, William Crooks to William Halton, 14 May 1816; RG1, E3, vol. 12, John Chisholm, Collector of Customs, n.d. [1824].

15PAC, RG11, A1, vol. I, William J. Kerr to the Board of Works, 28 November 1842; RG1, L3, vol. 226, Richard Hatt to the Lieutenant Governor in Council, 31 January 1809; RG5, A1, vol. 85, An Account of Produce Shipped and Merchandize Received from the First Day of April till the Fourth Day of December 1826 by A.J. Kerby and James Davy Forwarding at Burlington Outlet.

16PAC, RG5, A1, vol. 75, James Crooks and William Chisholm to Major Hillier, 12 December 1823.

17PAC, RG5, A1, vol. 71, Report of Canal Commissioners, 7 May 1825; Report Relative to the Works at Burlington Beach for September 1825; vol. 76, Francis Hall, Engineer, to Commissioners for Making a Canal and Piers at Burlington Beach, 1 January 1826; Francis Hall, Engineer, . . . 20 February 1826; vol. 85, Report of the Canal Commissioner, 29 September 1827; vol. 89, William J. Kerr to Arbitrators, 7 May 1828.

18*Western Mercury*, 13 October 1831; 21 July 1832; 11 April 1833; 18 July 1833; 19 September 1833; *Christian Guardian*, 7 August 1833; Patrick Sherriff, *A Tour Through North America* (Reprint of 1835 edition, New York: Blom, 1971), p. 148; Edwin C. Guillet, *Pioneer Travel in Upper Canada* (Toronto: University of Toronto Press, 1963), p. 90.

19Andrew Picken, *The Canadas: As They at Present Commend Themselves to the Enterprise of Emigrants, Colonists, and Capitalists* (London: Wilson, 1832), p. 254. For land-clearing practices and wages see *Western Mercury*, 17 November 1831. There are reports on wages paid on public-works projects in PAC, RG19, B2(a), vol. 1135; RG5, B21, vol. 1, Answers for the Information of Emigrants with Capital Willing to Settle on Land [1840]; vol. 3, Information for Immigrants [1843]. On merchants and settlement frontiers see PAO, Gilkison Papers, Jasper to William, 10 December 1832.

20PAC, MG24, D16, Isaac Buchanan Papers, vol. 3, James Bickel to Isaac Buchanan, 11 June 1835; vol. 63, Buchanan to ———, 22 October 1840; Buchanan to Peter Buchanan, 20 October 1840; 4 November 1840. "Colin Ferrie," *Dictionary of Hamilton Biography*, ed. Melville Bailey et al. (Hamilton, 1981), vol. 1.

21PAO, RG22, Gore District Court Records, files 1835-1837, Colin Ferrie vs. John Vollick, 27 April 1835; Gore District Gaol Records, 1832-1839.

22PAO, William Lyon Mackenzie Papers, J.M.A. Cameron to Mackenzie, 23 September 1830.

23 PAO, RG22, Gore District Court Records, Notebook for 1845-46, p. 56.

24HPL, Ferrie Papers, Adam Ferrie to Robert Ferrie, 13 August 1838.

25Queen's University, Douglas Library, Special Collections, Cartwright Family Papers, Allan MacNab to John Solomon Cartwright, 6 June 1832.

26PAO, Samuel Street Papers, Statement of the Real and Personal Estate and its Value Belonging to Peter Hunter Hamilton, 18 June 1835; Allan MacNab to Street, 23 December 1835.

27PAO, MacNab Papers, William Notman to Sir Allan MacNab, 7 May 1838.

28Edwin Guillet, *Pioneer Travel*, pp. 90-1; PAO, Gilkison Papers, Jasper to William, 18 August 1832; 1 January 1833; PAC, MG24, D16, vol. 64, Isaac Buchanan to Peter Buchanan, 25 June 1840; MLSC, Hamilton Police Village Minutes, 11 November 1844; 24 October 1846.

29Guillet, *Pioneer Travel*, pp. 184-9; Talbot, *Five Years Residence*, p. 126; MLSC, Hamilton Police Village Minutes, 26 February 1843.

30John Weaver, "The Iron Trades in Hamilton: A Study of Industrial Location, 1830–1890" (Paper given at the 2nd Conference, Canadian Science and Technology Historical Association, November, 1981).

31R.S. Longley, "Emigration and the Crisis of 1837 in Upper Canada," *Canadian Historical Review*, vol. 17 (March, 1936), pp. 29-40.

32PAC, RG5, C1, vol. 2, Petition from Gore District, 30 January 1837; RG5, B3, vol. 9, Petition of the Inhabitants of the Town of Hamilton . . . Respecting the Exportation of Bread Stuffs 1837; *Hamilton Gazette*, 10 June 1839; PAC, RG5, A1, vol. 226, William J. Kerr to ———, 15 August 1839; "Colin Ferrie," *Dictionary of Hamilton Biography*, vol. 1.

33PAC, RG5, B26, vol. 3, p. 597; PAO, RG20, Gore District Gaol Records, 1832-1851.

34William Cattermole, *Emigration: The Advantages of Emigration to Canada* (London: Simpkin and Marshall, 1831); *Western Mercury*, 3 July 1834; PAC, RG5, A1, vol. 99, Cattermole to Lieutenant-Governor Colborne, 23 April 1834; vol. 106, form for employers of immigrants dated November,

1839; vol. 235, Cattermole to Sir George Arthur, 30 December 1839.

[35]Charlotte Erickson, *Invisible Immigrants: The Adaptation of English and Scottish Immigrants in Nineteenth-Century America* (London: Weidenfeld and Nicolson, 1972), pp. 279-82.

[36]PAC, RG5, A1, vol. 250, Cartwright-Thomas, editor of *Hamilton Journal*, to Sir George Arthur, 16 December 1840.

[37]*Western Mercury*, 11 August 1831.

[38]PAC, RG5, B26, vol. 3-5, Gore District Population and Assessment Returns; MLSC, Hamilton Police Village Minutes, 1834 and 1835; *Western Mercury*, 16 May 1833; 30 May 1833; 16 June 1833.

[39]*Western Mercury*, 28 April 1834.

[40]Ibid., 11 April 1833 and 7 July 1831.

[41]See *Western Mercury* for July and August, 1832; PAO, Gilkison Papers, Jasper to William, 18 August 1832; PAC, RG1, E3, vol. 16, Report of William Chisholm to Peter Robinson on the state of emigrants, 11 March 1833. On the 1834 epidemic and the concern about allowing indigents into town see RG5, A1, vol. 144, John Law to Colonel Rowan, 5 August 1834.

[42]PAO, McQuesten Papers, Catherine W. Fisher to Calvin McQuesten, 29 November 1838.

[43]Report of A.C. Buchanan, Emigration Agent, "Annual Report on Emigration to the Canadas ... 1838," *British Sessional Papers*, vol. 39 (Readex microprint 1961); George Arthur, *The Arthur Papers*, ed. Charles R. Sanderson (Toronto: University of Toronto Press, 1959), vol. 3, p. 102.

[44]PAC, RG5, C1, vol. 3, Allan MacNab to Civil Secretary, 11 March 1837; *Arthur Papers*, vol. 2, p. 119; PAC, RG5, A1, vol. 235, Cattermole to Sir George Arthur, 30 December 1839.

[45]*Hamilton Gazette*, 7 December 1840; PAC, RG5, B26, vols. 3-5.

[46]*Western Mercury*, 6 October 1831.

[47]PAO, Gilkison Papers, Jasper to William, 18 August 1832; PAC, MG24, D16, Isaac Buchanan to Peter Buchanan, 25 June 1840; Edward Allen Talbot, *Five Years Residence*, vol. 2, p. 264; Patrick Sherriff, *A Tour Through North America*, p. 148.

[48]*Western Mercury*, 7 June 1832.

[49]Durand, *Reminiscences*, pp. 217-19. Also see *Western Mercury*, 14 February 1833; 21 February 1833; 21 March 1833.

[50]Durand, *Reminiscences*, p. 219; *Western Mercury*, 2 February 1832; 1 November 1832. Fire and destitution were frequent concerns of the village as indicated by the Police Village Minutes. PAO, Diaries Collection, Diary of Major Glegg, n.p.

[51]PAO, Samuel Street Papers, Statement of Real and Personal Estate ... June 18, 1835; RG1, A-1-6, vol. 10, Thomas Taylor to Peter Robinson, 28 June 1831.

[52]PAO, Macaulay Papers, John Macaulay to Ann Macaulay, 22 March 1837.

[53]PAO, Samuel Street Papers, Burley to Samuel Street, 3 November 1836.

[54]MLSC, Maps of Hamilton, Accession numbers 7453, 7537, 7677; *Western Mercury*, 26 June 1834. There are scattered references to drainage in Corktown in MLSC, Hamilton Police Village Minutes, 1833-1846. Concerning attitudes about elevation, drainage and health see James Dixon, *Personal Narrative of a Tour through a Part of the United States and Canada* (New York: Land and Scott, 1849), p. 128.

[55]PAO, Diaries Collection, Diary of Major Glegg, n.p.

[56]C. Vance, "Early Trade Unionism in Canada, 1833-1834: The Carpenters' and Joiners' General Strike in Montreal," *The Marxist Quarterly* (Summer, 1962), pp. 28-30; *Western Mercury*, 2 February 1832; MLSC, Hamilton Police Village Minutes, 16 March 1835; 20 July 1836; 8 July 1839. On violence see PAC, RG5, A1, vol. 170, John Macaulay to Colonel Rowan, 4 August 1834.

[57]Erickson, *Invisible Immigrants*, p. 288.

[58]Ibid., p. 287.

[59]Ibid., p. 286.

[60]PAO, Diaries Collection, Unidentified, Tour through Upper Canada 1837, p. 8; HPL, Adam Hope Papers, Adam Hope to his father, 1 March 1837.

[61]PAC, RG4, B26, vols. 3-5, Gore District Assessment and Population Returns. For the increase in shops and warehouses see PAC, RG5, B26, Gore District Assessment and Population Returns, vols. 5-7.

[62]MLSC, Hamilton Police Village Minutes, 1 September 1835; 19 December 1836; 18 May 1840; 5 October 1840; 6 October 1840; 17 April 1843; 22 June 1843. For the expulsion of prostitutes see 10 April 1843.

[63]Ibid, 8 July 1844.

[64]"Edwin Furman," *Dictionary of Hamilton Biography*; John Weaver, "Unlawful Acts in Upper Canada: The Case of the Gore District, 1816–1851" (Paper presented at the Conference of the Canadian Historical Association, 1981).

[65]MLSC, Hamilton Police Village Minutes, 27 July 1837; 24 August 1843.

[66]Durand, *Reminiscences*, passim; MLSC, Katrina Lamont, "Recreation and Leisure Activity in Hamilton, 1830–1860"; PAO, RG1, A-1-6, Hamilton to Peter Robinson, 2 February 1834.

[67]PAC, RG1, E3, vol. 36, Nehemiah Ford to Sir George Arthur, n.d. [1839]; MLSC, Hamilton Police Village Minutes, 22 March 1842.

[68]Travelling circuses and entertainers had to apply for licences to work in Hamilton. Such applications were discussed often in the town council. Durand, *Reminiscences*, pp. 284-5. Lotteries were common advertising features in the *Gore Gazette*, *Western Mercury*, and *Hamilton Gazette*. Concerning Miller's lottery see *Western Mercury*, 28 February 1833.

[69]Durand, *Reminiscences*, p. 265; *Christian Guardian*, 28 March 1832; 10

October 1832; Dundas Museum, James Lesslie Diary, 21 March 1832; C.A. Hagerman to Sir George Arthur, 9 July 1838; *Arthur Papers*, vol. 1, p. 229.

[70]Durand, *Reminiscences*, p. 452.

[71]PAO, McQuesten Papers, John Fisher to Calvin McQuesten, 29 May 1838.

[72]HPL, Adam Hope Papers, Adam Hope to his father, 24 December 1837.

[73]PAO, MacNab Papers, Pay of the Warriors of the Six Nations Indians of Upper Canada under the Command of Colonel, The Honourable A.N. MacNab.

[74]3 William 4 c. 16.

[75]MLSC, Typescript of Hamilton Police Village Minutes, 4 March 1835; 11 May 1835; 9 and 10 March 1836; 26 August 1836.

[76]MLSC, Typescript of Hamilton Police Village Minutes, 9 April 1838.

CHAPTER TWO

[1]*Hamilton Gazette*, 23 March 1840.

[2]Thomas F. McIlwraith, "The Logistical Geography of the Great Lakes Grain Trade, 1820-1850" (University of Wisconsin, Ph.D. dissertation, 1973), pp. 101-107, 334-5; PAC, RG16, A1, vol. 108, Port of Hamilton, Statement on the Number of Steamers . . . for the year 1847; RG16, A2, vol. 498, Port of Hamilton, Returns of the Quantity and Denomination of all Goods for 1843 and 1844.

[3]PAC, RG16, A1, vol. 108; Guillet, *Pioneer Travel*, pp. 90-1, 107-110.

[4]HPL, John Young Papers, James McIntyre to John Young, 15 April 1861.

[5]Report of the Board of Works, Appendix Q, *SPC 1843*; PAC, RG11, A1, vol. 4, Reports to Board of Works, 20 June 1844 to 15 November 1844. On Bethune's complaints see RG11, A2, vol. 94, Donald Bethune to Board of Works, 24 June 1843; 1 April 1845; RG11, A1, vol. 5, Bethune to Board of Works, 29 April 1845.

[6]On Robert Stinson's bank see "Robert Stinson," *Dictionary of Hamilton Biography*. For Robert J. Hamilton's activity see HPL, Miles O'Reilly to Robert J. Hamilton, 8 October 1864.

[7]PAC, RG19, B2(a), vol. 1138, A. Steven, Cashier, to Receiver General, 6 October 1836; vol. 1141, Colin Ferrie to J.H. Dunn, 12 November 1841; A. Steven to J.H. Dunn, 26 August 1843; vol. 1144, A. Steven to Receiver General, 11 May 1844.

[8]*Since 1847: The Canada Life Story* (Toronto, n.d.), pp. 5-22.

[9]HPL, Keefer Pamphlet Collection, vol. 7, *Report of the Engineer upon the Preliminary Surveys for the London and Gore Rail Road* (Toronto, 1836); PAC, RG1, E3, vol. 39, Report of the Executive Council of Upper Canada, 19 October 1837; RG5, C1, vol. 214, Board of Directors of the Great Western Railway to Civil Secretary, 3 December 1847.

[10]PAC, MG24, D16, vol. 64, Isaac Buchanan to Peter Buchanan, 4 February 1841.

[11]Peter A. Baskerville, "The Boardroom and Beyond: Aspects of the Upper Canadian Railroad Community" (Queen's University, Ph.D. dissertation, 1973), pp. 21-130, 306-7.

[12]PAC, MG24, D16, vol. 46, W. O'Brien, Secretary of the Corresponding Committee of the Great Western Railroad, London, to Sir Allan MacNab, 29 November 1845 (copy).

[13]PAC, RG5, C1, vol. 214, Board of Directors to Civil Secretary, 3 December 1847; vol. 222, Petition of Board of Directors, 13 March 1848.

[14]PAC, MG24, D16, vol. 46, MacNab to Isaac Buchanan, 29 July 1848; PAO, Gilkison Papers, Address of the Directors of the Great Western Rail Road Company . . . at a Public Meeting of the Inhabitants of Hamilton on the 22nd April, 1850.

[15]PAC, MG24, D16, vol. 94. Clipping from *Journal and Express*, 17 August 1849; PAO, Gilkison Papers, Draft of letter by Gilkison to various gentlemen, 12 March 1850.

[16]*Journal and Express*, 17 August 1849.

[17]MLSC, Minutes of Hamilton City Council, 20 August 1849; Report of Committee on Finance, 8 August 1849. For the quotation see Hamilton City Council, Report of Committee on Finance, 8 August 1849.

[18]PAC, RG16, A1, vol. 110, item 889, Moore, McElroy and Pierson to Francis Hincks, 16 April 1851; vol. 111, item 651, Sam Farwell to Francis Hincks, 24 March 1851; item 1142, file on exempted materials for GWR. See also PAC, RG30, vol. 93, GWR Construction Ledger, 1851-54; MG24, D16, vol. 94, pp. 65441-67, Report on Engineering Department [1852].

[19]Craill Papers, provenance of T. Melville Bailey, Peter Craill to his brother, 23 October 1852.

[20]*Christian Guardian*, 12 October 1853; PAC, MG24, D80, John Young Papers, vol. I, Memorandum on Contract for Rolling Stock, 20 April 1850; RG16, A1, vol. 110, item 2112, Petition of Benjamin F. Smith, 6 August 1851. Concerning the patents see Canada, *List of Canadian Patents . . . June 1824 to 31st of August 1872* (Ottawa, 1882).

[21]Ernie Main, "Grandpa Main," provenance of Mrs. Mary J. Graves, now deposited with MLSC.

[22]Isabella Lucy Bird, *The Englishwoman in America* (Madison: University of Wisconsin Press, 1966), p. 191.

[23]PAO, Merritt Papers, Package 35, Suspension Bridge, Meeting of Board, 31 March 1847; W.O. Buchanan to W.H. Merritt, 18 January 1849; Statements on tolls, various reports from 1848 to 1859.

[24]Report of A.C. Buchanan, Chief Agent for the Superintendent of Emigration to Canada, Appendix D.D.D., *SPC 1854-5*; Sessional Paper

44, *SPC 1856*; Sessional Paper 41, *SPC 1858*; PAC, RG16, A1, vol. 114, C. Brydges to Commissioners of Customs, 27 May 1857; NA, Consul General Reports, microfilm T222, American Consul General at Montreal to Secretary of State, 5 July 1862. On immigrant cars see PAC, MG28, D80, John Young Papers, vol. I, Memorandum on Contract for Rolling Stock. For accidents see HPL, Keefer Pamphlet Collection, vol. 4, *Great Western Railway of Canada, Special Report of the Board of Directors to the English Shareholders* (Hamilton: Spectator, 1853), pp. 11-14; H.B. Willson, *The Great Western Railway of Canada* (London, 1854); *Reports of the Commissioners Appointed to Inquire into a Series of Accidents and Detensions on the Great Western Railway* (Quebec, 1855); PAC, MG24, D16, vol. 2, Brackstone Baker to Isaac Buchanan, 18 June 1856; 24 June 1856; 1 July 1856. On hinterland opposition to GWR see Walter Neutel, "From 'Southern' Concept to Canada Southern Railway, 1835-1873" (University of Western Ontario, M.A. thesis, 1968), pp. 25-28.

[25]PAC, MG24, D16, vol. 94, pp. 65441-67, Report on Engineering Department [1852]; MG24, D80, vol. 1, Allan MacNab to John Young, 5 December 1851; MG24, D16, vol. 2, Brackstone Baker to Peter Buchanan, 26 January 1857; Baskerville, "The Boardroom and Beyond," pp. 84-121.

[26]PAC, MG24, D16, vol. 94, To the Shareholders in Great Britain of the Great Western Railway of Canada, 14 August 1856; John H. Greer to Buchanan, 15 September 1856; vol. 63, Marcus Smith to Thomas Ridout, 15 June 1857; vol. 22, James Cummings, Mayor of Hamilton, to Buchanan, 28 August 1856.

[27]PAC, MG24, D16, vol. 21, Isaac Buchanan to James Comrie, 8 March 1862; PAO, Gilkison Papers, Jasper Gilkison to James Cummings, Mayor of Hamilton, 29 December 1856; 2 January 1857.

[28]PAC, MG24, D16, vol. 113, To the Holders of the Debentures of the City of Hamilton, 15 January 1862; James McIntyre quoted in MLSC, Perry J. Poirier, "A City in Crisis: Hamilton, 1857-1863," p. 6; MG24, D16, vol. 21, Buchanan to Comrie, 8 March 1862.

[29]PAC, RG17, AIII, vol. 2393, Petition of William Fruehauf, German Agent at Hamilton, 20 September 1861; Poirier, "A City in Crisis," pp. 20-1; quoted p. 20.

[30]PAC, MG27, I, D8, Alexander T. Galt Papers, A.T. Galt to Baring Brothers, 14 June 1861; MG24, D16, vol. 113, To the Holders of the Debentures of the City of Hamilton, 15 January 1862.

[31]There are many accounts of this affair, but the best appears in "Grant vs. Hamilton," *Upper Canada Law Journal 1866*.

[32]"William E. Sanford," *Dictionary of Hamilton Biography*.

[33]Report on the Immigration into Canada for the Year 1864, Sessional Paper 32, *SPC 1864*; Sessional Paper 6, *SPC 1865*.

[34]J.A. Bryce, "Patterns of Profit and Power: Business, Community and Industrialization in a Nineteenth Century City," Working Paper 28, *York Social History Project, Third Report*, February, 1978, Project Director, Michael Katz, p. 369.

[35]Quoted in ibid., p. 371.

[36]See the business and real-estate advertisements in the *Journal and Express*. Scattered issues are held by the National Library and HPL.

[37]PAC, RG5, C1, vol. 234, A.B. Hawke to Provincial Secretary, 8 September 1848. Also see vol. 235, Hawke to Provincial Secretary, 7 October 1848.

[38]MLSC, Typescript Minutes of Hamilton City Council, 3 May 1847 to 22 May 1848.

[39]PAC, RG5, C1, vol. 235, A.B. Hawke to Provincial Secretary, 7 October 1848.

[40]PAC, RG5, C1, vol. 208, Extract of a Report of a Committee of the Executive Council of Canada, 24 August 1847.

[41]MLSC, Typescript Minutes of Hamilton City Council, Report of the Police Committee, 7 February 1848.

[42]Ibid., Report of the Police Committee on Paupers, 22 May 1848.

[43]PAC, RG5, C1, vol. 225, George S. Tiffany to Civil Secretary, 8 June 1848; vol. 221, Hamilton Emigrant Hospital Report for the Week Ending 22 July 1848; MLSC, Minutes of Hamilton City Council, 16 July 1849 to 20 August 1849.

[44]PAC, MG24, D16, vol. 28, John H. Greer to Isaac Buchanan, 3 September 1856; MLSC, Bob Mahler, "German Immigration: Hamilton 1850s-1860s"; *Christian Guardian*, 29 May 1861.

[45]*Census of Canada 1871*, vol. 4, summary tables of 1848 census, tables 1 and 5. Michael Doucet, "Working Class Housing in a Small Nineteenth Century Canadian City: Hamilton, Ontario, 1852-1881," *Essays in Canadian Working Class History*, ed. Gregory S. Kealey and Peter Warrian (Toronto: McClelland and Stewart, 1976), p. 90.

[46]*Journal of Commerce*, 12 May 1857. Michael Katz, *The People of Hamilton, Canada West: Family and Class in a Mid-Nineteenth Century City* (Cambridge, Massachusetts: Harvard University Press, 1975), passim.

[47]MLSC, Hamilton Council Minutes, 8 March 1847; 16 July 1849.

[48]McMaster University, Department of Geography, Map Library, Marcus Smith, Map of the City of Hamilton, 1850-51. Charles MacKay, *Life and Liberty*, quoted in Gerald Craig, ed., *Early Travellers in the Canadas, 1791-1867* (Toronto: Macmillan, 1955), p. 228; James Dixon, *Personal Narrative*, p. 128; A. Lillie, *Canada: Physical, Economic and Social* (Toronto: Maclear and Co., 1855), p. 162.

[49]MLSC, Typescript of Hamilton Council Minutes, 28 January 1847; 8 February 1847; 8 March 1847; 12 April 1847; 12 June 1848.

[50]Ian Davey and Michael Doucet, "The Social Geography of a Commercial City, ca. 1853," *The People of Hamilton, Canada West*, p. 331.

[51]Typescript of Hamilton Council Minutes, 9 August 1847. Alexander G. McKay, *Victorian Architecture in Hamilton* (The Architectural Conser-

vancy of Ontario, 1967), p. 8; PAC, MG24, D16, vol. 48, Samuel Mills to Isaac Buchanan, 3 November 1852.

52MLSC, Judy Eror, "School Reform and the Hamilton Central School"; McKay, *Victorian Architecture*, p. 14; PAC, RG5, C1, vol. 98, Dr. William Craigie to Civil Secretary, 15 November 1842; MG24, D16, vol. 22, Craigie to Isaac Buchanan, 21 February 1859; clipping from *Evening Times*, 11 August 1863.

53HPL, Robert J. Hamilton Papers, file on Hamilton waterworks, W.B. Robinson to Robert J. Hamilton, 6 November 1852. Concerning cholera see PAC, RG5, C1, vol. 417, Petition of the Council of the City of Hamilton, 21 August 1854.

54William and Evelyn James, *"A Sufficient Quantity of Pure and Wholesome Water": The Story of Hamilton's Old Pumphouse* (London: Phelps Publishing, 1978), passim.

55PAC, MG26, D16, vol. 10, Isaac Buchanan to Peter Buchanan, 3 October 1859.

56*Canadian Illustrated News*, 14 February 1863; Campbell, *A Mountain and a City*, p. 209.

57PAC, RG5, B21, vol. 1, Answers for the Information of Emigrants with Capital, Intending to Settle on Land [1840]; vol. 3, Information to Immigrants [1843]; R.H. Rae, Emigration Agent at Hamilton, to A.C. Buchanan, Statement showing the demand for the different class of labor in the various sections of the western country, visited . . . in March 1865; James G. Snell, "The Cost of Living in Canada in 1870," *Histoire sociale/Social History*, vol. 12 (May, 1979), pp. 190-1.

58Quoted in Poirier, "A City in Crisis," p. 10.

59Doucet, "Working Class Housing," p. 91.

60*Census of Canada 1871*, vol. 4, summary tables of 1848 census, tables 1 and 5; Katz, *The People of Hamilton, Canada West*, p. 87.

619 Vic. c. 73.

62*Hamilton Bee*, 8 April 1845; PAC, RG16, A1, vol. 109, William Higman to Francis Hincks, 8 August 1850; Higman to Dunscomb, 28 October 1850; RG5, C1, vol. 317, Petition from the Inhabitants of the City of Hamilton in Public Meeting, 12 February 1851; MLSC, Typescript of Hamilton Council Minutes, 11 April 1851.

63*Hamilton Spectator*, 20 February 1858, quoted in Poirier, "A City in Crisis," p. 11.

64John Battye, "'The Nine Hour Pioneers': The Genesis of the Canadian Labour Movement," *Labour/Le Travailleur*, vol. 4 (1979), pp. 25-56.

65"Colin Ferrie," *Dictionary of Hamilton Biography*.

66PAC, RG17, AIII, vol. 2393, Jasper Gilkison to P. Vankoughnet, 10 August 1859.

67HPL, John Young Papers, Daniel Gunn to John Young, 17 January 1861; W.C. Stephens to Young, 6 April 1861.

68Baskerville, "The Boardroom and Beyond," pp. 106-136.

69Campbell, *A Mountain and a City*, pp. 130-31; Bryan D. Palmer, *A Culture in Conflict: Skilled Workers and Industrial Capitalism in Hamilton, Ontario, 1860-1914* (Montreal: McGill-Queen's University Press, 1979), pp. 52-55, 269; HPL, John Young Papers, James Law to John Young, 24 October 1860; Richard Juson to Young, n.d. [1862]; PAC, Library, *Rules and Regulations of the Victoria Club* (Hamilton: Times, 1877); RG16, A1, vol. 115, Returns on Publications Imported into Hamilton, 1851-1855.

70HPL, Young Papers, Barbara MacNab to the Young Family, 21 May 1862.

71Report Relative to the General Working of the Tavern and Shop Licenses Acts, *OSP 1874*; Battye, "The Nine Hour Pioneers," p. 27.

72MLSC, Sheila Turcon, "Popular Entertainment in Hamilton in the Late Nineteenth Century"; MLSC, J. Martin Lawlor, "The Hamilton Independent Labour Party, 1919-1925."

73Charles M. Johnston, *The Head of the Lake: A History of Wentworth County* (Hamilton: Wentworth County Council, 1967), pp. 229-33; HPL, Joseph Tinsley's articles on Hamilton theatre; *Hamilton Association for the Advancement of Literature, Science and Art, 1857-1932* (Hamilton, 1932).

74MLSC, Stephen Davies, "The Railway as an Employer in Canada"; MTPL, L'Armitage, *The Great International Confederacy of Thieves, Burglars and Incendiaries on the Canadian Frontier* (n.p., 1865).

CHAPTER THREE

1A. St. L. Trigge, *A History of the Canadian Bank of Commerce*, vol. 3 (Toronto: The Canadian Bank of Commerce, 1934), pp. 60-76. HPL, *Building Society Statutes and Rules, The Hamilton Provident and Loan Society* (Hamilton, 1880), p. 3.

2HPL, *Prospectus, Hamilton and North-Western Railway* (Hamilton: Times, 1874); PAC, RG30, CNR Papers, vols. 120-21, Minutebooks of the Hamilton and North Western Railway, 1873-1880.

3Norman Helm, *In the Shadow of Giants: The Story of the Toronto, Hamilton & Buffalo Railway* (Cheltenham: Boston Mills Press, 1978), pp. 32-77.

4NA, RG84, Hamilton Consular Office Records, "The Iron and Steel Industry in the Hamilton, Ontario, Consular District, 15 December 1927."

5HPL, *Times Scrapbooks*, 01 Part 1, clipping of 25 November 1913; HPL, John Young Papers, William Leitch to John Young, 4 May 1861; 10 August 1861; Alan Birch, *The Economic History of the British Iron and Steel Industry, 1784-1879* (London: Frank Cass and Co., 1967), pp. 235-42.

6Victor S. Clark, *A History of Manufacturers in the United States* (New York: McGraw-Hill, 1929) vol. 3, p. 150.

7NA, RG84, Hamilton Consular Office Records, microfilm T470, reel 5, "Trade and Commerce of Hamilton, October 31 1882."

8For the decline of the stove industry see Craig Heron, "The Crisis of the Craftsman: Hamilton's Metal Workers in the Early Twentieth

Century," *Labour/Le Travailleur*, vol. 6 (Autumn, 1980), pp. 16-18. On the hardware jobbers see *Hamilton Herald*, 21 February 1913; Wood Vallance Papers, Letterbook, 1889-1898, provenance of Mrs. David Newlands.

[9]Ibid., Vallance to Jim, 9 April 1897.

[10]HPL, Ontario Rolling Mill Co. Ltd. Papers, Minutebooks 1879-1899, Accounts; *Hamilton, The Birmingham of Canada* (Hamilton: Times, 1892), n.p. Juson is discussed in Baskerville, "The Boardroom and Beyond," p. 306. On wire, nail and screw manufacture see Clark, *A History of Manufacturers in the United States*, vol. 2, pp. 348-57. The local manufacturers are described in HPL, Greening Wire Papers, *Wire, Its Manufacture, Antiquity and Relation to Modern Use*, n.d. [1900]; profile of Ontario Tack Company in *Hamilton Spectator*, Carnival Edition of 1903, n.p.; "100 Years of Fastener Pioneering," *Bits and Pieces, Special Issue* (1966), pp. 1-5.

[11]William Kilbourn, *The Elements Combined: A History of the Steel Company of Canada* (Toronto: Clarke, Irwin and Co., 1960), pp. 42-50; HPL, *The Hamilton Steel and Iron Company Catalogue and Price List* (1906), pp. 12-16.

[12]Campbell, *A Mountain and a City*, pp. 210-12.

[13]PAC, RG33, Royal Commissions, number 20, Royal Commission on Textile Industry, vol. 26, files 975-6; HPL, John Young Papers, James Farish to John Young, 30 July 1861; Douglas McCalla, "John Young," *Dictionary of Canadian Biography*; NA, RG84, Hamilton Consular Office Records, microfilm T470, reel 5, "Report on Hamilton Cotton Mills, December 8, 1885."

[14]Clark, *A History of Manufacturers in the United States*, vol. 2, pp. 443-4; HPL, *Hamilton the Birmingham of Canada* (1892), n.p.; NA, RG84, Hamilton Consular Office Records, "The Knit Goods Industry in the Hamilton Canada Consular District, March 20, 1928."

[15]*Postal Census of Manufacturers 1917* (for 1915); W.G. Phillips, *The Agricultural Implements Industry in Canada: A Study of Competition* (Toronto: University of Toronto Press, 1956), pp. 38-9.

[16]Clark, *A History of Manufacturers in the United States*, vol. 3, p. 146; Robert Ozanne, *A Century of Labor-Management Relations at McCormick and International Harvester* (Madison: University of Wisconsin Press, 1967), pp. 70-83; HPL, *International Harvester Scrapbook*, vol. I; *Times Scrapbooks*, vol. H4, part 1, May and June, 1911.

[17]*Hamilton Herald* quoted in Heron, "The Crisis of the Craftsman," p. 20.

[18]HPL, *International Harvester Scrapbook*, vol. I, undated clippings; *Spectator*, 29 April 1902; 1 March 1919.

[19]*Hamilton Herald*, 26 February 1910; 4 May 1911.

[20]*Hamilton Herald*, 26 February 1910; 17 May 1910; 4 May 1911; 16 April 1914.

[21]PAC, RG27, vol. I, Reports on Unemployment, Hamilton, 1914-1916, William T. Cooper to Department of Labour, 16 September 1914. See also PAC, Laurier Papers, Hamilton City Works Department to Central Information Office, Liberal Party, 6 March 1914.

[22]PAC, RG27, vol. I, Reports of 15 January and 15 February 1915; Ontario Government Public Employment Bureau, *OSP 1918*, pp. 20-2; HPL, *Times Scrapbook*, vol. R03, 4 September 1914; vol. II, 24 May 1915; 28 June 1915; *International Harvester Scrapbook*, vol. I, clipping from *Spectator*, 28 December 1957.

[23]PAC, MG28, I, 230, Canadian Manufacturers Association, vol. 16, Hamilton Branch Minutebook, 1914-1915, Articles that can be Supplied by Hamilton Manufacturers for War Office Equipment [insert]; RG16, Business Profits War Tax, vol. 1011, files 363, 366, 368, 391, 414, 422; vol. 1012, files 496, 509.

[24]Reports of the Inspectors of Factories, *OSP 1916-1919*. Concerning postwar employment problems see PAC, MG28, I, 280, vol. 17, Minutebook, 1919-1920, 26 September 1919, Statement of Captain Piercy of the Soldiers' Civil Re-establishment Department.

[25]Wood Vallance, Letterbook, 1889-1898. On mergers see *Hamilton Herald*, 4 May 1911; 8 August 1911; 30 May 1912; 30 January 1913; HPL, *A Brief History of Otis Elevator Company* (n.d.), pp. 2-10; Canada, *Royal Commission on Price Spreads*, vol. I, pp. 990-94; *Canadian Grocer*, 3 January 1930; 17 January 1930.

[26]Kilbourn, *The Elements Combined*, pp. 63-78.

[27]On Tuckett and Sanford see *Hamilton Herald*, 5 December 1889; 27 September 1895.

[28]HPL, *Times Scrapbooks*, vol. II, undated clipping 1914; *Census of Canada 1901*, vol. I, table 17.

[29]*Times Scrapbooks*, vol. II, undated clipping 1914; Reports of the Registrar General, *OSP 1900-1915*; *Hamilton Herald*, 26 February 1910; 17 May 1910. *Census of Canada 1921*, vol. 2, table 64.

[30]HPL, *Times Scrapbooks*, vol. II, 7 May 1912.

[31]*Times Scrapbooks*, vol. 55, 17 November 1913; *Census of Canada 1911*, vol. I, table 15; *Times Scrapbooks*, vol. M2, 2 June 1915. On the Polish population see *Hamilton Herald*, 31 August 1912.

[32]*Hamilton Herald*, 26 July 1895; HPL, *International Harvester Scrapbook*, vol. I; NA, RG84, Hamilton Consular Office Records, Consul Olivares to Secretary of State, 16 May 1917; RG27, vol. 294, file 2857; *Hamilton Herald*, 4 April 1910; 27 August 1912.

[33]*Hamilton Herald*, 18 April 1912; HPL, *Times Scrapbooks*, vol. P4, 23 September 1911; 16 December 1911.

[34]"Hamilton a Melting Pot for Many Races," *Hamilton Herald*, 31 August 1912.

[35]MLSC, "Italian National Catholic Churches of Hamilton"; HPL, *Times Scrapbooks*, vol. C4.6 (Churches), 8 May 1911; 26 September 1911; 28 December 1911.

[36]*Hamilton Herald*, 4 May 1911; HPL, *Times Scrapbooks*, vol. N, 19 November 1910; vol. R1, 15 November 1912.

[37]HPL, *Times Scrapbooks*, vol. N, 9 November 1910; vol. H1, 12 August

1919; *Hamilton Herald*, 20 May 1912. For descriptions of the blast furnace see *Hamilton Herald*, 15 June 1895; *Hamilton Spectator*, 31 December 1895.

[38]*Hamilton Herald*, 4 May 1911.

[39]For the development of the Hamilton Street Railway see Head Office HSR, Minutebooks 1C to 3C, 1873-1906. On the annexation and the allegations of conflict of interest see *Hamilton Herald*, 9 February 1910. The TH and B's achievement was reported in *Hamilton Herald*, 26 July 1895.

[40]HPL, *Times Scrapbooks*, vol. B3, 3 June 1911; 29 July 1911; 24 February 1912; *Hamilton Herald*, 21 December 1912. On the scale of development see *Hamilton Herald*, 16 December 1911; 30 December 1913.

[41]HPL, *Times Scrapbooks*, vol. R1, 5 June 1912; *Hamilton Herald*, 19 April 1911; 12, 13, 14, 16, 18, 19 November 1912; 10 July 1912. MLSC, Terry Naylor, "Ravenscliffe: Housing in an Elite District."

[42]Correspondence between Strathearn B. Thomson and W.A. Southam, published in *Hamilton Herald*, 24 December 1912.

[43]HPL, *Times Scrapbooks*, vol. R02, 5 February 1914; John C. Weaver, "From Land Assembly to Social Maturity: The Suburban Life of West-dale (Hamilton), Ontario, 1911-1951," *Histoire sociale/Social History*, vol. 11 (November, 1978), pp. 411-40.

[44]Ibid., pp. 420-25; PAC, RG27, vol. 32, Building Trades Reports; vol. 298, file 3343 (1911); file 2854 (1907).

[45]Rosemary Gagan, "Disease, Mortality and Public Health, Hamilton, 1900-1914" (McMaster University, MA thesis, 1981), passim, especially chapter 3.

[46]MLSC, Catherine L. Harris, "The Health of Hamilton, 1880-1905"; *Hamilton Herald*, 5 May 1910; 12 October 1912.

[47]Ibid., 26 February 1910; HPL, *Times Scrapbooks*, vol. H2, 24 January 1915; 11 February 1915; NA, RG84, Hamilton Consular Office Records, weekly health reports, 9 November 1918 to 27 March 1920.

[48]HPL, *Times Scrapbooks*, vol. P2, 6 April 1911.

[49]HPL, *Souvenir Number of the Hamilton Playgrounds Association* (1913), p. 4; *Times Scrapbooks*, vol. P2, 13 July 1916.

[50]PAC, MG30, C105, Noulan Cauchon Papers, vol. I, W.F. Tye and N. Cauchon, *The Railway Situation in Hamilton*; vol. 3, *Scrapbook 1912-21*.

[51]*Hamilton Herald*, 9 November 1912; 26 March 1913; 11 August 1914. For working-class district complaints see 21 June 1912; 18 December 1912. HPL, *Times Scrapbooks*, vol. P1, 19 September 1917; *Hamilton Herald*, 22 August 1911; 5 September 1911.

[52]*Board of Inquiry into the Cost of Living, Report of the Board* (Ottawa: King's Printer, 1915), pp. 81-89, 457-73, 485-6, 399-517; G. Bertram and M. Percy, "Real Wage Trends in Canada, 1900-1926: Some Provisional Estimates," *Canadian Journal of Economics*, vol. 12 (May, 1979), pp. 299-311. For the housing scheme see *Hamilton Herald*, 23 May 1912; 4 June 1912; 25 June 1912; 4 September 1912; 21 December 1912.

[53]PAO, George H. Mills, "Random Sketches, 1887-1889," 6 April 1887.

[54]Ibid., 20 January 1889. Donald F. Warner, *The Idea of Continental Union* (Kentucky: University of Kentucky Press, 1960), pp. 190-1.

[55]*Board of Inquiry into the Cost of Living*, pp. 517-18.

[56]PAC, RG27, vol. 296, file 3124; vol. 299, file 3460; vol. 301, file 1913-14; file 1913-27; Craig Heron, "The Crisis of the Craftsman," pp. 7-20.

[57]Ibid., pp. 27-34; Myer Siemiatycki, "Munitions and Labour Militancy: The 1916 Hamilton Machinists' Strike," *Labour/Le Travailleur*, vol. 3 (1978), pp. 131-51; PAC, RG27, vol. 304, file 1916-19; file 1916-27a.

[58]Mabel Burkholder, *The Course of Impatience Carningham* (Toronto: Musson, 1911), p. 280.

[59]PAC, RG27, vol. 304, file 1916-27a; Canada, Department of Labour, Library, *Minutes of Evidence Taken by Royal Commission on Industrial Relations, 1919*, vol. 4, evidence of J.R. Pruden, Procter and Gamble Superintendent, p. 2493.

[60]For skilled labour's complaint about immigrants see PAC, Laurier Papers, E. Madden, Corresponding Secretary of the Hamilton Trade and Labour Council, to Sir Wilford [sic] Laurier, 6 April 1908. On the militancy of "foreign labour" see PAC, RG27, vol. 294, files 2857 and 2868; vol. 296, file 3153; *Hamilton Herald*, 27 August 1912.

[61]For evidence of discrimination see PAC, RG27, I, Reports on unemployment, Hamilton, 1914-1916, Report of 15 October 1915. On the matter of radicalism see *Minutes of Evidence . . . 1919*, evidence of Fester of the Cigar Makers, pp. 2406-7.

[62]PAC, MG28, I, 230, vol. 16, Minutebook, 1910-1911, 5 April 1911; vol. 18, Minutebook of Executive Committee, 1926-1930, 31 May 1927; 8 December 1927; Burkholder, *The Course of Impatience Carningham*, passim.

[63]HPL, advertisement for Eaton's in *History of the Hamilton Fire Department* (Firemen's Benefit Fund, 1920), p. 50.

[64]*Minutes of Evidence . . . 1919*, evidence of J.R. Pruden, Procter and Gamble Superintendent, pp. 2470-93; evidence of A.L. Page, President of Frost Steel and Wire Fence Co., pp. 2508-14.

[65]Ibid., evidence of G. Emery, skilled labourer at International Harvester, p. 2538; evidence of William McKinley, representative of unorganized workers, member of International Harvester Council, p. 2338.

[66]HPL, Colin G. Snider, *Judge Snider's Report on Civic Investigation* (1914), pp. 4-13; *Times Scrapbooks*, vol. E1. 1, 4 January 1910; vol. B, 22 August 1917; *Hamilton Herald*, 26 September 1911; 11 December 1911; 21 December 1912.

[67]*Hamilton Herald*, 18 November 1912; Richard Lucas, "The Conflict over Public Power in Hamilton, Ontario, 1906-1914," *Ontario History*, vol. 68 (December, 1976), pp. 236-46; *Hamilton Herald*, 22, 25, 26 July 1911. For industry's interest in competition see PAC, MG28, I, 230, vol. 16, Minutebook, 1910-1911, 27 February 1911.

[68]For Studholme's career see Palmer, *A Culture in Conflict*, pp. 227-31; *Hamilton Herald*, 26 March 1913; 18 June 1914; HPL, *Times Scrapbooks*, vol.

E1.2 Part 1, 30 November 1911; 26 June 1914; 6 July 1914; Part 2, 30 July 1919. On the ILP Platform (1914) see *Times Scrapbooks*, vol. E1.2, Part 1, 31 October 1914. On elections see ibid., Part 2, 19 November 1914; Part 3, 15 December 1917.

⁶⁹W. Craig Heron, "Working-Class Hamilton, 1896-1930" (Dalhousie University, Ph.D. dissertation, 1981), pp. 494-564.

⁷⁰*Hamilton Herald*, 3 June 1890; HPL, *Official Programme and Souvenir of the Labour Day Demonstration Held at Dundurn Park, September 6, 1897*; HPL, *Times Scrapbooks*, vol. C2, 13 August 1913; 16 August 1913.

⁷¹PAC, MG28, I, vol. 16, *Minutebook 1911-1912*, 5 August 1911.

⁷²HPL, *Times Scrapbooks*, vol. H4, Part 1, 22 May 1911; F.W. Wodell, *Official Text-Book and Programme of the Queen's Jubilee Musical Festival at the Crystal Palace, Hamilton, June 21st and 22nd 1887* (Hamilton, 1887), pp. 12-25; *Hamilton Herald*, 1 August 1891.

⁷³For a history of rugby see *Hamilton Herald*, 21 December 1912; HPL, *Times Scrapbooks*, vol. S4.03, Part 2. On the Tigers see *Spectator*, 15 October 1979. Bicycling history was recounted in *Hamilton Herald*, 11 July 1891. Running was covered in ibid., 3 September 1895, and *Times Scrapbooks*, vol. S4.04.

⁷⁴HPL, Joseph Tinsley's articles on Hamilton theatre. See especially *Hamilton Herald*, 28 November 1908.

⁷⁵Johnston, *The Head of the Lake*, pp. 229-35; MLSC, Gloria Nardi, "The Hamilton Council of Women, 1893-1939."

⁷⁶PAC, Library, *The Recruiting League of Hamilton* (n.d.), pp. 1-24.

⁷⁷HPL, *Times Scrapbooks*, vol. S4.01, Part 2, 11 March 1916; 10 April 1916; 29 April 1916.

⁷⁸The political information was drawn from Parliamentary guidebooks. The estimate on casualties is derived from HPL, Honour Roll (of World War I dead).

⁷⁹*Times Scrapbooks*, 10 March 1914; vol. R1, 5 July 1919.

⁸⁰HPL, *Times Scrapbooks*, vol. A4, 5 August 1911; 22 April 1913; 22 July 1913; 19 January 1914.

CHAPTER FOUR

¹NA, RG84, Hamilton Consular Office Records, George C. Coppley to Consular Office, 25 September 1921. On unemployment generally see monthly reports in the *Labour Gazette*.

²*Herald*, 2 August 1930; 15 January 1935; *Spectator*, 3 March 1937; *Financial Post*, 8 May 1938; *Globe Magazine*, 30 January 1960. For Procter and Gamble see HPL, Procter and Gamble, *Galaxy: 60 Years in Hamilton* (1975).

³*Census of Canada 1931*, vol. 5, tables 18 and 23. The plight of the building trades was reported in HPL, *Brief of Submissions of the Corporation of the City of Hamilton to the Royal Commission on Dominion and Provincial Relations* (Hamilton,

May, 1938), p. 6. The collapse of the heavy industries is detailed in NA, RG84, Hamilton Consular Office Records, "Review of Commerce and Industry for Year Ended, December 31, 1930"; "Review of Commerce and Industry for Quarter Ended, March 31, 1931"; "Review of Commerce and Industry for the Quarter Ended, June 30, 1931."

⁴*Census of Canada 1931*, vol. 5, table 23; NA, RG84, Hamilton Consular Office Records, "Review of Commerce and Industry for Year Ended, December 31, 1930" and comparable reports for the year ending 31 December 1932; 12 January 1934; 9 January 1935; "Current Commercial and Industrial Developments, November, 1934" and comparable special reports dated 4 March 1936, October, 1936, April, 1938, January and February, 1939. On boarders see *Census of Canada 1931*, vol. 5, table 58.

⁵For wages in 1931 see *Census of Canada 1931*, vol. 5, table 18; NA, RG84, Hamilton Consular Office Records, annual and special reports on commerce and industry. On the war orders and steel recovery see especially "Commercial and Industrial Developments during January and February 1940."

⁶NG, RG84, Hamilton Consular Office Records, annual and special reports.

⁷MLSC, Russell Geddes, "Hamilton: A Case Study in Local Relief and Public Welfare during the Depression."

⁸PAC, RG64, Wartime Prices and Trade Board, vol. 146, Tables on Employment and Payrolls in Eight Leading Industries; NA, RG84, Hamilton Consular Office Records, "Movement of Industry, Hamilton (Ontario) Consular District, September 4, 1942"; Reports of the Department of Labour, *OSP 1940-1946*; MLSC, Terrence Hourigan, "Labour's Reactions in Canada and Hamilton to the Government Wartime Policies, 1939-1945," pp. 11-14.

⁹Registrar General's Reports, 1921 to 1947, *OSP; Census of Canada 1951*, vol. 1, table 48; *Census of Canada 1921*, vol. 2, table 70; *1931*, vol. 4, table 26. The details about immigration came from NA, RG84, Hamilton Consular Office Records. The estimates on the number of arrivals in the late 1920s is based on *Census of Canada 1931*, vol. 4, table 26.

¹⁰NA, RG84, Hamilton Consular Office, file on issue of fraudulent passports; Hamilton Consul to Director of Immigration, Buffalo, 5 November 1924; Vice Consul at Prague to Hamilton Consul, 10 December 1924; List of Aliens who Have Applied for Visas at Hamilton, 2 February 1925; Hamilton Consul to Secretary of State, 15 November 1924 and 26 January 1925; "Annual Report for 1926 on Commerce and Industry for Hamilton Consular District"; "Report on Smuggling of Aliens, February 19, 1927."

¹¹Registrar General's Reports, 1921 to 1931, *OSP*; HPL, *A Survey of Health Activities in the City of Hamilton* (1933), p. 41.

¹²HPL, Birth Control Society of Hamilton, *An Outline of the Work and Aims* (1933). Registrar General's Reports, 1921 to 1941, *OSP*. Immigration

policy is mentioned in Alan Green, *Immigration and the Postwar Canadian Economy* (Toronto: Macmillan, 1976), pp. 12-54.

[13]On early Hamilton apartments see HPL, *Hamilton Times Scrapbooks*, vol. RO.2, 25 February 1911; 10 March 1914; *Hamilton Herald*, 6 April 1912. The causes for the construction boom of the mid-1920s were discussed in NA, RG84, Hamilton Consular Office Records, "Annual Report of Commerce and Industries in Hamilton, Ontario Consular District for the Year 1925." MLSC, Kevin Braybrook, "The First Apartment Dwellers in the City of Hamilton: A Social Profile."

[14]On Canadian housing legislation see John Christopher Bacher, "The Origins of a Non-Policy; The Development of the Assumption of a Housing Responsibility by the Canadian Federal Government" (McMaster University, MA thesis, 1980); *Census of Canada 1941*, vol. 9, table 9c; *1951*, vol. 3, table 100; *1961*, Bulletin 2.2-8; *1966*, vol. 2, table 51.

[15]Claudius Gregory, *Forgotten Men* (Hamilton: Davis-Lisson, 1933), p. 394.

[16]Leo Haak, "A Housing Survey in Hamilton," *Social Welfare* (March, 1937), pp. 5-6; Dominion Bureau of Statistics, *Hamilton Housing Atlas* (1946).

[17]PAC, RG19, vol. 3979, F.W. Nicolls to W.C. Clark, 17 June 1940; vol. 3980, F.W. Nicolls to Lesslie Thomson, 11 January 1941; F.W. Nicolls to W.C. Clark, 8 February 1941; Advisory Committee on Reconstruction, *Housing and Community Planning, Final Report of the Subcommittee* (Ottawa: King's Printer, 1944), p. 245.

[18]PAC, RG83, vol. 70, Minutebook I of Wartime Housing Limited, entries for 26 May 1941; RG35, number 4, vol. 2, Interdepartmental Committee on Housing, file IHC6, "Wartime Housing Limited Tenancy Report, August 31, 1946."

[19]PAC, RG83, vol. 70, Minutebook 1, entries for 4 March 1942; Minutebook 2, entries for 12 January 1943; "Summary Report to the Members of the Board: Tenants' Relations Department," 10 August 1943; 29 May 1945.

[20]For a review of sports in 1925 see *Spectator*, 27 January 1951.

[21]Ibid., 27 January 1951; 15 October 1979. HPL, Hamilton Collection, subject index; HPL, *Dual Track and Field Meet: Oxford-Cambridge vs. Hamilton Olympic Club — 1929*; MLSC, Carol McNeil, "Hamilton, Ontario, 1930: The Setting for the First British Empire Games."

[22]HPL, *Players' Guild, 1874-1974* (Hamilton, 1974); Canada, Department of Labour, *An Investigation into an Alleged Combine in the Motion Picture Industry in Canada*, pp. 47-8, 103, 153.

[23]HPL, File on Radio Station CKOC, *Its the Character of a Radio Station which Counts* (1947); *Census of Canada 1931*, vol. 5, table 58; *1961*; Bulletin 2.2-4, table 58; Campbell, *A Mountain and a City*, p. 286.

[24]NA, RG84, Hamilton Consular Office Records, "Newspapers of Importance in the Hamilton (Ontario) Consular District, August 19, 1941."

[25]*Hamilton Herald*, 20 November 1924; 22 November 1924; 3 December 1924; Bill Freeman and Marsha Hewitt, eds., *Their Town: The Mafia, the Media, and the Party Machine* (Toronto: James Lorimer and Company, 1979), pp. 74-88.

[26]*The Argyll and Sutherland Highlanders of Canada (Princess Louise's) 1928-1953* (Hamilton, 1953), passim; Bereton Greenhous, *Semper Paratus: The History of the Royal Hamilton Light Infantry (Wentworth Regiment) 1862-1977* (Hamilton, 1977), passim.

[27]For the career of Thomas Jutten see Campbell, *A Mountain and a City*, p. 248; *Spectator*, 15 June 1953; 11 April 1955. For Humphrey Mitchell see Johnston, *The Head of the Lake*, pp. 275-6.

[28]David Millar, "The Labour Movement of Hamilton, 1930-1956," *The Hamilton Working Class, 1820-1977: A Bibliography*, ed. Wayne Roberts (Hamilton: Labour Studies, McMaster, 1978), p. 35.

[29]NA, RG84, Hamilton Consular Office Records, "Current Commercial and Industrial Developments, August 1936"; "Iron and Steel Industry Developments, June 1938"; "Commercial and Industrial Developments, July and August 1939."

[30]AFL organizer John Noble, quoted in Hamilton *Labour News*, 27 May 1937.

[31]NA, RG84, Hamilton Consular Office Records, "Labour Unrest in the Hamilton District, June 1943."

[32]MLSC, Terrence Hourigan, "Labour's Reaction in Canada and Hamilton to the Government Wartime Policies, 1939-1945," pp. 7-11.

[33]PAC, RG36, 4, vol. 116, Ontario Labour Court Decisions and Summary of the Activities of the Labour Court, June 14 to December 31, 1943.

[34]The American Consular Office prepared detailed monthly "labour letters" beginning in 1945. They occasionally included reports on conversations with corporate executives and labour leaders. See especially 22 May 1945; 21 June 1945; 21 November 1945; 21 December 1945; 21 March 1946. The quote appears in NA, RG84, Paul Morgen, Labour Expert, U.S. Embassy, to American Consul Hamilton, 22 January 1946.

[35]NA, RG84, Hamilton Consular Office Records, Labour Letters, 23 January 1946; 21 February 1946; 23 April 1946; 8 July 1946; 17 July 1946; 22 August 1946; 28 August 1946; 22 November 1946; 20 December 1946.

[36]David Millar, p. 37; MLSC, Mark Skuse, "A Profile of City Council and Elections in the 1940s." NA, RG84, Hamilton Consular Office Records, "Political Complexion of Hamilton as Revealed by Municipal Election, December 12, 1946."

[37]Skuse, "A Profile of City Council"; NA, RG84, Hamilton Consular Office Records, Labour Letter, 23 April 1946; "Preliminary Survey of Communist Organizations in Hamilton (Ontario), March 6, 1947";

"Debate on Communism in Hamilton City Council, February 13, 1947";
"Communist and Socialist Setbacks in Hamilton (Ontario) Civic Election,
December 9, 1947."

[38]PAC, RG64, vol. 64, Wartime Prices and Trade Board, "The Fight
against Inflation: The Story of the Campaign in the Central Ontario
Region, 1941-1947."

[39]For Morrison see *Spectator*, 17 November 1939; 8 December 1942. On
the activities of Henderson see HPL, scrapbook on Nora Frances
Henderson.

CHAPTER FIVE

[1]Donald Kerr, "The Geography of the Canadian Iron and Steel Industry," *Economic Geography*, vol. 35 (1959), pp. 151-63.

[2]On the expansion of steel-making capacity at both companies see
Spectator, 5 January 1951; 10 December 1955; 12 November 1960. For
accidents see *Spectator*, 11 August 1966; 26 June 1971; 3 November 1971;
20 May 1972; 27 October 1972. Concerning pollution see *Spectator*, 9
November 1955; 12 June 1962; 9 June 1968; 6 October 1973.

[3]*Labour Gazette*, February, 1947, p. 248; March, 1947, p. 418; February,
1949, p. 201.

[4]*Spectator*, 15 April 1946; 20 October 1949; 15 December 1949; 21 June
1949; 11 May 1950; 24 August 1951; 25 August 1952; 12 June 1953; 13
September 1954; 21 November 1956; 22 October 1959; 6 June 1961; 8
June 1962; 21 January 1971.

[5]*Spectator*, 2 April 1948; 29 April 1948; 29 April 1949; 5 January 1951;
14 April 1955; 26 April 1955; 10 December 1955; 15 April 1957; 15 June
1962; 10 April 1963; 22 January 1968; 17 December 1971.

[6]*Spectator*, 21 October 1964; *Globe and Mail*, 27 October 1972.

[7]*Spectator*, 19 March 1968; 1 November 1968; 5 November 1968; 6
November 1968.

[8]See, for example, "The Dofasco Way," in *All that Our Hands Have Done*,
by Craig Heron, Shea Hoffmitz, Wayne Roberts, Robert Storey (Oakville:
Mosaic Press, 1981), pp. 145-6.

[9]*Submission of the Steel Company of Canada, Limited, to the Royal Commission on
Corporate Concentration* (November, 1975), passim.

[10]*Spectator*, 2 October 1948; HPL, Stelco Scrapbook, Stuart Armour to
Freda Waldon, 14 October 1948. Articles on Hoover and Westinghouse
appeared in the special edition of the *Spectator*, 12 November 1960.

[11]*Spectator*, 4 February 1949; 31 August 1953; 10 May 1959; 12 November 1960; 25 February 1964; 28 January 1967; 26 September 1972; 18
April 1980; 31 May 1980.

[12]*Spectator*, 3 June 1960; 12 November 1960; 27 January 1967; 4
November 1969; 17 April 1971; 24 January 1972; 26 February 1972.

[13]For the Austin venture see *Spectator*, 2 February 1967. Studebaker was
the subject of articles in the *Spectator*, 25 April 1947; 12 November 1960;
9 December 1963; 10 December 1963; 28 January 1967; 16 September
1967.

[14]*Spectator*, 12 July 1957; 1 February 1958; 8 March 1958; 4 April 1962;
6 November 1972.

[15]*Canada Yearbook, 1980-81*, tables 15.23 and 15.24.

[16]*Census of Canada 1941*, vol. 4, table 22; *Census of Canada 1951*, vol. 1,
table 48.

[17]Green, *Immigration and the Postwar Canadian Economy*, p. 24; *Census of Canada
1961*, Bulletin 1.2-8.

[18]*Spectator*, 25 February 1952; 20 March 1954; 28 February 1955; 13
March 1956; 14 December 1956; 6 June 1957; 15 December 1960.

[19]*Census of Canada 1951*, vol. 1, table 57; *1961*, Bulletin 1.2-8. *Spectator*,
13 April 1951; 9 December 1955; 25 January 1957. For the educational
pressures see *Spectator*, 3 March 1949; 2 February 1955; 15 February 1968.

[20]David B. Chandler, "The Residential Location of Occupational and
Ethnic Groups in Hamilton" (McMaster University, MA thesis, 1965),
pp. 76-81; MLSC, Anna Chiota, "A Study of the Hamilton Italian Community through its Social Institutions"; Devianee Caussy, "Residential
Mobility of Italian Immigrants in Hamilton" (McMaster University, MA
thesis, 1980), p. 64.

[21]PAC, RG19, vol. 4017, Memorandum re Rates of Demobilization as
Related to Need for Housing, July, 1945; *Census of Canada 1951*, vol. 1, table
65; *1951*, vol. 3, table 100 and table 117; HPL, Scrapbooks on Housing,
particularly *Spectator*, 3 January 1951; 22 May 1951; Lynn Livesey, "A
Study of the Spatial and Physical Characteristics of Urban and Suburban
Growth in Hamilton, 1946 to 1954"; Trevor Whiffen, "Postwar Suburban
Expansion: An Analysis of its Causes and Evolution in Hamilton and
Ancaster."

[22]HPL, Scrapbooks on Housing, *Spectator*, clipping, 2 February 1948.

[23]*Census of Canada 1951*, vol. 3, tables 70 and 100; *1961*, Bulletin 2.2-6,
table 65.

[24]*Census of Canada 1961*, Bulletin CT-8; *1941*, vol. 9, table 10a; *1951*, vol.
3, table 26; *1961*, Bulletin 2.2-4.

[25]*Census of Canada 1941*, vol. 9, table 17; *1951*, vol. 3, tables 38 and 42;
1961, Bulletin CT-8. *Hamilton Spectator*, Progress Edition, 12 November
1960. For women's occupations see *Census of Canada 1931*, vol. 7, table 57;
1941, vol. 7, table 22.

[26]*Census of Canada 1951*, vol. 3, table 89. Jackson's comment was reported
in the *Spectator*, 4 October 1951; HPL, Scrapbooks on Housing, particularly
the following *Spectator* clippings: 16 January 1948; 5 July 1948; 8 September
1948; 30 July 1949; 21 March 1950; 16 October 1951; 20 June 1952; 28
April 1954; 27 July 1954; 10 February 1955; 21 May 1958; *Daily News*, 25
February 1956.

[27] Statistics Canada, *Traveller Accommodation Statistics 1970*, table 13.

[28] For the mountain's population see *Globe and Mail*, 22 May 1948; *Spectator*, 19 March 1968. On land-use traits see *Globe and Mail*, 22 June 1959.

[29] *Spectator*, 17 November 1959; 23 October 1962; 18 December 1962; 5 December 1963; 19 March 1968; 2 June 1972; 2 September 1972.

[30] PAC, MG28, I, 280, vol. 18, Canadian Manufacturers Association, Hamilton Branch, Minutebook, Annual Report, 28 April 1925. UDC, *General Background Information*, p. 3. City Planning Committee, *Report on Existing Conditions*.

[31] UDC, *General Background Information*, p. 4.

[32] Freeman and Hewitt, eds., *Their Town*, pp. 120-135.

[33] Ann Faulkner, *Without our Past? A Handbook for the Preservation of Canada's Architectural Heritage* (Toronto: University of Toronto Press, 1977), p. 5.

[34] MLSC, Rose Csicsai, "The Hamilton Experiment with Neighbourhood Planning Groups."

[35] On the professionalization of football see *Spectator*, 10 April 1948; 24 February 1949; 25 October 1956; 14 September 1959; 15 December 1959; *Weekend Magazine*, 10 December 1966. Ivan Miller is quoted from the *Spectator*, 12 November 1960.

[36] *Census of Canada 1971*, Bulletin 2.4-4; Bulletin 703, table 7; *1941*, vol. 10, table 6; *1961*, Bulletin 6.102, table 7.

[37] Dominion Bureau of Statistics, *Motion Picture Theatres, Exhibitors, and Distributors 1950*, table 3; *Motion Picture Theatres and Film Distributors 1959*, table 5. *Spectator*, 5 August 1972; 11 October 1980; Canadian Radio and Television Commission, *Broadcasting Stations in Canada* (1970).

[38] HPL collection of theatre programs. The art gallery situation is discussed in *Herald*, 15 March 1923; *Spectator*, 23 October 1928; 20 December 1947; *Daily News*, 7 December 1953.

[39] *Spectator*, 8 December 1960.

[40] *Spectator*, 24 September 1967; 17 December 1968; 25 November 1969; 24 February 1970; 17 March 1970; 21 April 1973.

[41] For Warrender see *Spectator*, 27 February 1962; for Gisborn see 3 January 1981. Munro's career is pieced together from *Daily News*, 3 November 1954; *Globe Magazine*, 10 October 1966; *Globe and Mail*, 22 April 1968; 1 July 1974; 9 September 1978; *Spectator*, 22 February 1963; 17 June 1965; 23 April 1968.

[42] The situation of women in civic politics is drawn from a review of the *Spectator* for elections from 1946 to 1980. Fairclough's career is reconstructed from the *Spectator*, 8 April 1949; 16 May 1950; 18 December 1950; *Globe and Mail*, 22 June 1957; 22 February 1958. Conservative Quinto Martini from Hamilton East, elected in 1957, was the first MP of Italian descent.

[43] *Spectator*, 8 December 1949; Campbell, *A Mountain and a City*, pp. 255-56.

[44] *Spectator*, 8 December 1960; 10 December 1960; 30 October 1962; 15 November 1962; 22 November 1962; 30 September 1968.

[45] *Spectator*, 30 October 1962.

Suggestions for Further Reading and Research

Major Finding Aids and Repositories

The Hamilton Collection at the Hamilton Public Library contains family papers, local government documents, scrapbooks on industries and leading individuals, and pamphlets or books produced by corporations and organizations for anniversary celebrations. This collection is complemented by a Hamilton Collection in the Mills Library at McMaster University. An extensive listing of published material that can be secured without having to use either Hamilton Collection is listed in Alan Artibise and Gilbert Stelter, *Canada's Urban Past: A Bibliography to 1980 and a Guide to Canadian Urban Studies* (Vancouver: University of British Columbia Press, 1981).

The bulk of material for this book was drawn from over twenty manuscript collections, nearly as many government record groups and various newspapers. Serious research on Hamilton's past requires a consideration of the manuscript collections available at the Public Archives of Canada, the Public Archives of Ontario and the Hamilton Public Library. All repositories continue to add to their collections so that basic finding aids like the *Union List of Manuscripts in Canadian Repositories*, 2 vols. (Ottawa: Public Archives of Canada, 1975) and the supplements published in 1976 and 1979 or Russell G. Hann et al., *Primary Sources in Canadian Working Class History, 1860–1930* (Kitchener: Dumont Press, 1973) must be used in conjunction with inquiries at libraries and archives. The National Archives in Washington hold the records of many United States consular offices. The Hamilton office had compiled abundant reports on economic and labour matters during the 1930s and 1940s.

General Sources

As a community which had a historical society as early as 1889 and has seen the publication of an extensive list of promotional and centennial books (1913, 1946, 1967), Hamilton has accumulated layers of lore that are repetitive and of uneven quality. The publications of the Wentworth Historical Society and *Wentworth Bygones* produced by the Head-of-the-Lake Historical Society contain references to landmarks, families, congregations, civic departments and early settlers. Among early Hamilton titles it is worth mentioning the following: *Hamilton, The Birmingham of Canada* (Hamilton: Times, 1892); *Hamilton Spectator*, Carnival Edition (1903); *Hamilton, the electric city* (1906); *Hamilton, the electric city of Canada* (1910); *Hamilton, Canada: the city of 400 varied industries (1912)*. There were many more pieces of promotional history, but one of the most useful in recent years was a progress edition of the *Spectator*, 12 November 1960. Alexander Wingfield, ed., *Hamilton Centennial, 1846-1946* (Hamilton: Davis-Lisson, 1946) contains, among other items, a valuable article on churches and a brief but important contribution to sport history by Ivan Miller. Two detailed histories that have attempted to recount the city's past are Charles M. Johnston, *The Head of the Lake: A History of Wentworth County* (Hamilton, 1958; Reprinted 1967) and Marjorie Freeman Campbell, *A Mountain and a City: The Story of Hamilton* (Toronto: McClelland and Stewart, 1966). T. Melville Bailey et al., *Dictionary of Hamilton Biography*, vol. I, like Campbell's book, depends heavily on the public library's resources. Wayne Roberts et al., *All that Our Hands Have Done: A Pictorial History of the Hamilton Workers* (Oakville: Mosaic Press, 1981), is the largest of several labour-history publications produced by Roberts and the McMaster University Office of Labour Studies. Finally, no one working on Hamilton history can fail to appreciate the work produced by or under the direction of Michael Katz as reported in numerous collections of papers reproduced under the auspices of the Canadian Social History Project and later the York Social History Project.

The Founding and the Early Years

Since most of the early history concerns influential individuals or families, the following biographical studies are recommended: Bruce Wilson, "The Enterprises of Robert Hamilton: A Study of Wealth and Influence in Early Upper Canada, 1776-1812" (University of Toronto, Ph.D. dissertation, 1978); Nicholas Leblovic, "The Life and History of Richard Beasley Esquire," *Wentworth Bygones*, vol. 7 (1967); John Weaver, "James Durand's Eventful Careers, 1802-1834: An Adventurous Englishman on the Upper Canada Frontier," *Wentworth Bygones*, vol. 13 (1981), pp. 41-9. Pierre Berton's *The Invasion of Canada, 1812-1813* (Toronto: McClelland and Stewart, 1980) presents a colourful but sound account of the sparsely settled colony of which the Head of the Lake was a part. A bizarre and confusing book, Charles Durand's *Reminiscences of Charles Durand of Toronto, Barrister* (Toronto: Hunter Rose, 1897) is essential reading for an understanding of life around Dundas and Hamilton in the 1820s and 1830s. Research by many people went into the *Documentary Research Committee File, Dundurn Castle Restoration, 1964–1967* (mimeograph). Marion MacRae's *MacNab of Dundurn* (Toronto: Clarke, Irwin and Company, 1971) compresses much of the research collected for the restoration file. However, the best biography of MacNab to date is by Peter Baskerville in volume IX of the *Dictionary of Canadian Biography*.

Economic Growth

No economic history of Canada contains adequate references to Hamilton or to the city's industries. The *Labour Gazette* (1900-1978) presents valuable fragments; a serious reader will have to turn to numerous specialized studies on a particular commodity or company. In addition to his *The Upper Canada Trade, 1834-1872: A Study of the Buchanans' Business* (Toronto: University of Toronto Press, 1979), the following articles by Douglas McCalla are recommended: "The Wheat Staple and Upper Canadian Development," *Historical Papers, Canadian Historical Association, 1978*, pp. 34-45; "The Decline of Hamilton as a Wholesale Centre," *Ontario History*, vol. 65 (1973), pp. 247-54. For Hamilton's place in the trade networks of the mid-nineteenth century, one also should see Thomas F. McIlwraith, "The Logistical Geography of the Great Lakes Grain Trade, 1820-1850" (University of Wisconsin, Ph.D. dissertation, 1973) and Gerald Tulchinsky, *The River Barons: Montreal Businessmen and the Growth of Industry and Transportation, 1837–53* (Toronto: University of Toronto Press, 1977). An overview of the railway situation is provided by Peter Baskerville, "The Boardroom and Beyond: Aspects of the Upper Canadian Railroad Community" (Queen's University, PhD. dissertation, 1973). J.M. and Edward Trout, *The Railways of Canada* (Toronto, 1871; Coles Canadiana Collection, 1974) and Gustavus Myers, *A History of Canadian Wealth* (Chicago, 1914; James Lewis and Samuel Limited, 1972) are worth reading for aspects of the Great Western Railway. Norman Helm, *In the Shadow of Giants: The Story of the Toronto, Hamilton and Buffalo Railway* (Cheltenham: Boston Mills Press, 1978) is primarily written for railway buffs. The history of the Gore Bank is well served by Victor Ross, *A History of the Canadian Bank of Commerce*, vol. I (Toronto: Oxford University Press, 1920); the Bank of Hamilton receives lengthy treatment in A. St. L. Trigge, *A History of the Canadian Bank of Commerce*, vol. 3 (Toronto: The Canadian Bank of Commerce, 1934). The Canada Life Assurance Company has produced *Since 1847: The Canada Life Story* (n.p., n.d.).

Histories of the iron trades, farm implements, machine tools, and steel manufacture are sorely needed to complement the growing literature on labour history. An examination of the Government of Canada's *List of Patents . . . 1824 to . . . 1874* (Ottawa, 1882; reprinted by Gordon Publication, 1979) along with a reading of American and British studies on early industries is an interim means of understanding how the initial foundries and machine shops functioned in Hamilton. Of particular value is Victor S. Clark, *A History of Manufacturing in the United States*, 3 vols. (New York: McGraw-Hill, 1929). A background to the farm-implements industry can be found in W.G. Phillips, *The Agricultural Implements Industry in Canada: A Study of Competition* (Toronto: University of Toronto Press, 1956). Some insight into practices in the early foundries is gained by reading Alan Birch, *The Economic History of the British Iron and Steel Industry* (London: Frank Cass, 1967). Many leading companies have produced corporate histories or anniversary volumes. The most informative and scholarly remains William Kilbourn, *The Elements Combined: A History of the Steel Company of Canada* (Toronto: Clarke, Irwin and Company, 1960). The following company histories vary in quality: International Harvester Company of Canada, *Manufacturing Operations in Canada of Hamilton Works, Hamilton Twine Mills, Chatham Works* (Hamilton, 1946); Otis Elevator Company, *A Brief History of Otis Elevator Company (U.S.A.) and Otis Elevator Company Limited (Canada)* (n.p., 1950); John Forbes Robinson, *Oh Christopher!* (Hamilton, 1959), a history of Greening Wire; *Wire, Its Manufacture, Antiquity and Relation to Modern Use* (1900); "100 Years of Fastener Pioneering," *Bits and Pieces*, Special Issue (1966). There are fragments on newspaper competition in Southam Press, *A Century of Southam* (n.p., 1977).

Research on the local economy since 1950 is facilitated by the public library's clipping files and scrapbooks on individual companies. The Dominion Bureau of Statistics (now Statistics Canada) collected and printed a wealth of economic information. A listing of publications, *Historical Catalogue of Dominion Bureau of Statistics Publications, 1918–1960* (Ottawa, 1966), contains sections on manufacturing, commerce, construction, employment and labour income.

Population

Aggregate population data for the 1830s was collected and published in the *Appendices of the Sessional Papers for Upper Canada*. Decennial enumerations have been taken since 1842 (1852, 1861-1981). Annual estimates appeared in the Reports of the Registrar General of Ontario from 1878 (for the year 1876) to the present. The ethnic composition of the population is difficult to reconstruct because of the underenumeration of immigrants; this is a major problem with the *Census of Canada, 1911*. Despite Hamilton's reputation as a city with ethnic diversity, studies of most constituent groups are lacking. The publication of *New Perspective*, an occasional journal from the Hamilton Multicultural Centre, and a series of interviews with Italians by a researcher from the Ontario Multicultural History Society have begun to provide data. Pending more research, there are a few studies that hold interesting details: Eugene Rapp, *100th Anniversary of the Germania Club* (Hamilton, 1967); Louis Greenspan, "The Governance of the Jewish Community of Hamilton" (paper prepared for the Center for Jewish Community Studies, 1974); Maria Campanella, ed., *Italian Canadian Federation of Hamilton, Symposium '77: On the Economic, Social, and Cultural Conditions of the Italian Canadian in the Hamilton-Wentworth Region* (Hamilton, 1978). The clipping files at the public library should be consulted when examining immigration since 1945. The spatial context of the immigrants has been the subject of several theses: David Chandler, "The Residential Location of Occupational and Ethnic Groups in Hamilton" (McMaster University, MA thesis, 1965); M.J. Foster, "Ethnic Settlement in the Barton Street Region of Hamilton" (McMaster University, MA thesis, 1965); Devianee Caussy, "Residential Mobility of Italian Immigrants in Hamilton" (McMaster University, MA thesis, 1980).

Social History

Commencing in the early 1970s, Michael Katz introduced qualitative social history to Canadian scholarly writing. He selected Hamilton as the community for an extended review of social stratification, mobility (both social and geographic) and family. The first book, *The People of Hamilton, Canada West: Family and Class in a Mid-Nineteenth Century City* (Cambridge, Massachusetts: Harvard University Press, 1975) depicted a society with a great deal of transiency, a concentration of property and a disproportionate number of Irish Roman Catholics among the city's poor. The companion volume, coauthored with Michael Doucet and Mark Stern, is concerned with urban society in Buffalo and Hamilton in the 1860s and 1870s: *The Social Origins of Early Industrial Capitalism* (Cambridge: Harvard University Press, 1982). Class conflict, recreation, leisure and a political economy of the working class are subjects in Bryan Palmer's *A Culture in Conflict: Skilled Workers and Industrial Capitalism in Hamilton, Ontario, 1860–1914* (Montreal: McGill-Queen's, 1979). Craig Heron, "Working-Class Hamilton, 1896–1930" (Dalhousie University, Ph.D. dissertation, 1981) is an outstanding contribution to labour and social history.

There is very little in the way of social-history reading available for the pre-1850 decades. John Weaver, "Crime, Violence, and Immorality in a Pre-Industrial Society: Unlawful Acts and Law Enforcement in the Gore District of Upper Canada from Settlement to the Railway Era" (paper given at the Canadian Historical Association Annual Meeting, 1981) covers pathological and repressive aspects of early Hamilton society. Concerning the twentieth century, Jayne Synge's manuscript on the nature of family life in the city from 1900 to 1920 promises to be a methodical and literate portrait of domestic activity in the industrial age. Rosemary Gagan, "Disease, Mortality, and Public Health, Hamilton, 1900-1914" (McMaster University, MA thesis, 1981), makes a singular contribution to an understanding of the crises in health in an industrial city. The Dominion Bureau of Statistis/Statistics Canada provides the essential starting point for the study of households, occupations and amenities. Fictional accounts of life in Hamilton are disappointing. Mabel Burkholder, *The Course of Impatience Carningham* (Toronto: Musson, 1911) and Claudius Gregory, *Forgotten Men* (Hamilton: David-Lisson, 1933) are trite novels. Sylvia Fraser's *Pandora* (Toronto: McClelland and Stewart, 1972) provides a sensitive account of growing up in an Anglo-Saxon working-class neighbourhood during the Second World War.

The Urban Landscape

Land development, land use, urban services and architecture have been the subjects of published and unpublished work. The residential landscape of Victorian Hamilton receives excellent scholarly treatment in two studies by Michael Doucet: "Building the Victorian City: The

Process of Land Development in Hamilton, Ontario, 1847–1881" (University of Toronto, Ph.D. dissertation, 1977); "Working Class Housing in a Small Nineteenth Century Canadian City: Hamilton, Ontario, 1852–1881," *Essays in Canadian Working Class History*, edited by Gregory S. Kealey and Peter Warrian (Toronto: McClelland and Stewart, 1976), pp. 83-105. Land development and residential characteristics also are reviewed in John C. Weaver, "From Land Assembly to Social Maturity: The Suburban Life of Westdale (Hamilton), Ontario, 1911–1951," *Histoire social/Social History*, vol. 11 (November, 1978), pp. 411-40. Several short studies have been published: Leo Haak, "A Housing Survey in Hamilton," *Social Welfare* (March, 1937), pp. 5-6; City of Hamilton, Planning Committee, *Report on Existing Conditions Proposed as Basic Materials for Planning* (Hamilton, 1945); Department of Political Economy, McMaster University, *Hamilton Housing Survey 1955* (Hamilton, 1955). The federal government produced invaluable studies: Advisory Committee on Reconstruction, *Housing and Community Planning, Final Report of the Subcommittee* (Ottawa: King's Printer, 1944) and Dominion Bureau of Statistics, *Hamilton Housing Atlas* (Ottawa, 1946). The Social Planning and Research Council of Hamilton and District has prepared briefs and papers on housing, socioeconomic conditions and politics. Noteworthy as a spatial study is Mike Pennock, *A Socio-Economic Atlas of the City of Hamilton* (Hamilton, 1977). Grant Thrall, "Spatial Inequalities in Tax Assessment: A Case Study of Hamilton, Ontario," *Economic Geography*, vol. 55 (April, 1979), pp. 124-34, includes a short discussion of housing market values in sixteen Hamilton districts. The city has produced a number of reports on land use with respect to urban renewal schemes. The City of Hamilton, *Data Book: Hamilton, Burlington, Wentworth Local Government Review* (Hamilton, 1968) contains land-use and annexation maps as well as population tables. The highrise phenomenon of the early 1960s is the subject of J. Mercer, "Some Aspects of the Spatial Pattern of Multiple Residential Structures in Hamilton" (McMaster University, MA thesis, 1966).

William and Evelyn James, *"A Sufficient Quantity of Pure and Wholesome Water": The Story of Hamilton's Old Pumphouse* (London: Phelps Publishing Company, 1978) examines the origins and construction of the waterworks. Mabel Burkholder wrote an unpublished history of the Hamilton Street Railway which is held by the Hamilton Public Library. A photographic account of local radial lines can be found in John M. Mills, *Cataract Traction: The Railways of Hamilton* (Toronto: Upper Canada Railway Society, 1971). On the Cataract Power Company there is Richard Lucas, "The Conflict over Public Power in Hamilton, Ontario, 1906-1914," *Ontario History*, vol. 67 (December, 1976), pp. 236-46. The *City Engineer's Report*, especially from 1904 to 1914, gives evidence of the prewar boom. The Building Inspector's Reports published in the *City Council Minutes* from 1897 to 1925 capture the housing construction trends. Except for Alexander G. McKay, *Victorian Architecture in Hamilton* (Hamilton: The

Architectural Conservancy of Ontario, 1967), there is nothing readily available that records and celebrates Hamilton structures.

Labour History

Hamilton has attracted the interest of a handful of young and able labour historians. Some of this activity is reflected in the bibliographic essays in Wayne Roberts, ed., *The Hamilton Working Class, 1820 to 1977: A Bibliography* (Hamilton: McMaster Labour Studies, 1978). The nine-hours movement of 1872 is covered by John Battye, "'The Nine Hour Pioneers': The Genesis of the Canadian Labour Movement," *Labour/Le Travailleur*, vol. 4 (1979), pp. 25-56 and again in Palmer, *A Culture in Conflict*. The background to this episode has been developed in Robert H. Storey, "Industrialization in Canada: The Emergence of the Hamilton Working Class, 1850-1870" (Dalhousie University, MA thesis, 1976). *A Culture in Conflict* is at its best covering the Knights of Labor in the 1880s. The authority on industrial technology and labour for the late nineteenth and early twentieth century is Craig Heron. His article "The Crisis of the Craftsman: Hamilton's Metal Workers in the Early Twentieth Century," *Labour/Le Travailleur*, vol. 6 (Autumn, 1980), pp. 7-48, is highly recommended, as is Myer Siemiatycki, "Munitions and Labour Militancy: The 1916 Hamilton Machinists' Strike," *Labour/Le Travailleur*, vol. 3 (1978), pp. 131-51. Wayne Roberts has edited *Organizing Westinghouse: Alf Ready's Story* (Hamilton: McMaster Labour Studies, 1979).

Civic Politics

John M. McMenemy's "Lion in a Den of Daniels: A Study of Sam Lawrence, Labour in Politics" (McMaster, MA thesis, 1965) stands alone as a political biography. *Their Town: The Mafia, the Media, and the Party Machine*, edited by Bill Freeman and Marsha Hewitt (Toronto: James Lorimer, 1979) attempted to explain through a series of articles on politics, the media and urban planning the inability of democratic socialism to influence greatly the development of a working-class city. A realistic analysis of politics is advanced in Henry Jacek, John McDonough, Ronald Skimizu and Patrick Smith, "Social Articulation and Aggregation in Political Party Organization in a Large Canadian City," *Canadian Journal of Political Science*, vol. 8 (June, 1975), pp. 274-98. A similar appreciation for the local political setting characterizes Henry Jacek, "Central Government Planning *versus* Conflicting Local Elites: Regional Government in Hamilton-Wentworth," *Government and Politics of Ontario*, edited Donald C. MacDonald (Toronto: MacMillan, 1975), pp. 48-63.

Index